INFINITY INCOMING!

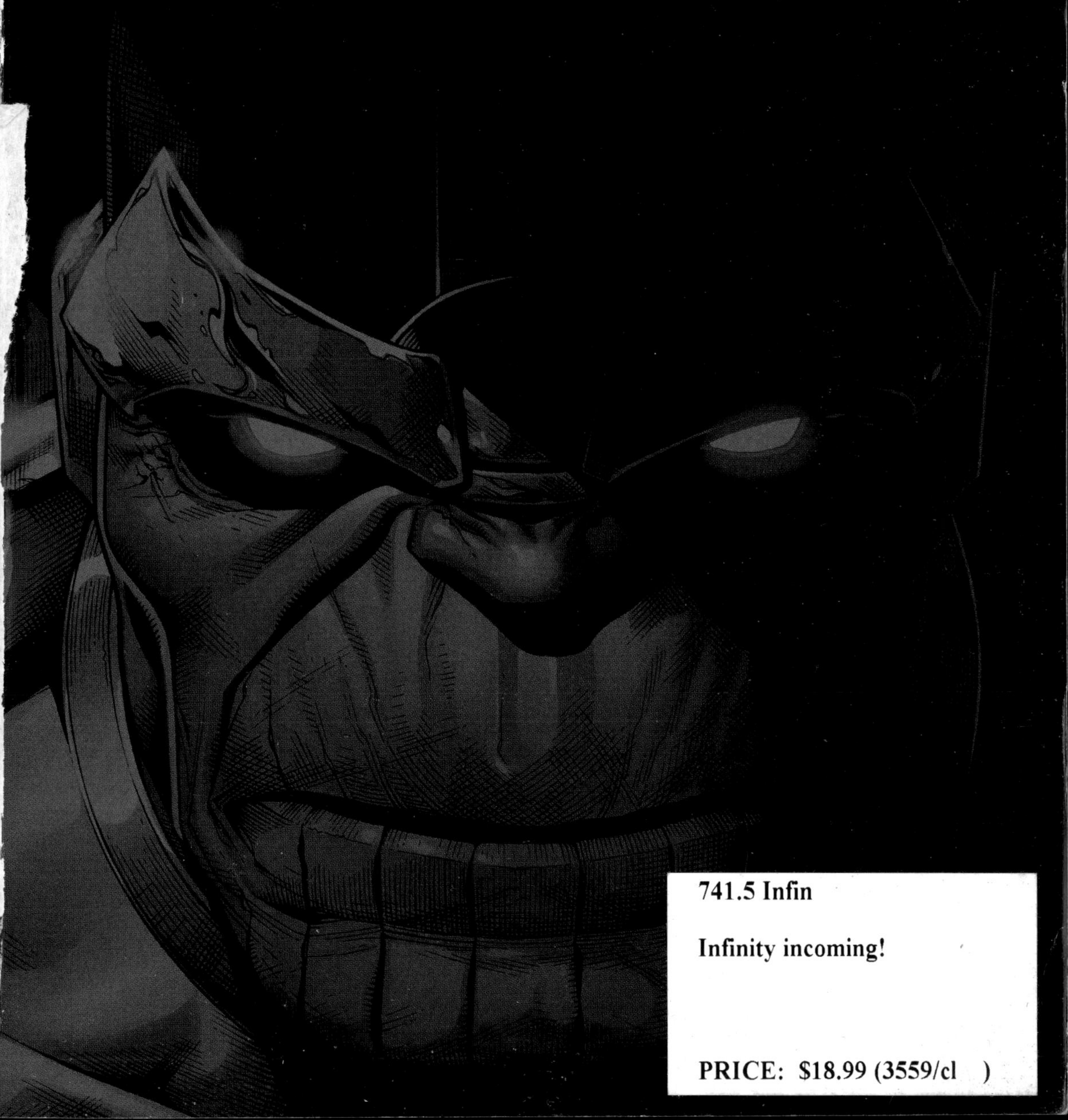

INFINITY

INCOMING!

"THE ORIGIN OF: THE INCOMPARABLE INHUMANS!"
FROM *THOR* (1966) #146-149

WRITER: **STAN LEE**

PENCILER: **JACK KIRBY**

INKER: **JOE SINNOTT**

LETTERER: **ART SIMEK** & **SAM ROSEN**

COLOR RECONSTRUCTION: **MICHAEL KELLEHER**
& **KELLUSTRATION**

ART RECONSTRUCTION: **CHRIS FAMA**

"GENOTYPICAL"
FROM *INHUMANS* (1998) #2

WRITER: **PAUL JENKINS**

ARTIST: **JAE LEE**

COLOR ARTIST: **AVALON'S DAVE KEMP**

LETTERER: **RICHARD STARKINGS** & **COMICRAFT'S
DAVE LANPHEAR**

COVER ART: **JAE LEE** & **AVALON STUDIOS**

EDITORS: **JOE QUESADA** & **JIMMY PALMIOTTI**

THANOS RISING #1

WRITER: **JASON AARON**

ARTIST: **SIMONE BIANCHI**

COLOR ARTIST: **SIMONE PERUZZI**

LETTERER: **VC'S CLAYTON COWLES**

COVER ART: **SIMONE BIANCHI**

ASSISTANT EDITOR: **ELLIE PYLE**

ASSOCIATE EDITOR: **SANA AMANAT**

EDITOR: **STEPHEN WACKER**

"WAKE THE WORLD" & **"WE WERE AVENGERS"**
FROM *AVENGERS* (2012) #1-2

WRITER: **JONATHAN HICKMAN**

ARTIST: **JEROME OPEÑA**

COLOR ARTISTS: **DEAN WHITE**
WITH **JUSTIN PONSOR** & **MORRY HOLLOWELL** (#2)

LETTERER: **VC'S CORY PETIT**

COVER ART: **DUSTIN WEAVER** & **JUSTIN PONSOR**

ASSISTANT EDITOR: **JAKE THOMAS**

EDITORS: **TOM BREVOORT**

WITH **LAUREN SANKOVITCH**

"IN SECRET THEY RULE"
FROM *NEW AVENGERS* (2013) #2

WRITER: **JONATHAN HICKMAN**

PENCILER: **STEVE EPTING**

INKERS: **RICK MAGYAR**
WITH **STEVE EPTING**

COLORIST: **FRANK D'ARMATA**

LETTERER: **VC'S JOE CARAMAGNA** • COVER ART: **JOCK**

ASSISTANT EDITOR: **JAKE THOMAS**

EDITORS: **TOM BREVOORT**

WITH **LAUREN SANKOVITCH**

COLLECTION EDITOR & DESIGN: CORY LEVINE • ASSISTANT EDITORS: ALEX STARBUCK & NELSON RIBEIRO
EDITORS, SPECIAL PROJECTS: JENNIFER GRÜNWALD & MARK D. BEAZLEY • SENIOR EDITOR, SPECIAL PROJECTS: JEFF YOUNGQUIST
MARVEL MASTERWORKS EDITOR: CORY SEDLMEIER • SVP OF PRINT & DIGITAL PUBLISHING SALES: DAVID GABRIEL
COLLECTION COVER BY JIM CHEUNG & JUSTIN PONSOR

EDITOR IN CHIEF: AXEL ALONSO • CHIEF CREATIVE OFFICER: JOE QUESADA
PUBLISHER: DAN BUCKLEY • EXECUTIVE PRODUCER: ALAN FINE

INFINITY INCOMING! Contains material originally published in magazine form as THOR #146-149, INHUMANS #2, THANOS RISING #1, AVENGERS #1-2 and NEW AVENGERS #2. First printing 2013. ISBN# 978-0-7851-8785-1. Published by MARVEL WORLDWIDE, INC., a subsidiary of MARVEL ENTERTAINMENT, LLC. OFFICE OF PUBLICATION: 135 West 50th Street, New York, NY 10020. Copyright © 1967, 1968, 1998, 2012 and 2013 Marvel Characters, Inc. All rights reserved. All characters featured in this issue and the distinctive names and likenesses thereof, and all related indicia are trademarks of Marvel Characters, Inc. No similarity between any of the names, characters, persons, and/or institutions in this magazine with those of any living or dead person or institution is intended, and any such similarity which may exist is purely coincidental. **Printed in the U.S.A.** ALAN FINE, EVP - Office of the President, Marvel Worldwide, Inc. and EVP & CMO Marvel Characters B.V.; DAN BUCKLEY, Publisher & President - Print, Animation & Digital Divisions; JOE QUESADA, Chief Creative Officer; TOM BREVOORT, SVP of Publishing; DAVID BOGART, SVP of Operations & Procurement, Publishing; C.B. CEBULSKI, SVP of Creator & Content Development; DAVID GABRIEL, SVP of Print & Digital Publishing Sales; JIM O'KEEFE, VP of Operations & Logistics; DAN CARR, Executive Director of Publishing Technology; SUSAN CRESPI, Editorial Operations Manager; ALEX MORALES, Publishing Operations Manager; STAN LEE, Chairman Emeritus. For information regarding advertising in Marvel Comics or on Marvel.com, please contact Niza Disla, Director of Marvel Partnerships, at ndisla@marvel.com. For Marvel subscription inquiries, please call 800-217-9158. **Manufactured between 5/31/2013 and 7/8/2013 by QUAD/GRAPHICS ST. CLOUD, ST. CLOUD, MN, USA.**

10 9 8 7 6 5 4 3 2 1

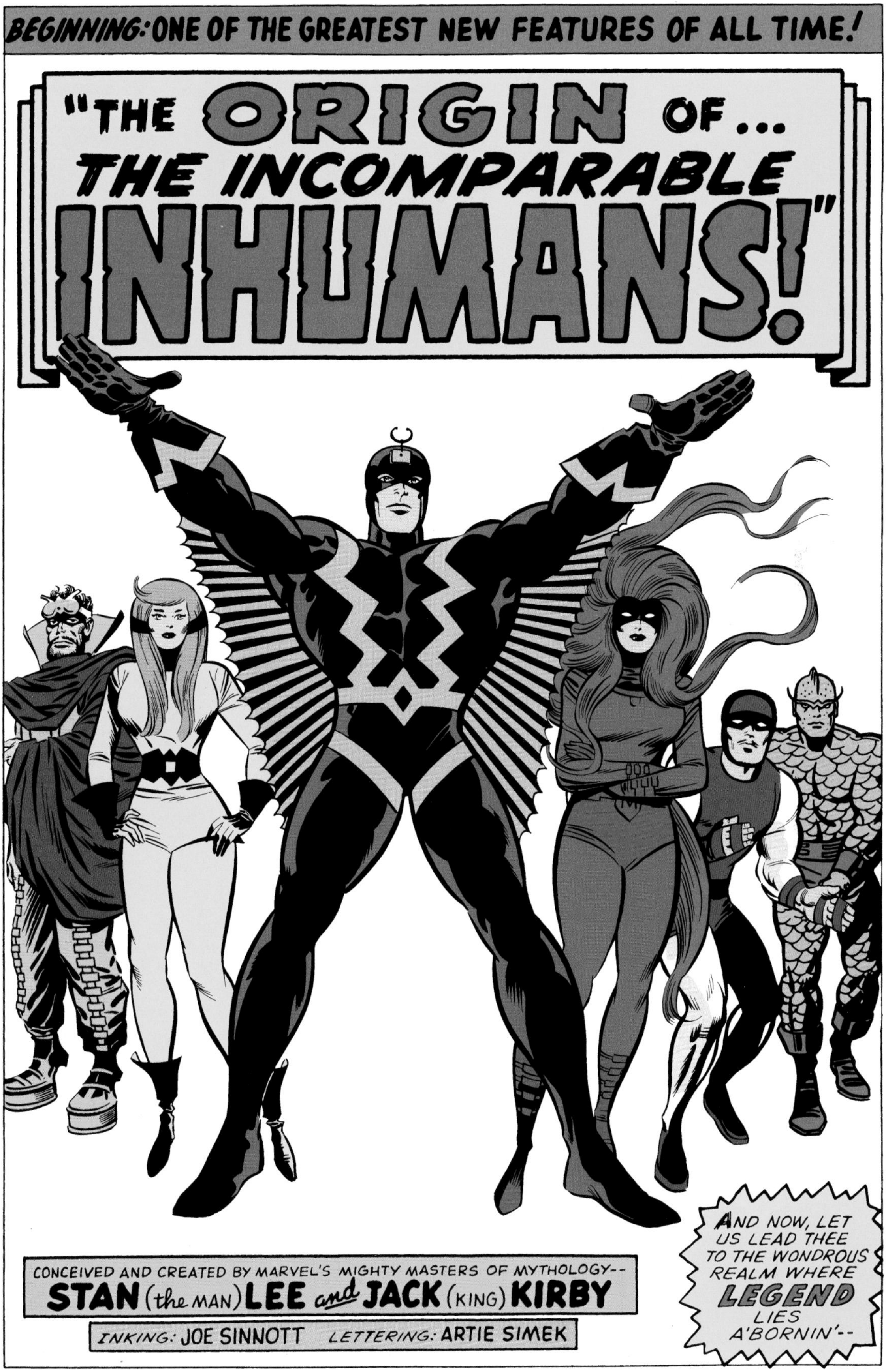

BEGINNING: ONE OF THE GREATEST NEW FEATURES OF ALL TIME!
"THE ORIGIN OF... THE INCOMPARABLE INHUMANS!"
AND NOW, LET US LEAD THEE TO THE WONDROUS REALM WHERE LEGEND LIES A'BORNIN'--
CONCEIVED AND CREATED BY MARVEL'S MIGHTY MASTERS OF MYTHOLOGY--
STAN (the MAN) LEE and JACK (KING) KIRBY
INKING: JOE SINNOTT LETTERING: ARTIE SIMEK

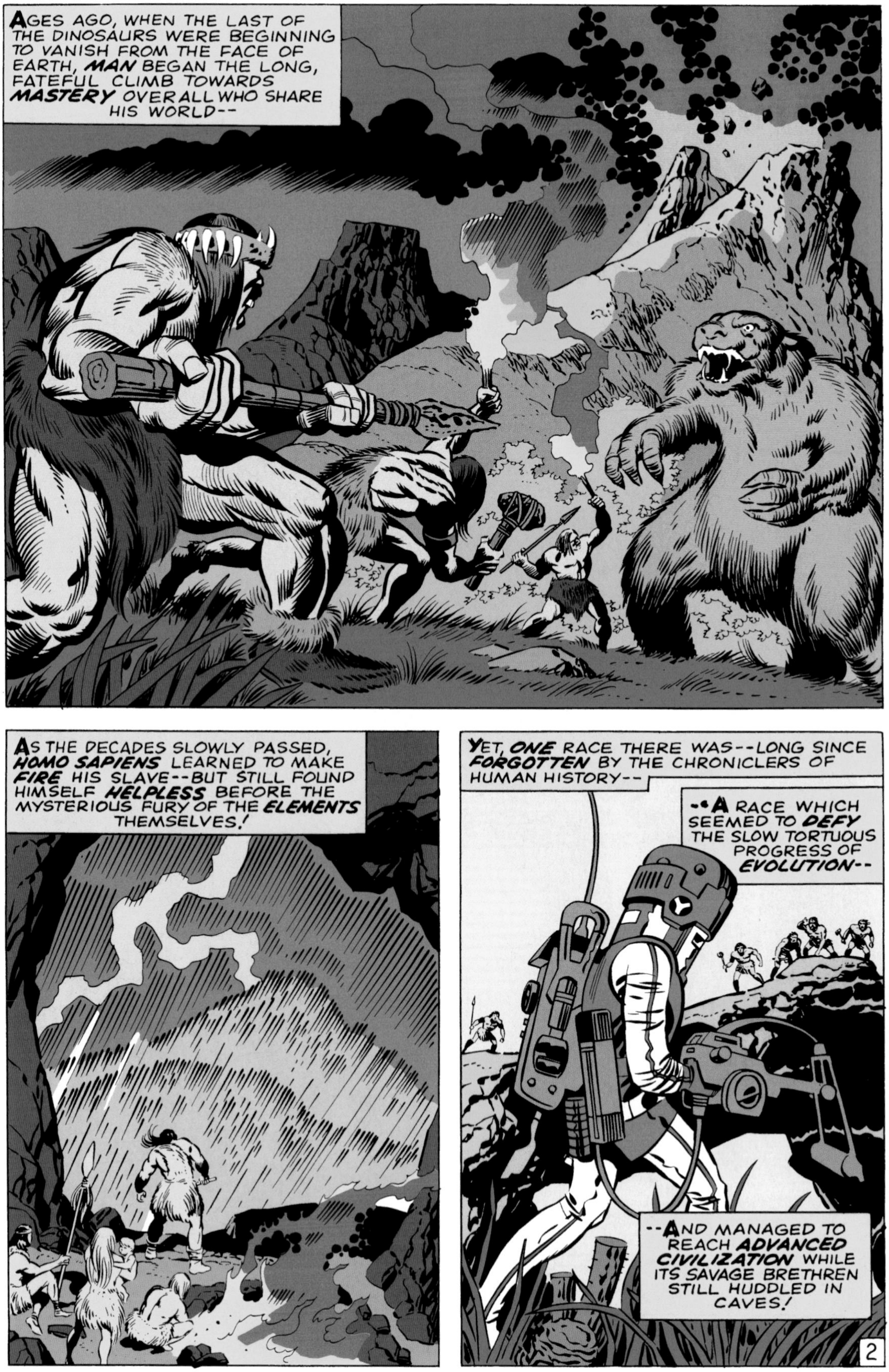
AGES AGO, WHEN THE LAST OF THE DINOSAURS WERE BEGINNING TO VANISH FROM THE FACE OF EARTH, MAN BEGAN THE LONG, FATEFUL CLIMB TOWARDS MASTERY OVER ALL WHO SHARE HIS WORLD--
AS THE DECADES SLOWLY PASSED, HOMO SAPIENS LEARNED TO MAKE FIRE HIS SLAVE--BUT STILL FOUND HIMSELF HELPLESS BEFORE THE MYSTERIOUS FURY OF THE ELEMENTS THEMSELVES!
YET, ONE RACE THERE WAS--LONG SINCE FORGOTTEN BY THE CHRONICLERS OF HUMAN HISTORY--
--A RACE WHICH SEEMED TO DEFY THE SLOW TORTUOUS PROGRESS OF EVOLUTION--
--AND MANAGED TO REACH ADVANCED CIVILIZATION WHILE ITS SAVAGE BRETHREN STILL HUDDLED IN CAVES!

POSSESSING WEAPONS WHICH COULD STUN A DEADLY **SABER-TOOTH** IN MID-LEAP, OR DROP A MONSTROUS **MASTODON** IN ITS TRACKS--

--THEY WERE REGARDED AS SUPERNATURAL **DEMONS** BY THE PRIMITIVE, BESTIAL BEINGS WHO WATCHED THEIR ACTIONS WITH BALEFUL, UNCOMPREHENDING EYES!

WITH THE PASSAGE OF TIME, AS THE PRIMITIVES GREW EVER MORE **NUMEROUS,** THOSE WHO HAD ADVANCED AGES **BEYOND** THEM WERE CONSTANTLY FORCED TO SEEK **NEW** REFUGE--AWAY FROM THE SAVAGES WHO SOUGHT TO **SLAY** WHAT THEY COULD NOT UNDERSTAND--!

AND, WHEREVER THEY FLED, THEY WOULD LOAD A MAGNETIC-POWERED **ARC** WITH LIVING **SPECIMENS** FOR THEIR EVER-CONTINUING RESEARCH--

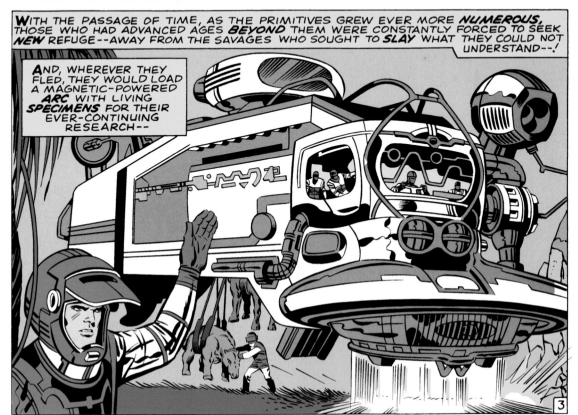

3

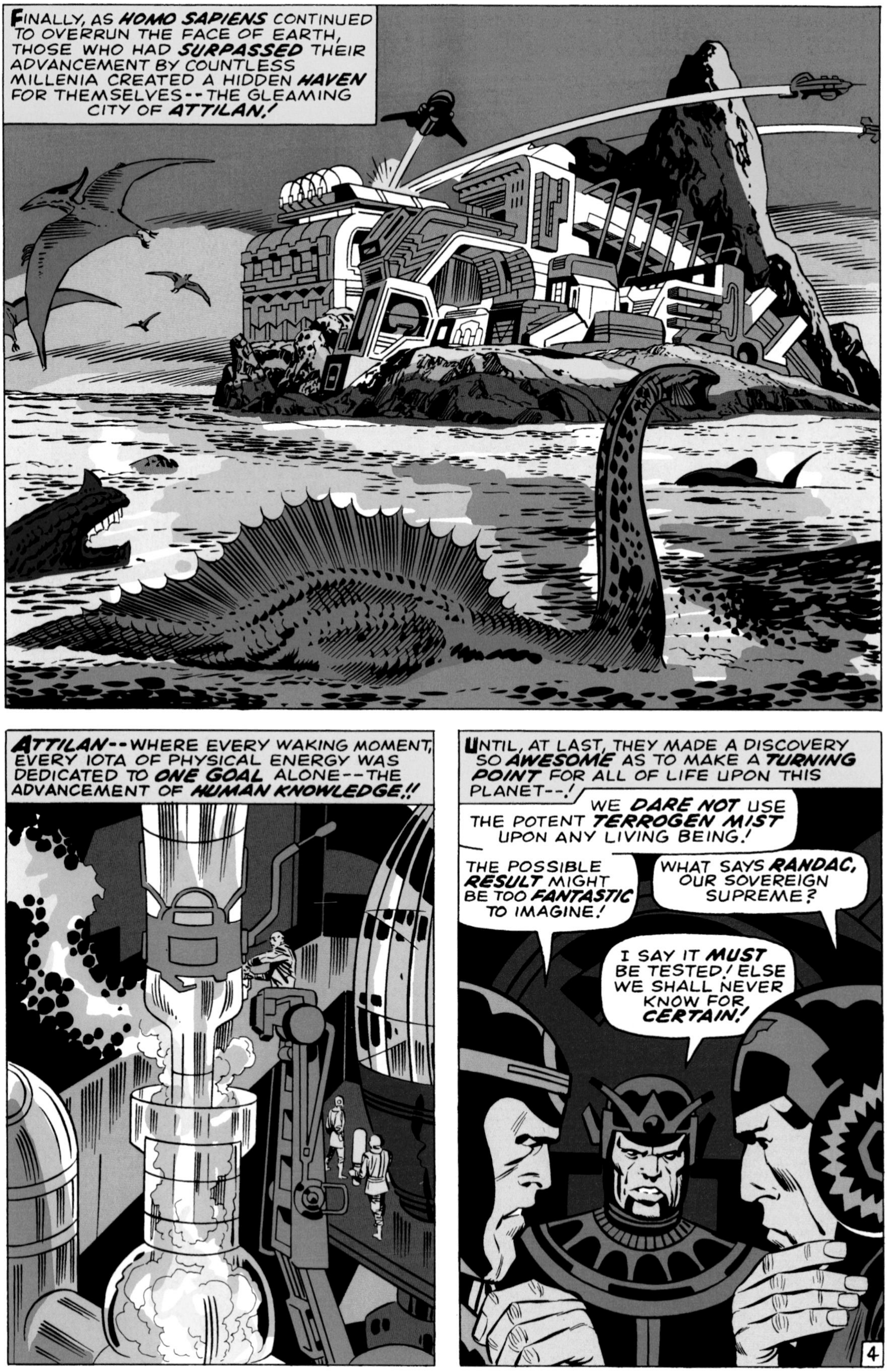

FINALLY, AS HOMO SAPIENS CONTINUED TO OVERRUN THE FACE OF EARTH, THOSE WHO HAD SURPASSED THEIR ADVANCEMENT BY COUNTLESS MILLENIA CREATED A HIDDEN HAVEN FOR THEMSELVES--THE GLEAMING CITY OF ATTILAN!
ATTILAN--WHERE EVERY WAKING MOMENT, EVERY IOTA OF PHYSICAL ENERGY WAS DEDICATED TO ONE GOAL ALONE--THE ADVANCEMENT OF HUMAN KNOWLEDGE!!
UNTIL, AT LAST, THEY MADE A DISCOVERY SO AWESOME AS TO MAKE A TURNING POINT FOR ALL OF LIFE UPON THIS PLANET--!
WE DARE NOT USE THE POTENT TERROGEN MIST UPON ANY LIVING BEING!
THE POSSIBLE RESULT MIGHT BE TOO FANTASTIC TO IMAGINE!
WHAT SAYS RANDAC, OUR SOVEREIGN SUPREME?
I SAY IT MUST BE TESTED! ELSE WE SHALL NEVER KNOW FOR CERTAIN!
4

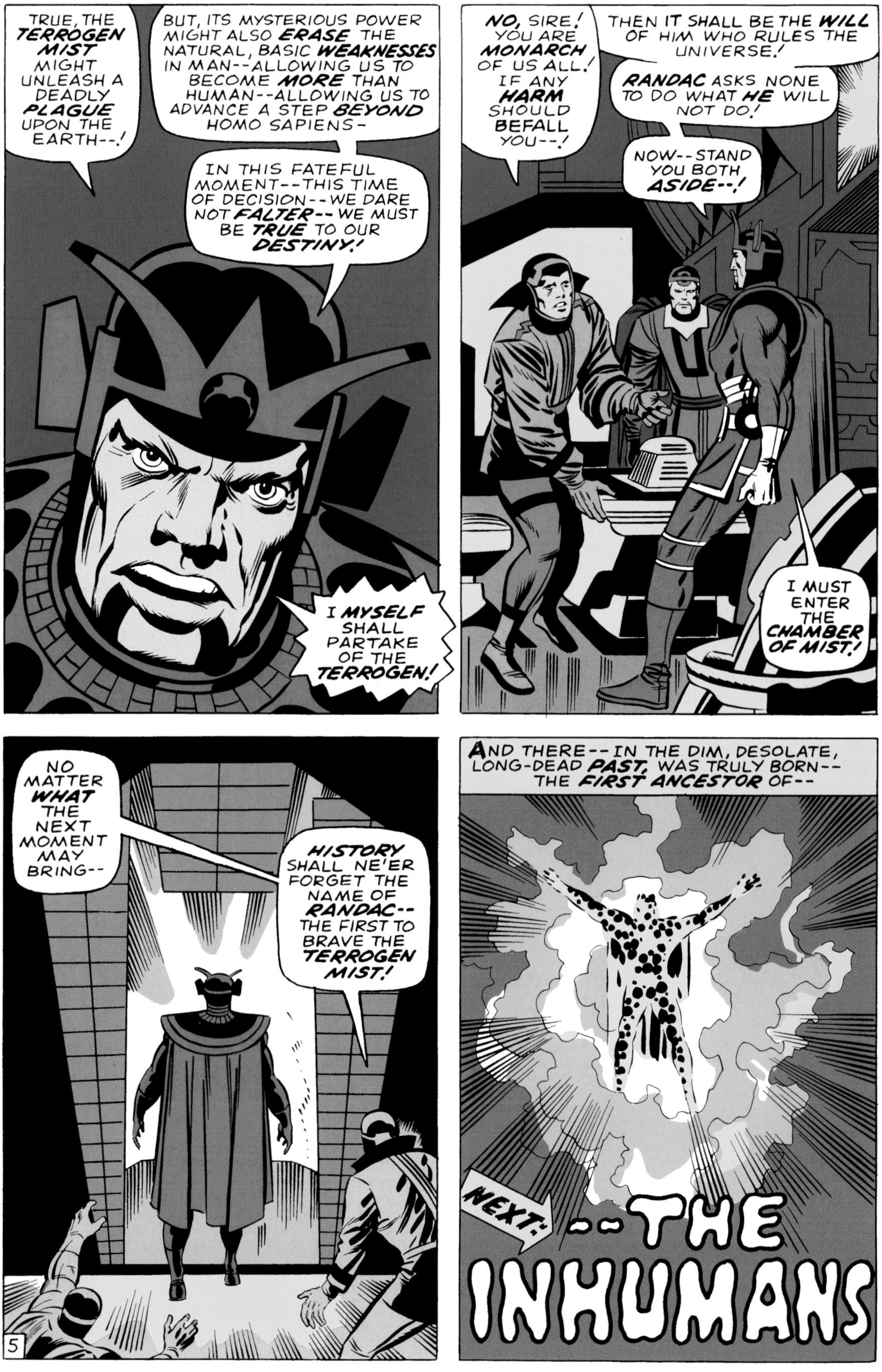
TRUE, THE TERROGEN MIST MIGHT UNLEASH A DEADLY PLAGUE UPON THE EARTH--!
BUT, ITS MYSTERIOUS POWER MIGHT ALSO ERASE THE NATURAL, BASIC WEAKNESSES IN MAN--ALLOWING US TO BECOME MORE THAN HUMAN--ALLOWING US TO ADVANCE A STEP BEYOND HOMO SAPIENS-
IN THIS FATEFUL MOMENT--THIS TIME OF DECISION--WE DARE NOT FALTER--WE MUST BE TRUE TO OUR DESTINY!
I MYSELF SHALL PARTAKE OF THE TERROGEN!
NO, SIRE! YOU ARE MONARCH OF US ALL! IF ANY HARM SHOULD BEFALL YOU--!
THEN IT SHALL BE THE WILL OF HIM WHO RULES THE UNIVERSE!
RANDAC ASKS NONE TO DO WHAT HE WILL NOT DO!
NOW--STAND YOU BOTH ASIDE--!
I MUST ENTER THE CHAMBER OF MIST!
NO MATTER WHAT THE NEXT MOMENT MAY BRING--
HISTORY SHALL NE'ER FORGET THE NAME OF RANDAC--THE FIRST TO BRAVE THE TERROGEN MIST!
5
AND THERE--IN THE DIM, DESOLATE, LONG-DEAD PAST, WAS TRULY BORN--THE FIRST ANCESTOR OF--
NEXT:
--THE INHUMANS

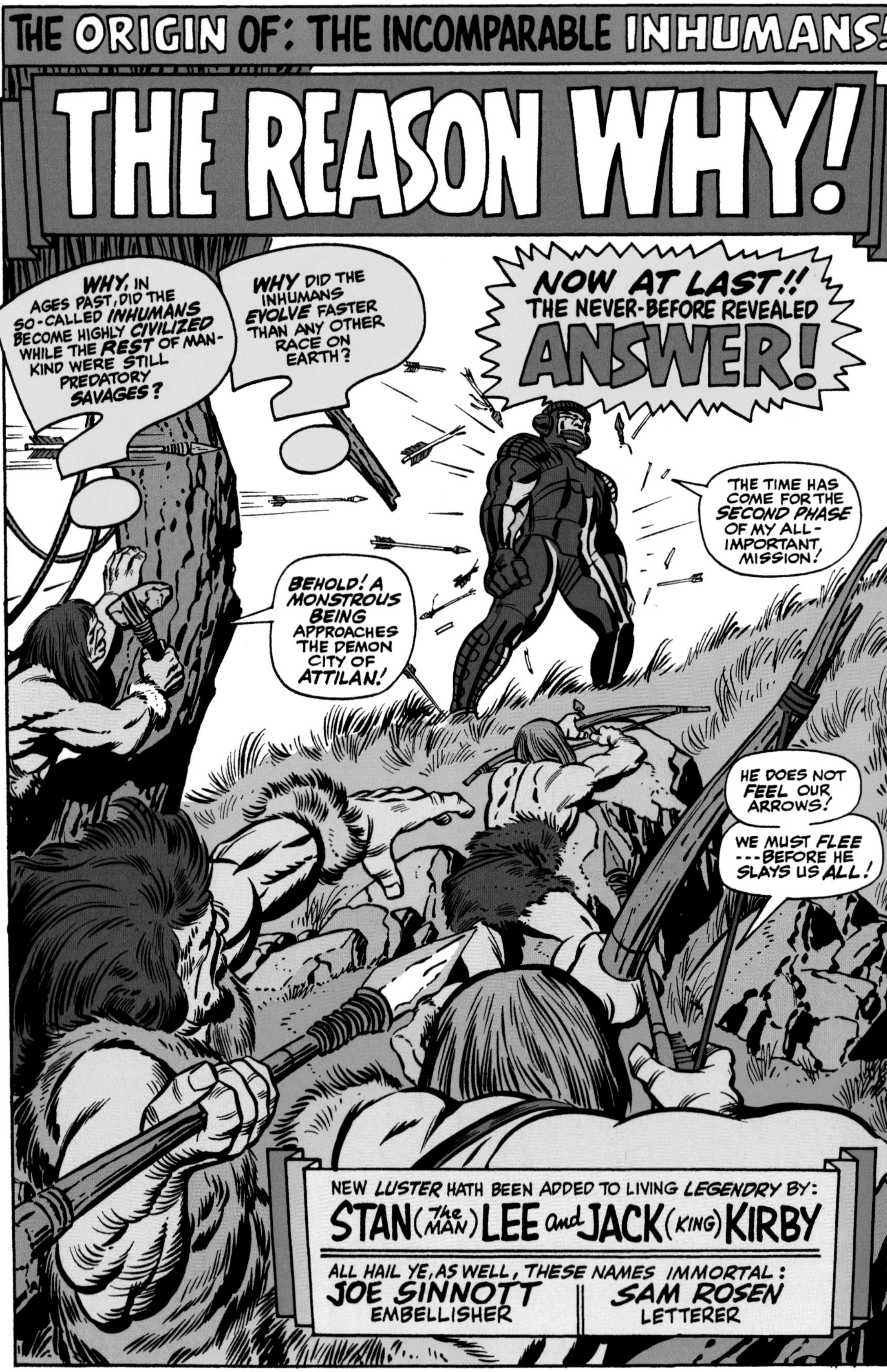
THE ORIGIN OF: THE INCOMPARABLE INHUMANS!
THE REASON WHY!
WHY, IN AGES PAST, DID THE SO-CALLED INHUMANS BECOME HIGHLY CIVILIZED WHILE THE REST OF MAN-KIND WERE STILL PREDATORY SAVAGES?
WHY DID THE INHUMANS EVOLVE FASTER THAN ANY OTHER RACE ON EARTH?
NOW AT LAST!! THE NEVER-BEFORE REVEALED ANSWER!
THE TIME HAS COME FOR THE SECOND PHASE OF MY ALL-IMPORTANT MISSION!
BEHOLD! A MONSTROUS BEING APPROACHES THE DEMON CITY OF ATTILAN!
HE DOES NOT FEEL OUR ARROWS!
WE MUST FLEE ---BEFORE HE SLAYS US ALL!
NEW LUSTER HATH BEEN ADDED TO LIVING LEGENDRY BY:
STAN (THE MAN) LEE and JACK (KING) KIRBY
ALL HAIL YE, AS WELL, THESE NAMES IMMORTAL:
JOE SINNOTT EMBELLISHER
SAM ROSEN LETTERER

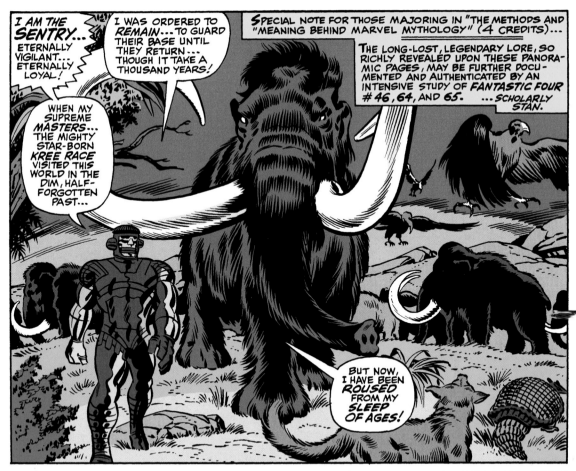

I AM THE *SENTRY*... ETERNALLY VIGILANT... ETERNALLY LOYAL!

I WAS ORDERED TO *REMAIN*...TO GUARD THEIR BASE UNTIL THEY RETURN... THOUGH IT TAKE A THOUSAND YEARS!

WHEN MY SUPREME *MASTERS*... THE MIGHTY STAR-BORN *KREE RACE* VISITED THIS WORLD IN THE DIM, HALF-FORGOTTEN PAST...

SPECIAL NOTE FOR THOSE MAJORING IN "THE METHODS AND "MEANING BEHIND MARVEL MYTHOLOGY" (4 CREDITS)...

THE LONG-LOST, LEGENDARY LORE, SO RICHLY REVEALED UPON THESE PANORAMIC PAGES, MAY BE FURTHER DOCUMENTED AND AUTHENTICATED BY AN INTENSIVE STUDY OF *FANTASTIC FOUR* #*46*, *64*, AND *65*. ...*SCHOLARLY STAN.*

BUT NOW, I HAVE BEEN *ROUSED* FROM MY *SLEEP OF AGES!*

ONLY AN EVENT OF THE GREATEST *MAGNITUDE* COULD HAVE... WAIT!

THAT IS WHAT I SEEK!

THERE, IN THE MIDST OF SAVAGE BEINGS, MORE *BEAST* THAN MAN, HAS RISEN A MIGHTY *CITY*...

A BASTION OF *SCIENTIFIC EVOLVEMENT*...A WELL-SPRING OF *CULTURE*, AND HIGHLY-ADVANCED *CIVILIZATION!*

IT CAN ONLY MEAN.. THE GREAT *EXPERIMENT* OF THE *KREE*...HAS BEEN *SUCCESSFUL!*

THEN, AS WE DULY WONDER *WHAT* EXPERIMENT THE MIGHTY ALIEN IS REFERRING TO, HE ACTIVATES HIS INBORN *HOVER POWER*, RISING ABOVE THE POUNDING SURF---

HERE, WITH MY OWN EYES, I MUST *BEHOLD* WHAT HAS TRANSPIRED!

2.

AND NOW, AS THE SENTRY'S *THOUGHTS* ARE THUS REVEALED TO US, WE FIND OURSELVES PRIVY TO THE *ANSWER* WE HAVE SO LONG BEEN SEEKING ...

WHEN FIRST THEY *LANDED* UPON THIS TINY PLANET...THIS *PRIMITIVE* WORLD, WHOSE VERY *DISCOVERY* WAS BUT A CASUAL ACCIDENT---

MY SUPREME MASTERS, THE ALL-POWERFUL *KREE*, ELECTED TO TEST THE *POWER-POTENTIAL* OF THE *SAVAGES* WHOM THEY FOUND INHABITING THIS HOSTILE WASTELAND!

THUS, THEY *ISOLATED* ONE SMALL TRIBE, SUBJECTING THE *EARTHLINGS* TO AN *EVOLUTIONARY SPEED-UP*, WHILE SLIGHTLY *ALTERING* THE BASIC PATTERN OF THEIR *GENES*!

BUT THEN, *OTHER* MATTERS SOON OCCUPIED THE ATTENTION OF THE *KREE* ...

AND I SUSPECT THEY COMPLETELY *LOST INTEREST* IN THE RESULTS OF SO *SIMPLE* A TEST!

HOWEVER, AS A DEDICATED *SENTRY*, IT IS MY *DUTY* TO INVESTIGATE FURTHER...

AND SO I *SHALL*!

ATTENTION, ALL SECURITY UNITS!

UNKNOWN ENTITY APPROACHING *ATTILAN*!

HE APPEARS TO BE OF *EXTRA-TERRESTRIAL* ORIGIN!

SO *HIGHLY-CIVILIZED* ARE THOSE WHO DWELL UPON THE ISLE OF *ATTILAN*, THAT THE COMING OF A STRANGER IS CAUSE FOR *PLEASURE*, RATHER THAN THE *FEAR* WHICH WOULD BE FELT BY LESSER TRIBES..!

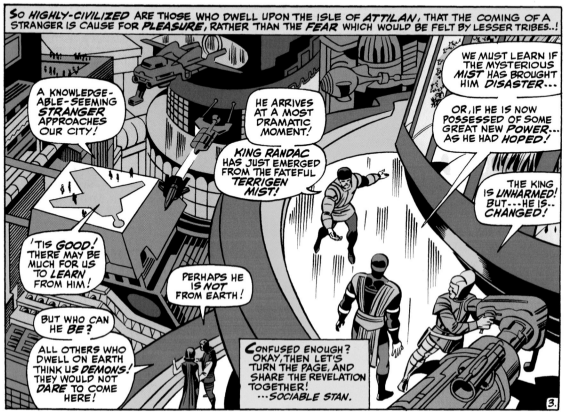

A KNOWLEDGE-ABLE-SEEMING *STRANGER* APPROACHES OUR CITY!

HE ARRIVES AT A MOST DRAMATIC MOMENT!

KING *RANDAC* HAS JUST EMERGED FROM THE FATEFUL *TERRIGEN MIST*!

WE MUST LEARN IF THE MYSTERIOUS *MIST* HAS BROUGHT HIM *DISASTER*...

OR, IF HE IS NOW POSSESSED OF SOME GREAT NEW *POWER*... AS HE HAD *HOPED*!

THE KING IS *UNHARMED*! BUT---HE IS.. *CHANGED*!

'TIS *GOOD*! THERE MAY BE MUCH FOR US TO *LEARN* FROM HIM!

PERHAPS HE IS *NOT* FROM EARTH!

BUT WHO CAN HE *BE*?

ALL OTHERS WHO DWELL ON EARTH THINK US *DEMONS*! THEY WOULD NOT *DARE* TO COME HERE!

CONFUSED ENOUGH? OKAY, THEN LET'S TURN THE PAGE, AND SHARE THE REVELATION TOGETHER! ...SOCIABLE STAN.

3.

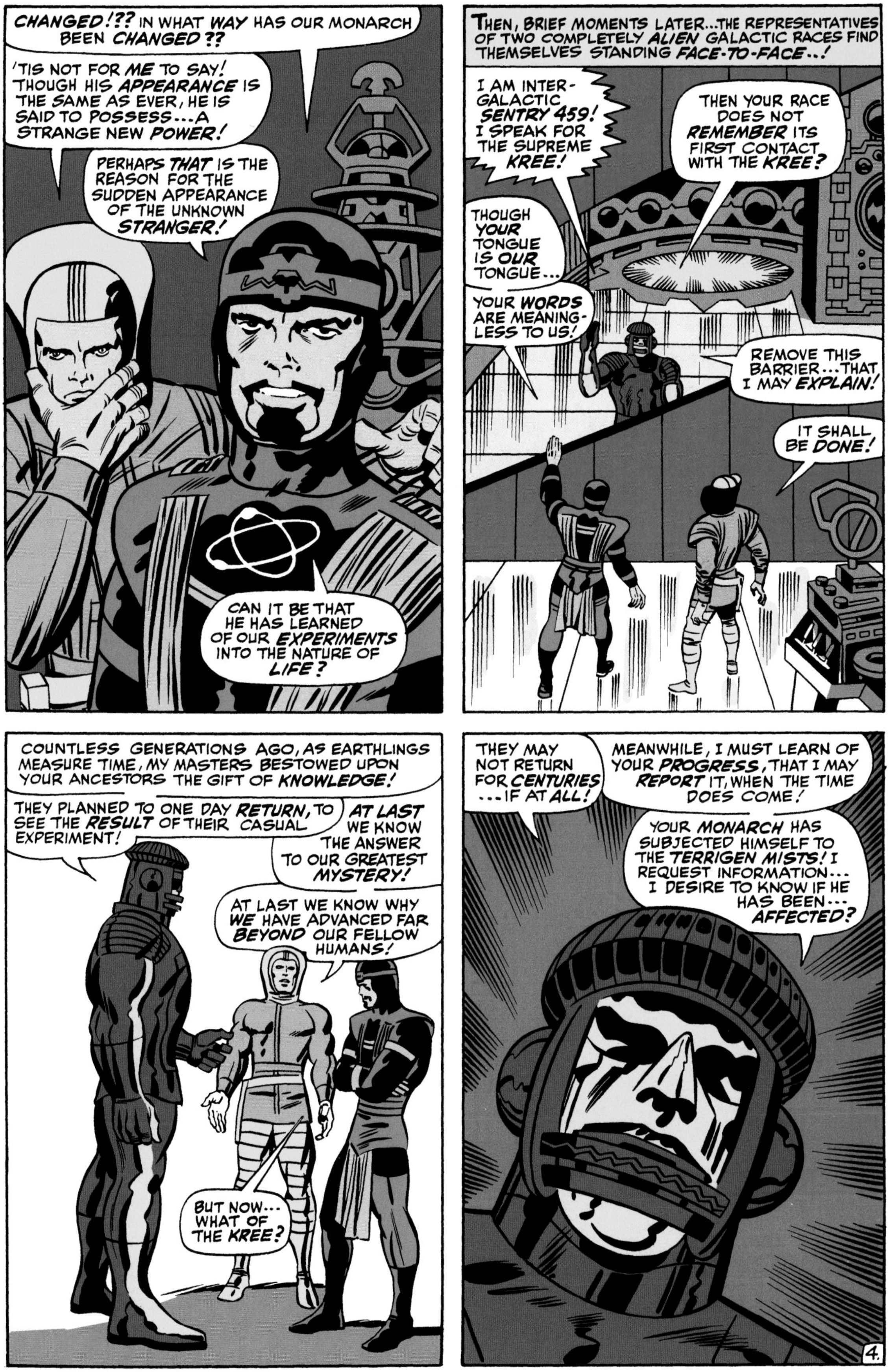
CHANGED!?? IN WHAT WAY HAS OUR MONARCH BEEN CHANGED??
'TIS NOT FOR ME TO SAY! THOUGH HIS APPEARANCE IS THE SAME AS EVER, HE IS SAID TO POSSESS...A STRANGE NEW POWER!
PERHAPS THAT IS THE REASON FOR THE SUDDEN APPEARANCE OF THE UNKNOWN STRANGER!
CAN IT BE THAT HE HAS LEARNED OF OUR EXPERIMENTS INTO THE NATURE OF LIFE?
THEN, BRIEF MOMENTS LATER...THE REPRESENTATIVES OF TWO COMPLETELY ALIEN GALACTIC RACES FIND THEMSELVES STANDING FACE-TO-FACE..!
I AM INTER-GALACTIC SENTRY 459! I SPEAK FOR THE SUPREME KREE!
THEN YOUR RACE DOES NOT REMEMBER ITS FIRST CONTACT WITH THE KREE?
THOUGH YOUR TONGUE IS OUR TONGUE...
YOUR WORDS ARE MEANING-LESS TO US!
REMOVE THIS BARRIER...THAT I MAY EXPLAIN!
IT SHALL BE DONE!
COUNTLESS GENERATIONS AGO, AS EARTHLINGS MEASURE TIME, MY MASTERS BESTOWED UPON YOUR ANCESTORS THE GIFT OF KNOWLEDGE!
THEY PLANNED TO ONE DAY RETURN, TO SEE THE RESULT OF THEIR CASUAL EXPERIMENT!
AT LAST WE KNOW THE ANSWER TO OUR GREATEST MYSTERY!
AT LAST WE KNOW WHY WE HAVE ADVANCED FAR BEYOND OUR FELLOW HUMANS!
BUT NOW... WHAT OF THE KREE?
THEY MAY NOT RETURN FOR CENTURIES ...IF AT ALL!
MEANWHILE, I MUST LEARN OF YOUR PROGRESS, THAT I MAY REPORT IT, WHEN THE TIME DOES COME!
YOUR MONARCH HAS SUBJECTED HIMSELF TO THE TERRIGEN MISTS! I REQUEST INFORMATION... I DESIRE TO KNOW IF HE HAS BEEN... AFFECTED?
4.

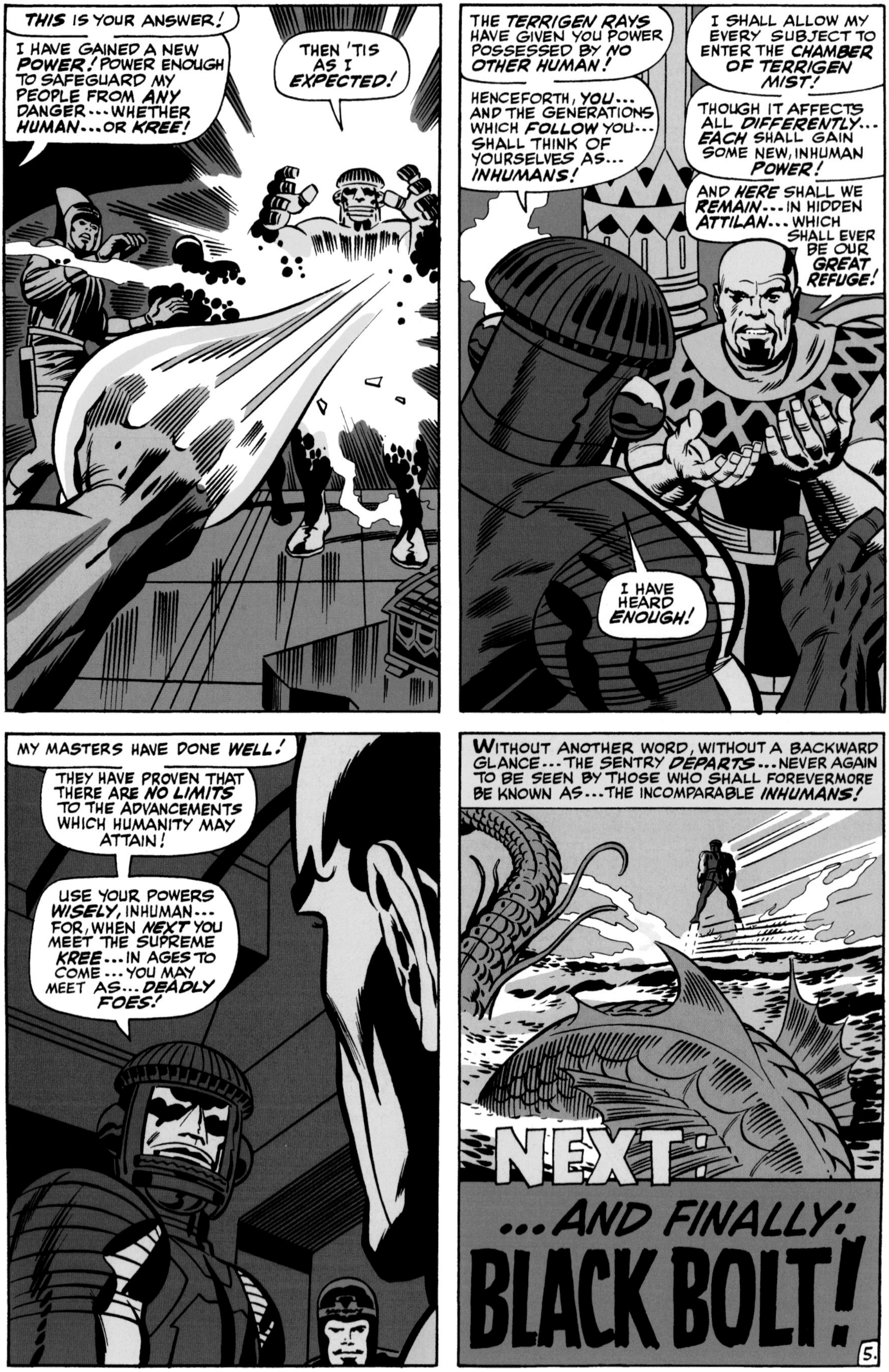
THIS IS YOUR ANSWER!
I HAVE GAINED A NEW POWER! POWER ENOUGH TO SAFEGUARD MY PEOPLE FROM ANY DANGER--WHETHER HUMAN...OR KREE!
THEN 'TIS AS I EXPECTED!
THE TERRIGEN RAYS HAVE GIVEN YOU POWER POSSESSED BY NO OTHER HUMAN!
HENCEFORTH, YOU... AND THE GENERATIONS WHICH FOLLOW YOU... SHALL THINK OF YOURSELVES AS... INHUMANS!
I SHALL ALLOW MY EVERY SUBJECT TO ENTER THE CHAMBER OF TERRIGEN MIST!
THOUGH IT AFFECTS ALL DIFFERENTLY... EACH SHALL GAIN SOME NEW, INHUMAN POWER!
AND HERE SHALL WE REMAIN... IN HIDDEN ATTILAN... WHICH SHALL EVER BE OUR GREAT REFUGE!
I HAVE HEARD ENOUGH!
MY MASTERS HAVE DONE WELL!
THEY HAVE PROVEN THAT THERE ARE NO LIMITS TO THE ADVANCEMENTS WHICH HUMANITY MAY ATTAIN!
USE YOUR POWERS WISELY, INHUMAN... FOR, WHEN NEXT YOU MEET THE SUPREME KREE... IN AGES TO COME... YOU MAY MEET AS... DEADLY FOES!
WITHOUT ANOTHER WORD, WITHOUT A BACKWARD GLANCE... THE SENTRY DEPARTS... NEVER AGAIN TO BE SEEN BY THOSE WHO SHALL FOREVERMORE BE KNOWN AS... THE INCOMPARABLE INHUMANS!
NEXT:
...AND FINALLY: BLACK BOLT!
5.

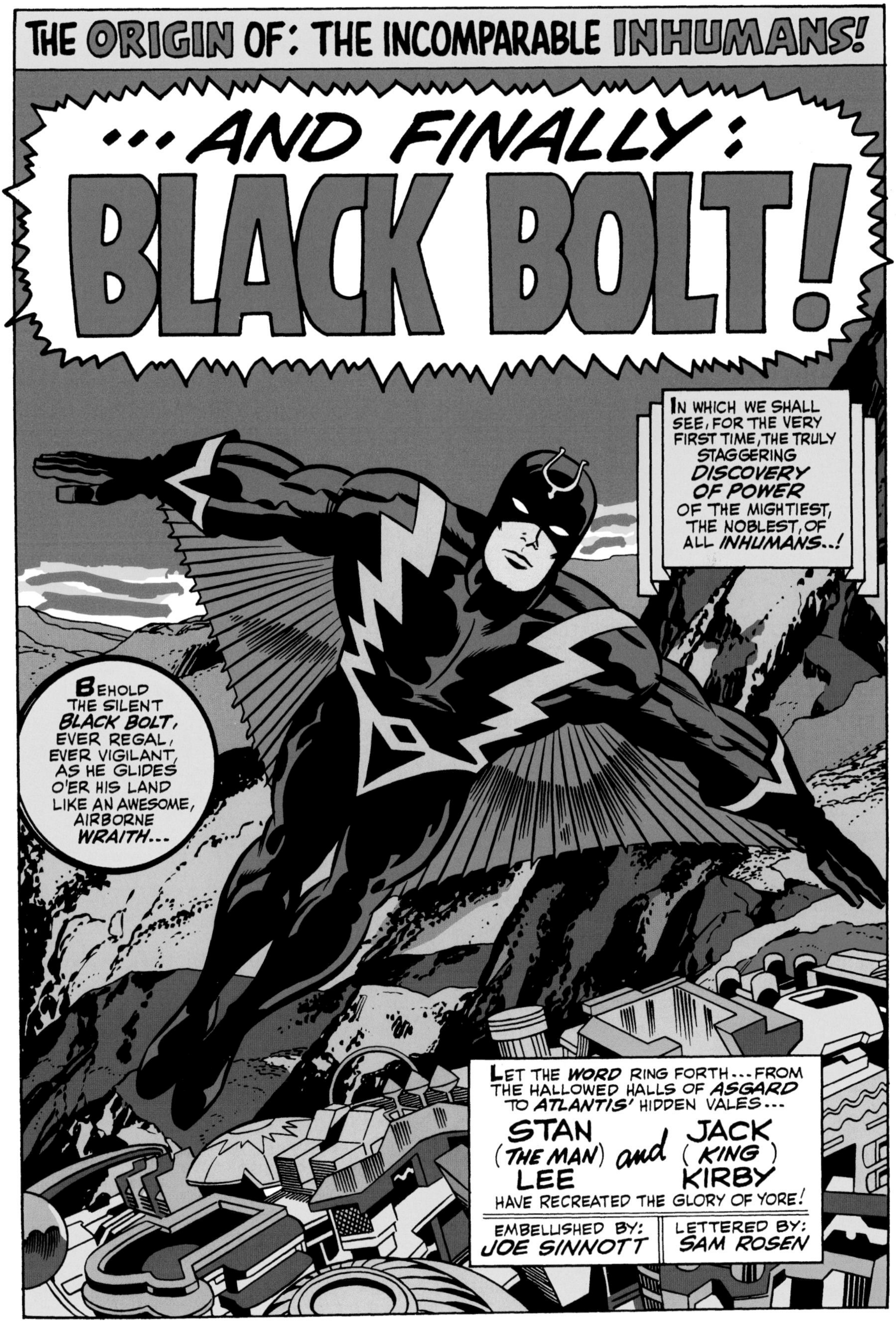
THE ORIGIN OF: THE INCOMPARABLE INHUMANS!
...AND FINALLY: BLACK BOLT!
IN WHICH WE SHALL SEE, FOR THE VERY FIRST TIME, THE TRULY STAGGERING DISCOVERY OF POWER OF THE MIGHTIEST, THE NOBLEST, OF ALL INHUMANS..!
BEHOLD THE SILENT BLACK BOLT, EVER REGAL, EVER VIGILANT, AS HE GLIDES O'ER HIS LAND LIKE AN AWESOME, AIRBORNE WRAITH...
LET THE WORD RING FORTH...FROM THE HALLOWED HALLS OF ASGARD TO ATLANTIS' HIDDEN VALES...
STAN (THE MAN) LEE and JACK (KING) KIRBY
HAVE RECREATED THE GLORY OF YORE!
EMBELLISHED BY: JOE SINNOTT
LETTERED BY: SAM ROSEN

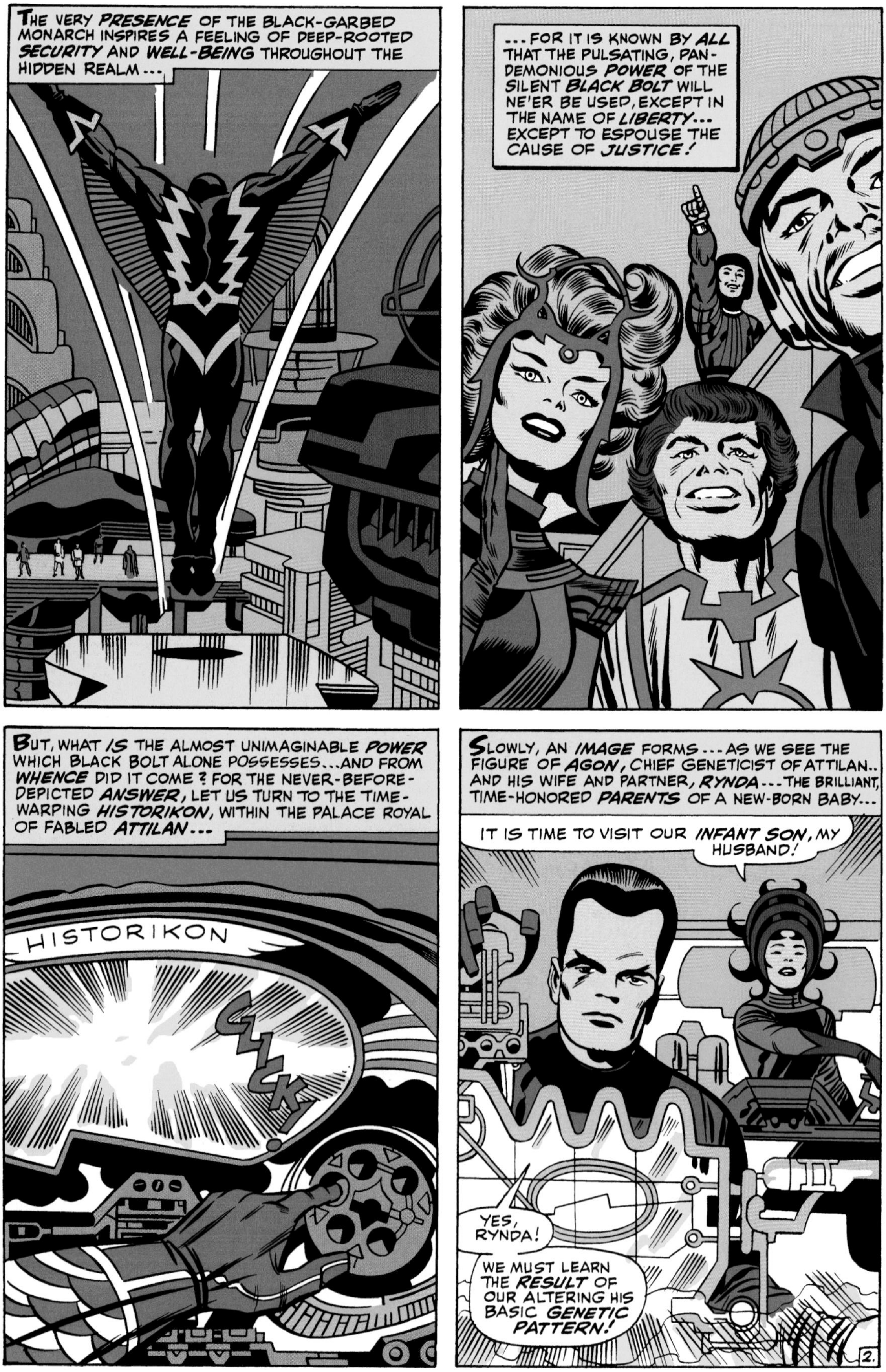
THE VERY PRESENCE OF THE BLACK-GARBED MONARCH INSPIRES A FEELING OF DEEP-ROOTED SECURITY AND WELL-BEING THROUGHOUT THE HIDDEN REALM...
...FOR IT IS KNOWN BY ALL THAT THE PULSATING, PAN-DEMONIOUS POWER OF THE SILENT BLACK BOLT WILL NE'ER BE USED, EXCEPT IN THE NAME OF LIBERTY... EXCEPT TO ESPOUSE THE CAUSE OF JUSTICE!
BUT, WHAT IS THE ALMOST UNIMAGINABLE POWER WHICH BLACK BOLT ALONE POSSESSES...AND FROM WHENCE DID IT COME? FOR THE NEVER-BEFORE-DEPICTED ANSWER, LET US TURN TO THE TIME-WARPING HISTORIKON, WITHIN THE PALACE ROYAL OF FABLED ATTILAN...
HISTORIKON
CLICK!
SLOWLY, AN IMAGE FORMS...AS WE SEE THE FIGURE OF AGON, CHIEF GENETICIST OF ATTILAN.. AND HIS WIFE AND PARTNER, RYNDA...THE BRILLIANT, TIME-HONORED PARENTS OF A NEW-BORN BABY...
IT IS TIME TO VISIT OUR INFANT SON, MY HUSBAND!
YES, RYNDA!
WE MUST LEARN THE RESULT OF OUR ALTERING HIS BASIC GENETIC PATTERN!
2.

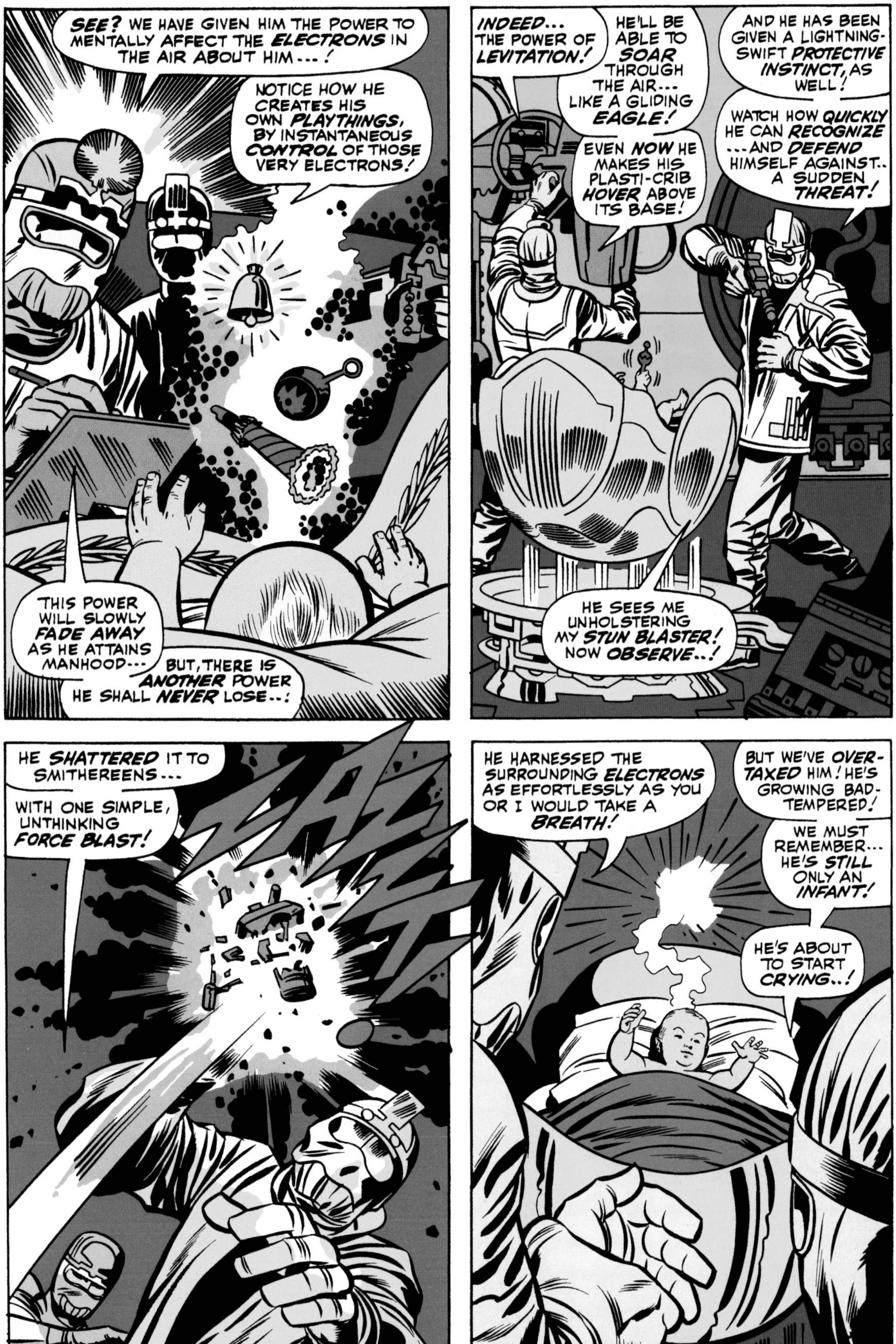
SEE? WE HAVE GIVEN HIM THE POWER TO MENTALLY AFFECT THE ELECTRONS IN THE AIR ABOUT HIM---!
NOTICE HOW HE CREATES HIS OWN PLAYTHINGS, BY INSTANTANEOUS CONTROL OF THOSE VERY ELECTRONS!
THIS POWER WILL SLOWLY FADE AWAY AS HE ATTAINS MANHOOD---
BUT, THERE IS ANOTHER POWER HE SHALL NEVER LOSE--!
INDEED... THE POWER OF LEVITATION!
HE'LL BE ABLE TO SOAR THROUGH THE AIR--- LIKE A GLIDING EAGLE!
EVEN NOW HE MAKES HIS PLASTI-CRIB HOVER ABOVE ITS BASE!
AND HE HAS BEEN GIVEN A LIGHTNING-SWIFT PROTECTIVE INSTINCT, AS WELL!
WATCH HOW QUICKLY HE CAN RECOGNIZE ---AND DEFEND HIMSELF AGAINST.. A SUDDEN THREAT!
HE SEES ME UNHOLSTERING MY STUN BLASTER! NOW OBSERVE..!
HE SHATTERED IT TO SMITHEREENS---
WITH ONE SIMPLE, UNTHINKING FORCE BLAST!
HE HARNESSED THE SURROUNDING ELECTRONS AS EFFORTLESSLY AS YOU OR I WOULD TAKE A BREATH!
BUT WE'VE OVER-TAXED HIM! HE'S GROWING BAD-TEMPERED!
WE MUST REMEMBER... HE'S STILL ONLY AN INFANT!
HE'S ABOUT TO START CRYING..!

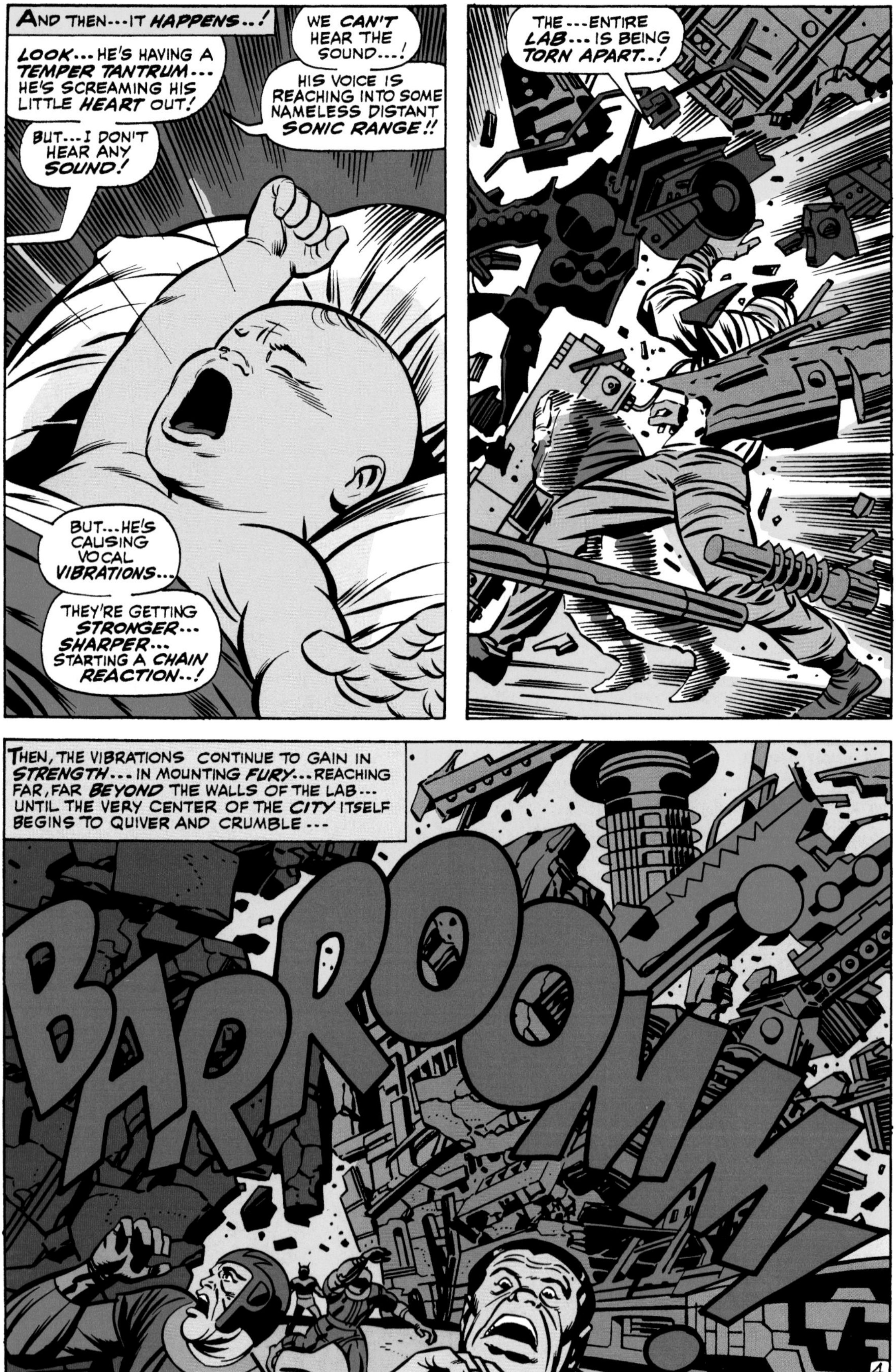

AND THEN---IT HAPPENS..!
LOOK... HE'S HAVING A TEMPER TANTRUM... HE'S SCREAMING HIS LITTLE HEART OUT!
BUT...I DON'T HEAR ANY SOUND!
WE CAN'T HEAR THE SOUND...!
HIS VOICE IS REACHING INTO SOME NAMELESS DISTANT SONIC RANGE!!
BUT...HE'S CAUSING VOCAL VIBRATIONS...
THEY'RE GETTING STRONGER... SHARPER... STARTING A CHAIN REACTION..!
THE---ENTIRE LAB... IS BEING TORN APART..!
THEN, THE VIBRATIONS CONTINUE TO GAIN IN STRENGTH... IN MOUNTING FURY... REACHING FAR, FAR BEYOND THE WALLS OF THE LAB--- UNTIL THE VERY CENTER OF THE CITY ITSELF BEGINS TO QUIVER AND CRUMBLE---
BARROOM!
4.

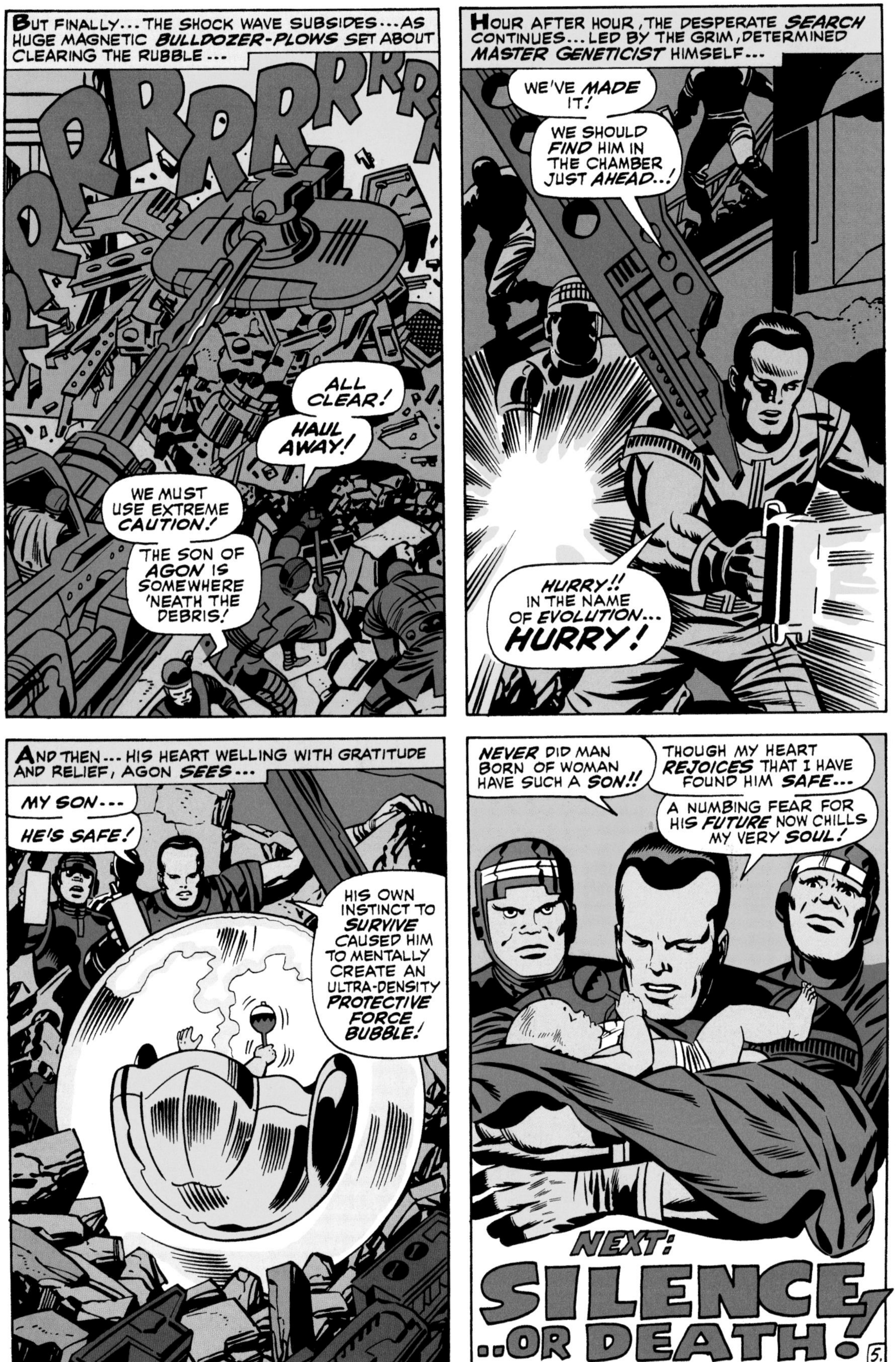
BUT FINALLY... THE SHOCK WAVE SUBSIDES... AS HUGE MAGNETIC BULLDOZER-PLOWS SET ABOUT CLEARING THE RUBBLE...
RRRRRRRRRR
ALL CLEAR!
HAUL AWAY!
WE MUST USE EXTREME CAUTION!
THE SON OF AGON IS SOMEWHERE 'NEATH THE DEBRIS!
HOUR AFTER HOUR, THE DESPERATE SEARCH CONTINUES... LED BY THE GRIM, DETERMINED MASTER GENETICIST HIMSELF...
WE'VE MADE IT!
WE SHOULD FIND HIM IN THE CHAMBER JUST AHEAD..!
HURRY!! IN THE NAME OF EVOLUTION... HURRY!
AND THEN... HIS HEART WELLING WITH GRATITUDE AND RELIEF, AGON SEES...
MY SON...
HE'S SAFE!
HIS OWN INSTINCT TO SURVIVE CAUSED HIM TO MENTALLY CREATE AN ULTRA-DENSITY PROTECTIVE FORCE BUBBLE!
NEVER DID MAN BORN OF WOMAN HAVE SUCH A SON!!
THOUGH MY HEART REJOICES THAT I HAVE FOUND HIM SAFE...
A NUMBING FEAR FOR HIS FUTURE NOW CHILLS MY VERY SOUL!
NEXT: SILENCE, ..OR DEATH!
5.

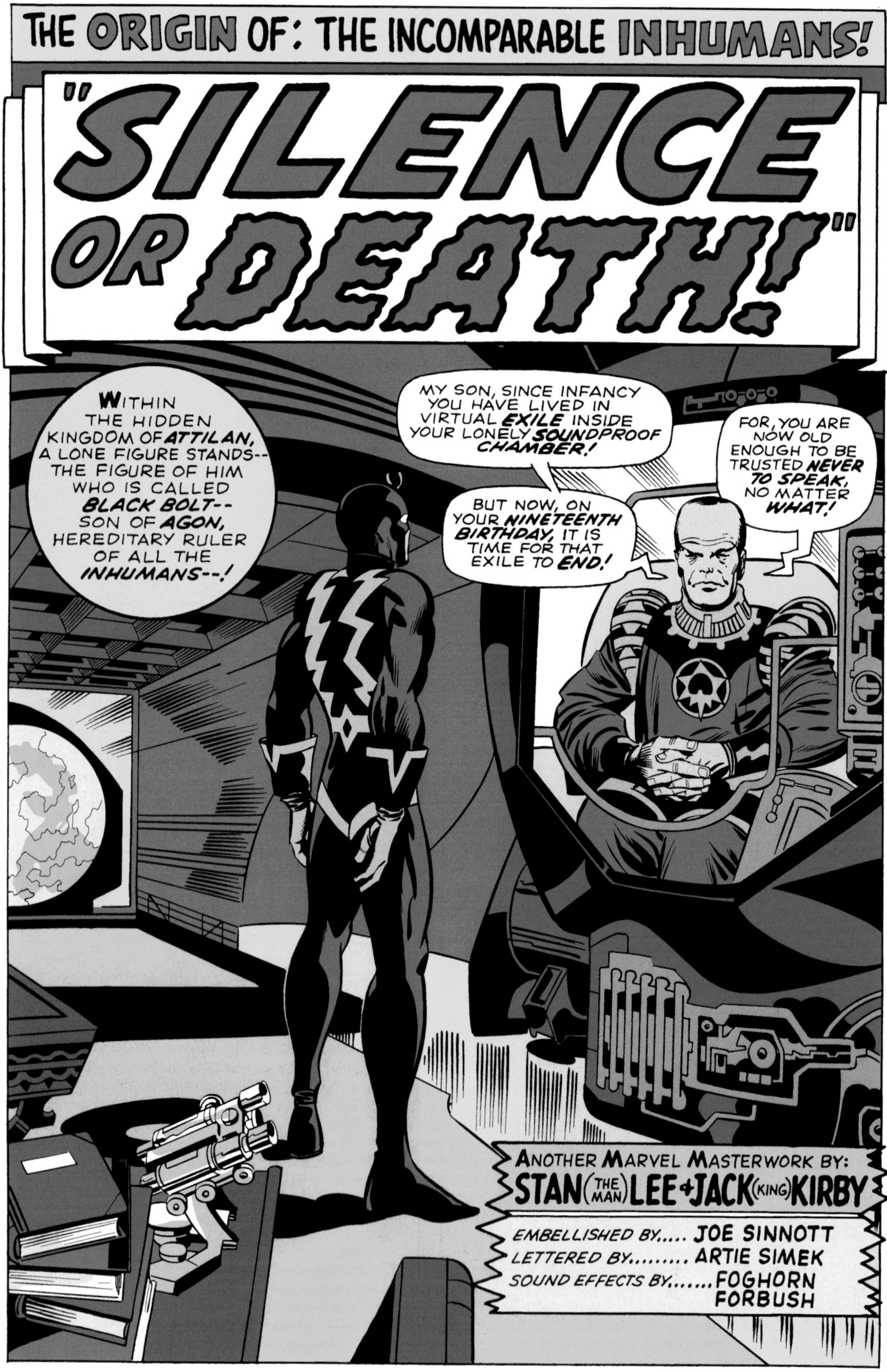
THE ORIGIN OF: THE INCOMPARABLE INHUMANS!
"SILENCE OR DEATH!"
WITHIN THE HIDDEN KINGDOM OF ATTILAN, A LONE FIGURE STANDS-- THE FIGURE OF HIM WHO IS CALLED BLACK BOLT-- SON OF AGON, HEREDITARY RULER OF ALL THE INHUMANS--!
MY SON, SINCE INFANCY YOU HAVE LIVED IN VIRTUAL EXILE INSIDE YOUR LONELY SOUNDPROOF CHAMBER!
BUT NOW, ON YOUR NINETEENTH BIRTHDAY, IT IS TIME FOR THAT EXILE TO END!
FOR, YOU ARE NOW OLD ENOUGH TO BE TRUSTED NEVER TO SPEAK, NO MATTER WHAT!
ANOTHER MARVEL MASTERWORK BY:
STAN (THE MAN) LEE + JACK (KING) KIRBY
EMBELLISHED BY..... JOE SINNOTT
LETTERED BY........ ARTIE SIMEK
SOUND EFFECTS BY...... FOGHORN FORBUSH

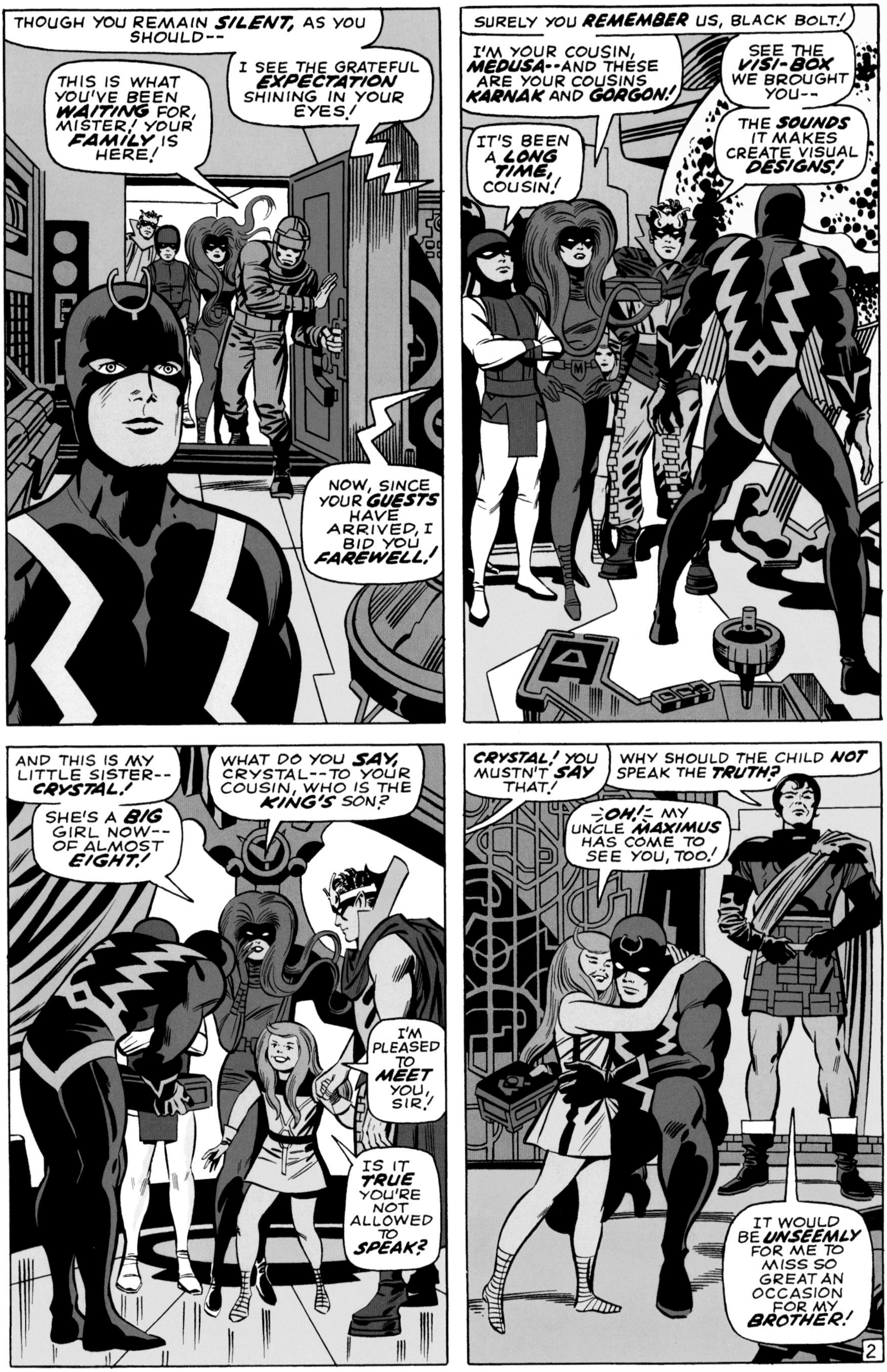
THOUGH YOU REMAIN SILENT, AS YOU SHOULD--
THIS IS WHAT YOU'VE BEEN WAITING FOR, MISTER! YOUR FAMILY IS HERE!
I SEE THE GRATEFUL EXPECTATION SHINING IN YOUR EYES!
NOW, SINCE YOUR GUESTS HAVE ARRIVED, I BID YOU FAREWELL!
SURELY YOU REMEMBER US, BLACK BOLT!
I'M YOUR COUSIN, MEDUSA--AND THESE ARE YOUR COUSINS KARNAK AND GORGON!
IT'S BEEN A LONG TIME, COUSIN!
SEE THE VISI-BOX WE BROUGHT YOU--
THE SOUNDS IT MAKES CREATE VISUAL DESIGNS!
AND THIS IS MY LITTLE SISTER--CRYSTAL!
SHE'S A BIG GIRL NOW--OF ALMOST EIGHT!
WHAT DO YOU SAY, CRYSTAL--TO YOUR COUSIN, WHO IS THE KING'S SON?
I'M PLEASED TO MEET YOU, SIR!
IS IT TRUE YOU'RE NOT ALLOWED TO SPEAK?
CRYSTAL! YOU MUSTN'T SAY THAT!
WHY SHOULD THE CHILD NOT SPEAK THE TRUTH?
OH! MY UNCLE MAXIMUS HAS COME TO SEE YOU, TOO!
IT WOULD BE UNSEEMLY FOR ME TO MISS SO GREAT AN OCCASION FOR MY BROTHER!
2

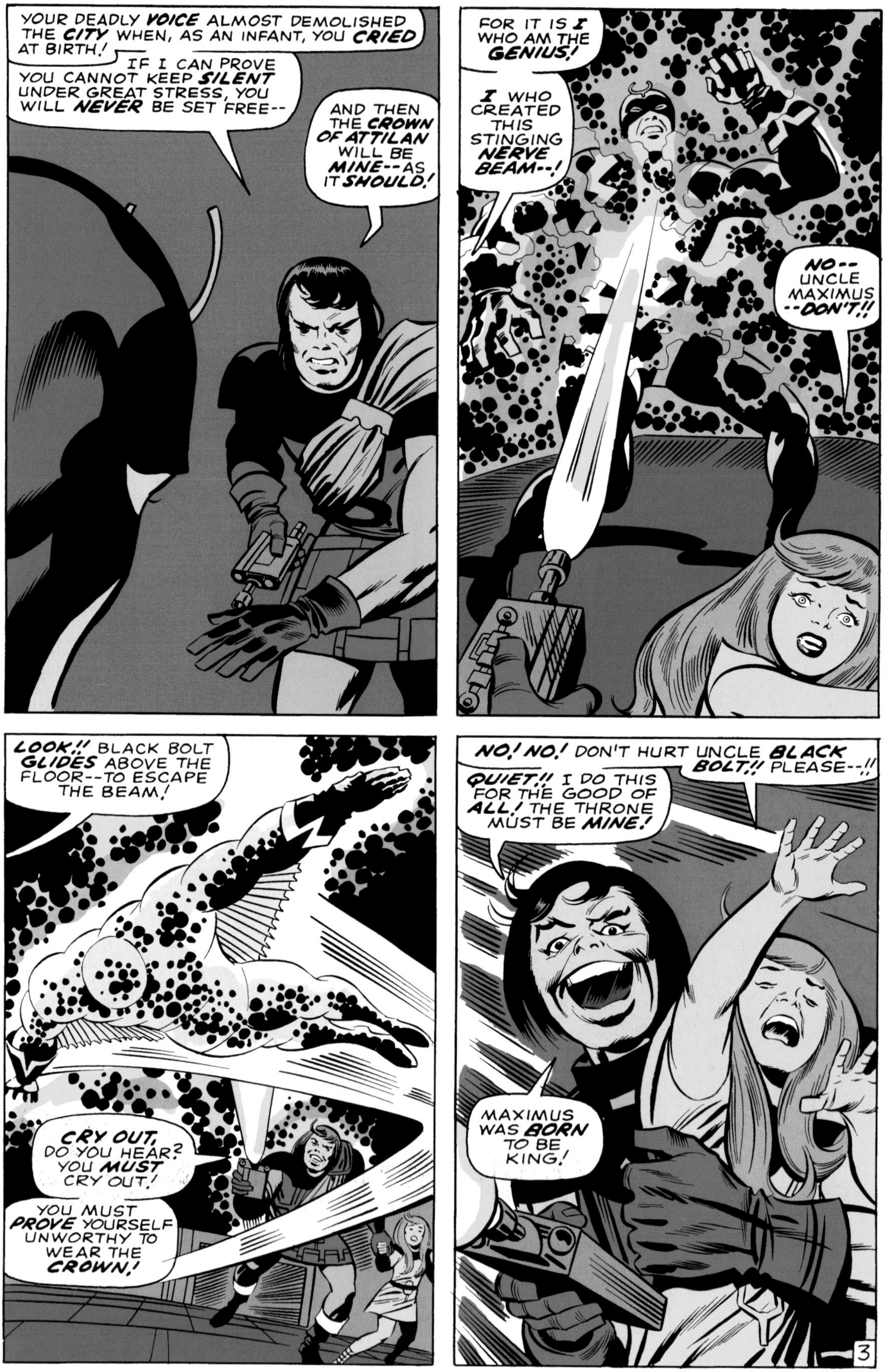
YOUR DEADLY VOICE ALMOST DEMOLISHED THE CITY WHEN, AS AN INFANT, YOU CRIED AT BIRTH!
IF I CAN PROVE YOU CANNOT KEEP SILENT UNDER GREAT STRESS, YOU WILL NEVER BE SET FREE--
AND THEN THE CROWN OF ATTILAN WILL BE MINE--AS IT SHOULD!
FOR IT IS I WHO AM THE GENIUS!
I WHO CREATED THIS STINGING NERVE BEAM--!
NO--UNCLE MAXIMUS --DON'T!!
LOOK!! BLACK BOLT GLIDES ABOVE THE FLOOR--TO ESCAPE THE BEAM!
CRY OUT, DO YOU HEAR? YOU MUST CRY OUT!
YOU MUST PROVE YOURSELF UNWORTHY TO WEAR THE CROWN!
NO! NO! DON'T HURT UNCLE BLACK BOLT!! PLEASE--!!
QUIET!! I DO THIS FOR THE GOOD OF ALL! THE THRONE MUST BE MINE!
MAXIMUS WAS BORN TO BE KING!

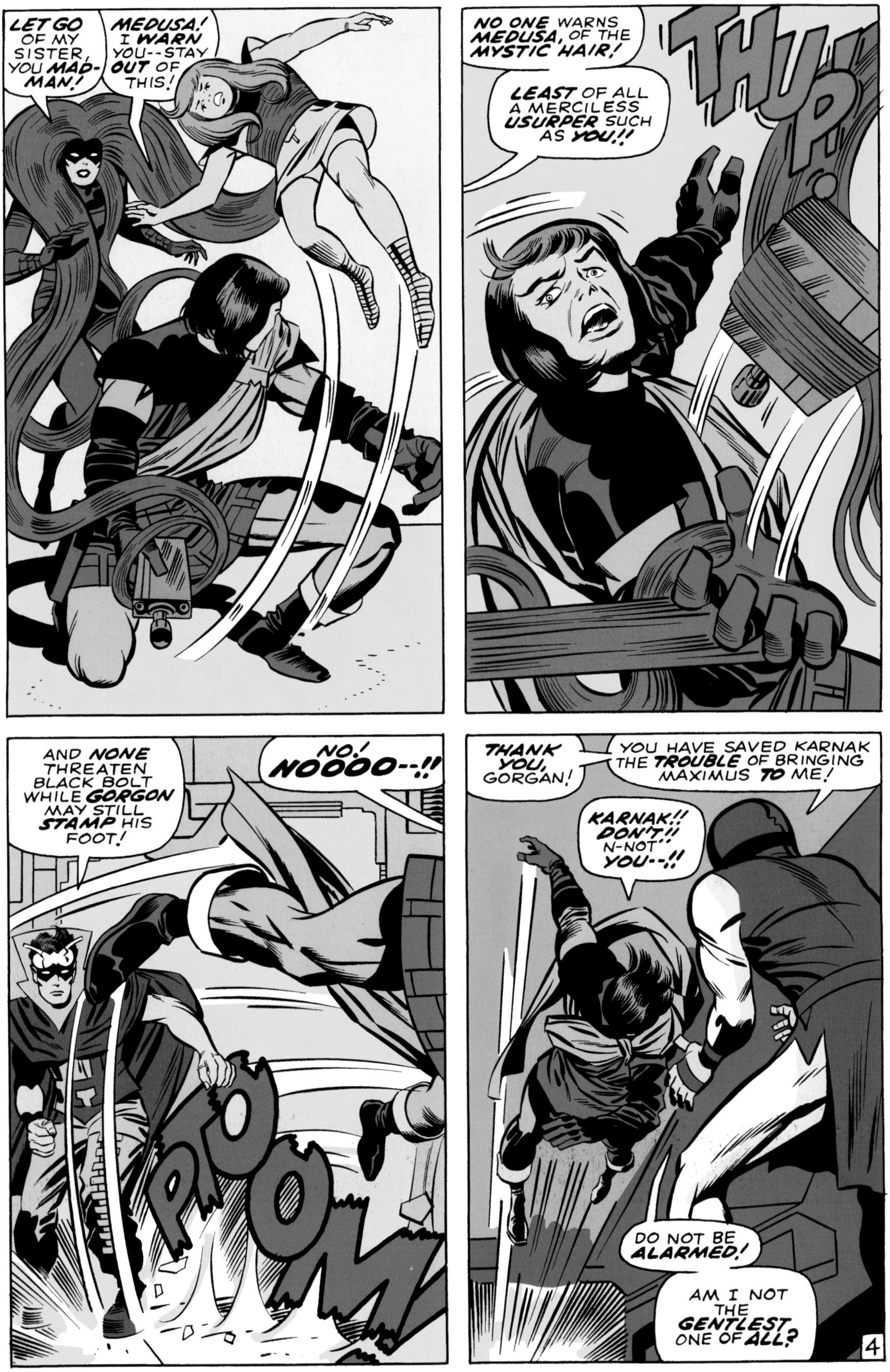
LET GO OF MY SISTER, YOU MAD-MAN!
MEDUSA! I WARN YOU--STAY OUT OF THIS!
NO ONE WARNS MEDUSA, OF THE MYSTIC HAIR!
LEAST OF ALL A MERCILESS USURPER SUCH AS YOU!!
THUP!
AND NONE THREATEN BLACK BOLT WHILE GORGON MAY STILL STAMP HIS FOOT!
NO! NOOOO--!!
PTOOM
THANK YOU, GORGAN!
YOU HAVE SAVED KARNAK THE TROUBLE OF BRINGING MAXIMUS TO ME!
KARNAK!! DON'T!! N-NOT YOU--!!
DO NOT BE ALARMED!
AM I NOT THE GENTLEST ONE OF ALL?
4

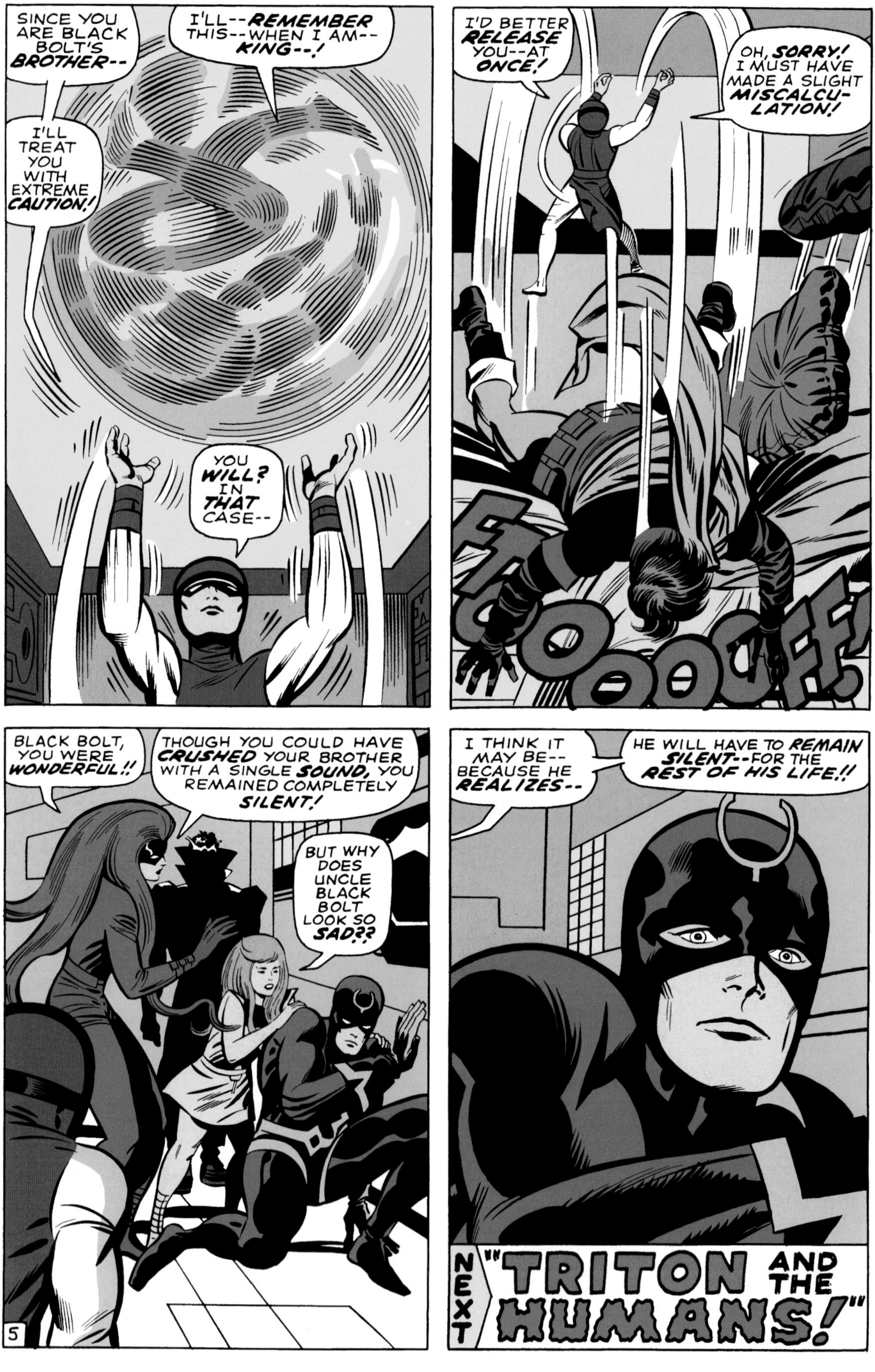

SINCE YOU ARE BLACK BOLT'S BROTHER--
I'LL TREAT YOU WITH EXTREME CAUTION!
I'LL--REMEMBER THIS--WHEN I AM--KING--!
YOU WILL? IN THAT CASE--
I'D BETTER RELEASE YOU--AT ONCE!
OH, SORRY! I MUST HAVE MADE A SLIGHT MISCALCULATION!
FTOOOOOF!
BLACK BOLT, YOU WERE WONDERFUL!!
THOUGH YOU COULD HAVE CRUSHED YOUR BROTHER WITH A SINGLE SOUND, YOU REMAINED COMPLETELY SILENT!
BUT WHY DOES UNCLE BLACK BOLT LOOK SO SAD??
5
I THINK IT MAY BE--BECAUSE HE REALIZES--
HE WILL HAVE TO REMAIN SILENT--FOR THE REST OF HIS LIFE!!
NEXT "TRITON AND THE HUMANS!"

CONTINUED IN *MARVEL MASTERWORKS: THE INHUMANS VOL. 1*

INHUMANS #2

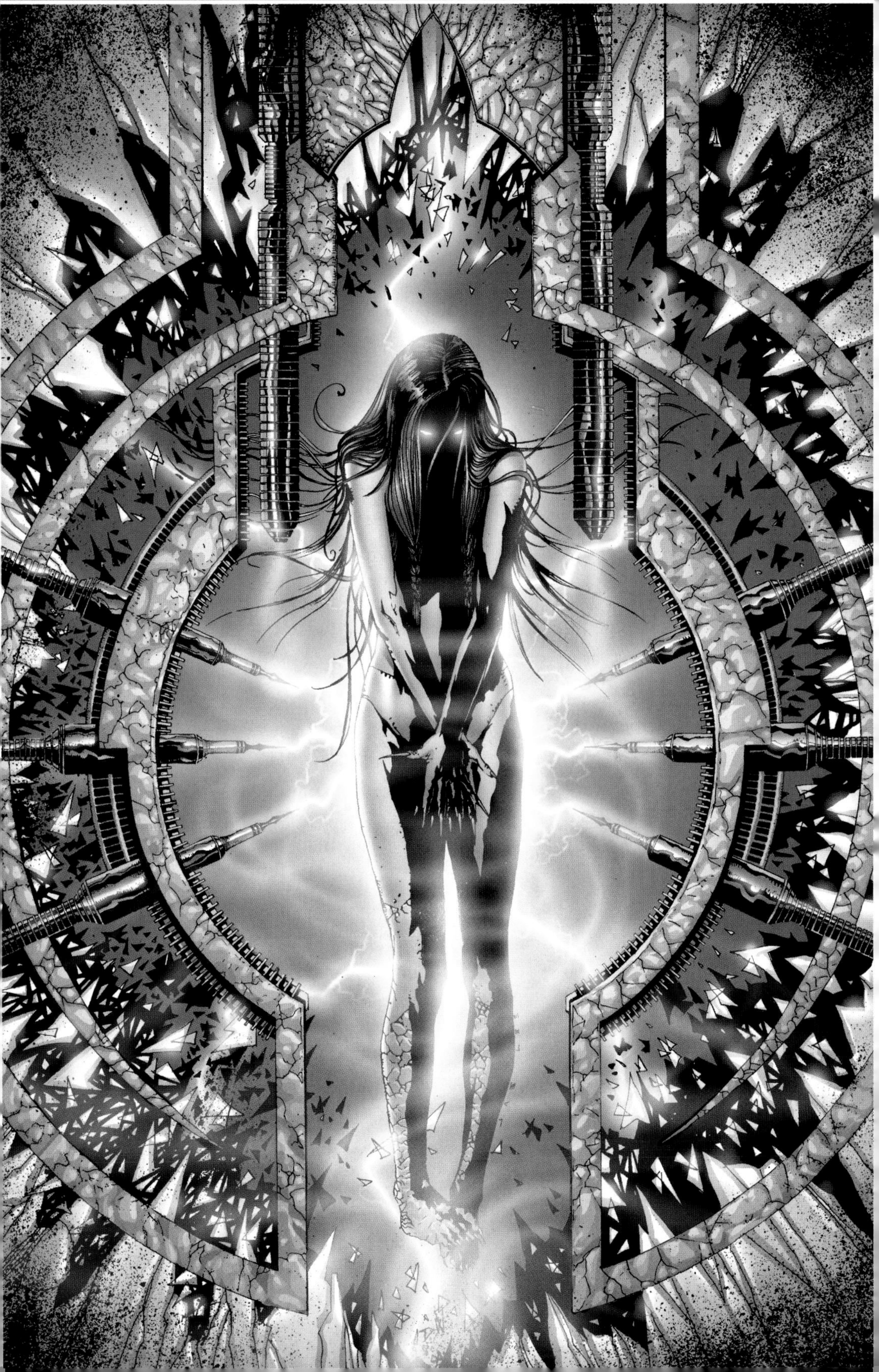

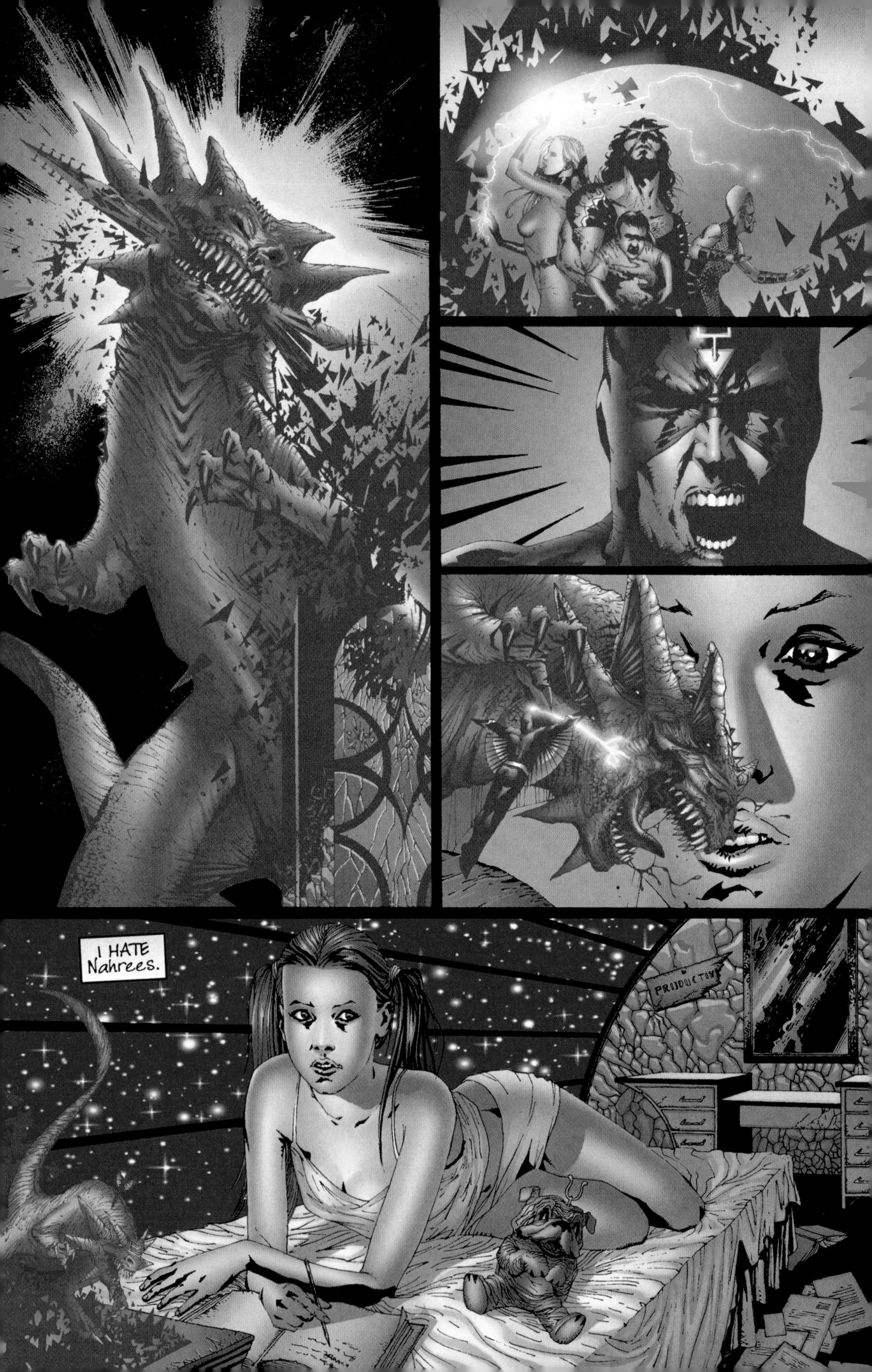
I HATE
Nahrees.

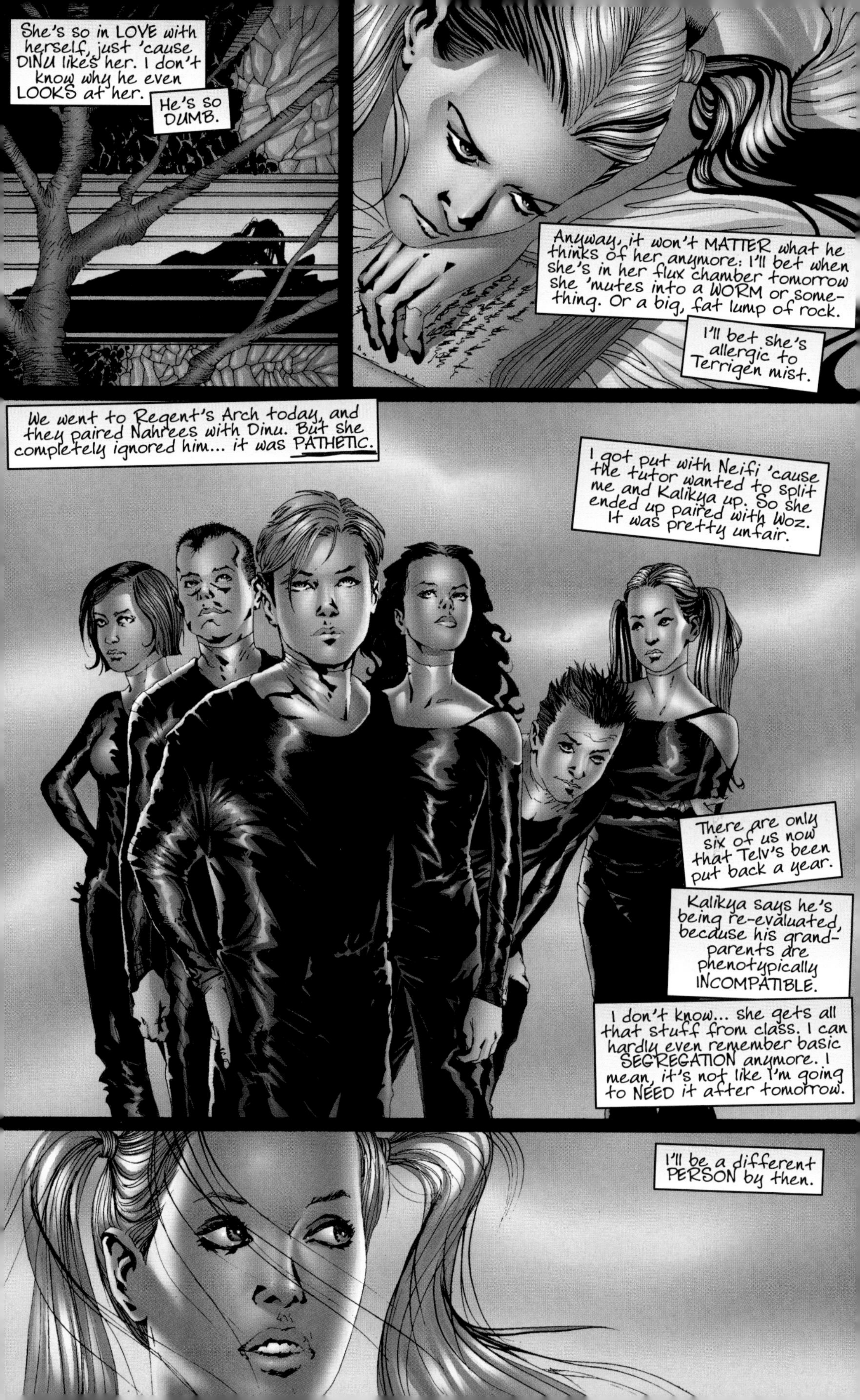

She's so in LOVE with herself, just 'cause DINU likes her. I don't know why he even LOOKS at her.
He's so DUMB.
Anyway, it won't MATTER what he thinks of her anymore: I'll bet when she's in her flux chamber tomorrow she 'mutes into a WORM or something. Or a big, fat lump of rock.
I'll bet she's allergic to Terrigen mist.
We went to Regent's Arch today, and they paired Nahrees with Dinu. But she completely ignored him... it was PATHETIC.
I got put with Neifi 'cause the tutor wanted to split me and Kalikya up. So she ended up paired with Woz. It was pretty unfair.
There are only six of us now that Telv's been put back a year.
Kalikya says he's being re-evaluated, because his grandparents are phenotypically INCOMPATIBLE.
I don't know... she gets all that stuff from class. I can hardly even remember basic SEGREGATION anymore. I mean, it's not like I'm going to NEED it after tomorrow.
I'll be a different PERSON by then.

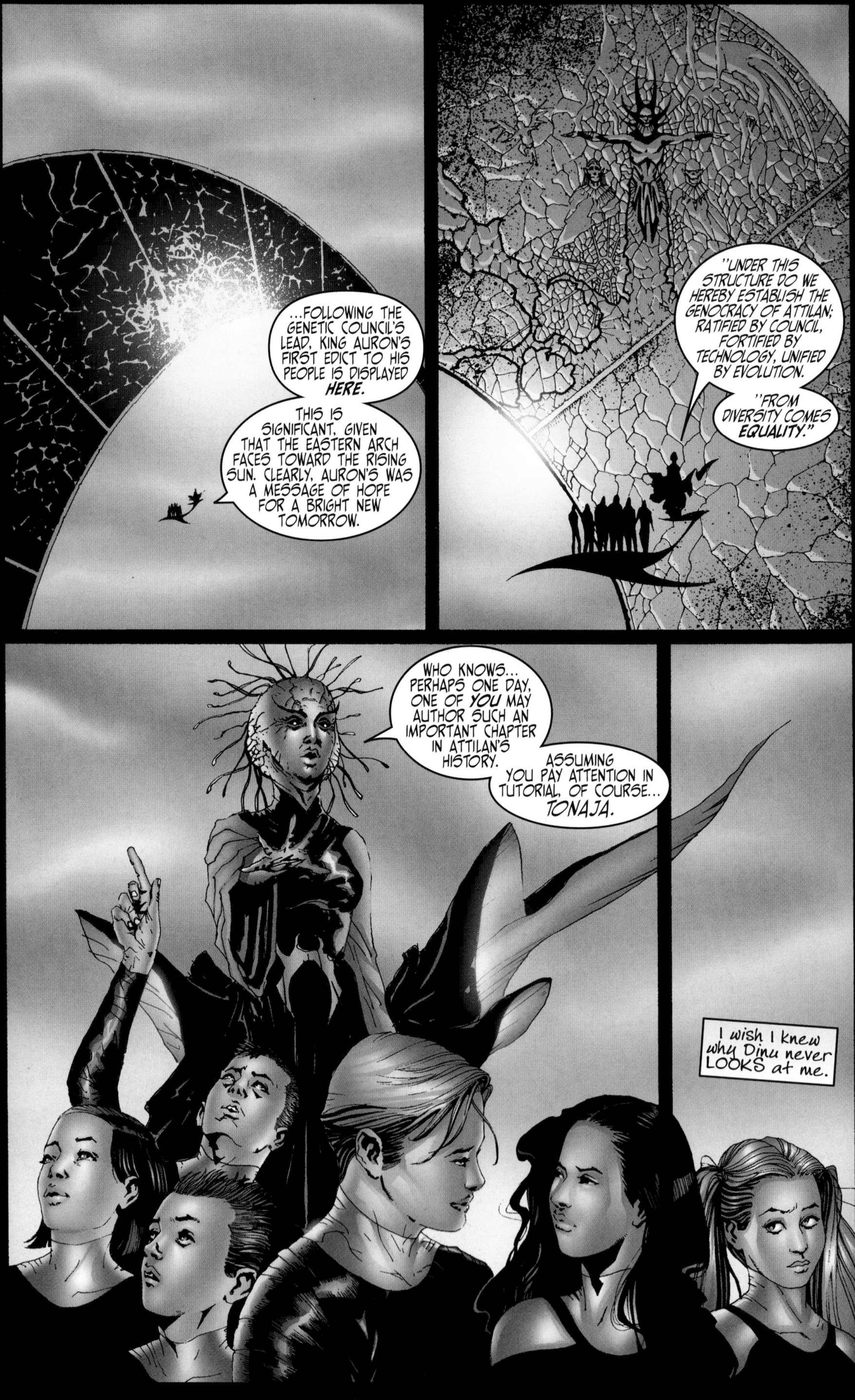
...FOLLOWING THE GENETIC COUNCIL'S LEAD, KING AURON'S FIRST EDICT TO HIS PEOPLE IS DISPLAYED **HERE**.
THIS IS SIGNIFICANT, GIVEN THAT THE EASTERN ARCH FACES TOWARD THE RISING SUN. CLEARLY, AURON'S WAS A MESSAGE OF HOPE FOR A BRIGHT NEW TOMORROW.
"UNDER THIS STRUCTURE DO WE HEREBY ESTABLISH THE GENOCRACY OF ATTILAN; RATIFIED BY COUNCIL, FORTIFIED BY TECHNOLOGY, UNIFIED BY EVOLUTION.
"FROM DIVERSITY COMES **EQUALITY**."
WHO KNOWS... PERHAPS ONE DAY, ONE OF **YOU** MAY AUTHOR SUCH AN IMPORTANT CHAPTER IN ATTILAN'S HISTORY.
ASSUMING YOU PAY ATTENTION IN TUTORIAL, OF COURSE... *TONAJA*.
I wish I knew why Dinu never LOOKS at me.

It's 'cause my nose is too big. Maybe I'll get lucky or something, and it'll disappedr completely.

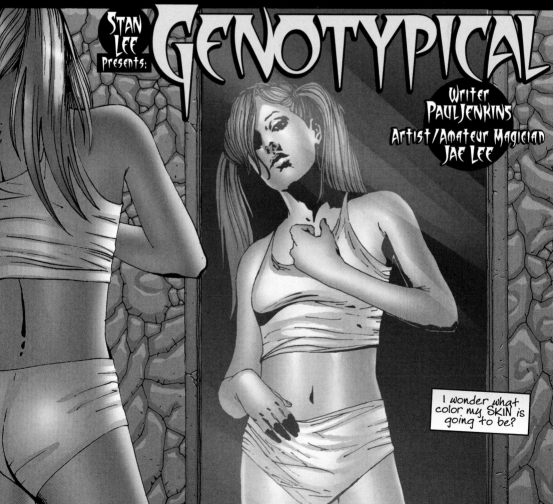

STAN LEE presents: **GENOTYPICAL**

Writer
Paul Jenkins

Artist/Amateur Magician
Jae Lee

I wonder what color my SKIN is going to be?

DAVE KEMP/AVALON
Colorist, Gent, Toff

RS&COMICRAFT/DL
Calligraphers

QUESADA & PALMIOTTI
Keepers of the Myth

NANCI DAKESIAN
Keeping Jae on his Toes

BOB HARRAS
High Priest

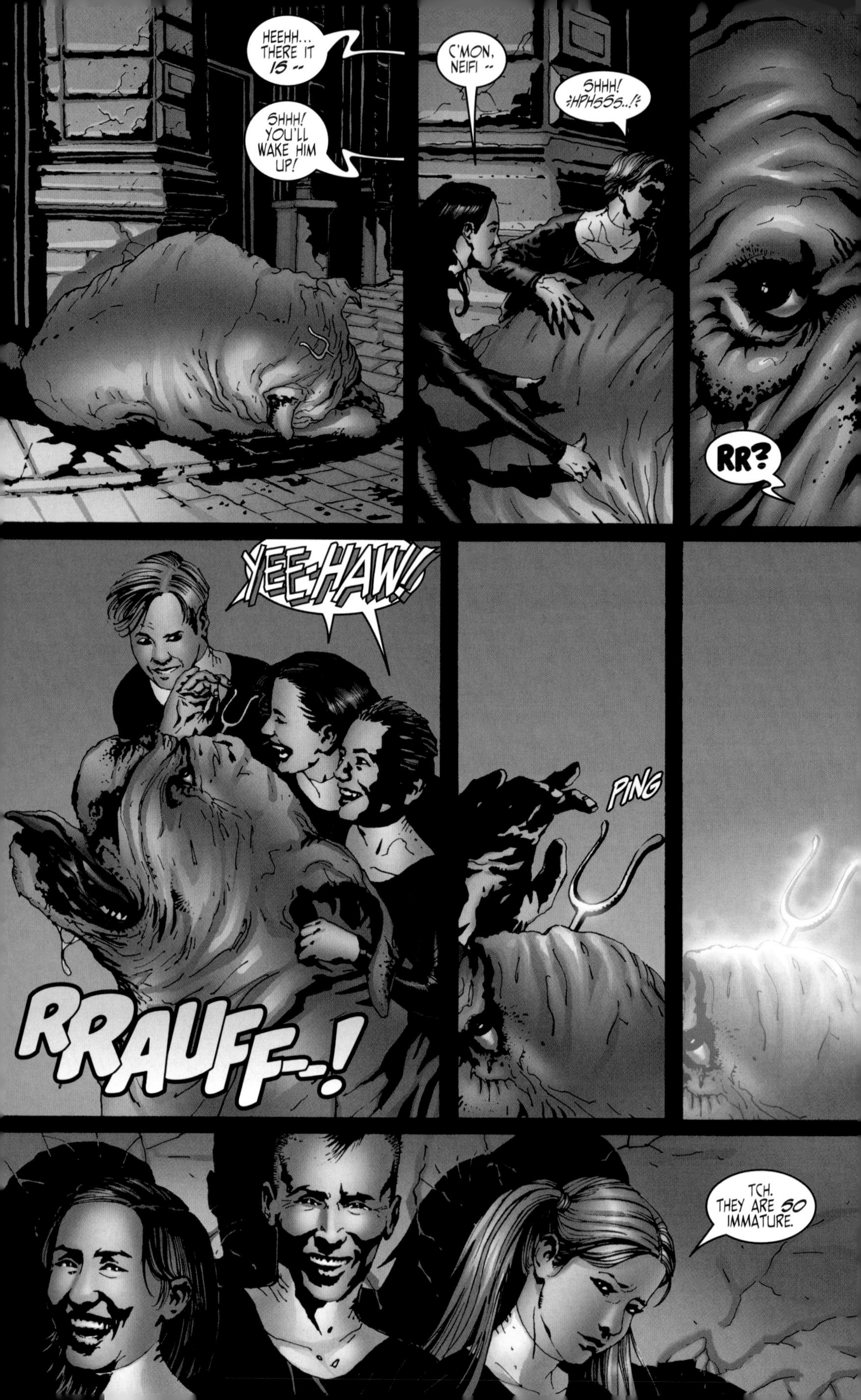
HEEHH... THERE IT IS --
SHHH! YOU'LL WAKE HIM UP!
C'MON, NEIFI --
SHHH! ≈HPHSSs..!≈
RR?
YEE-HAW!!
RRAUFF--!
PING
TCH. THEY ARE SO IMMATURE.

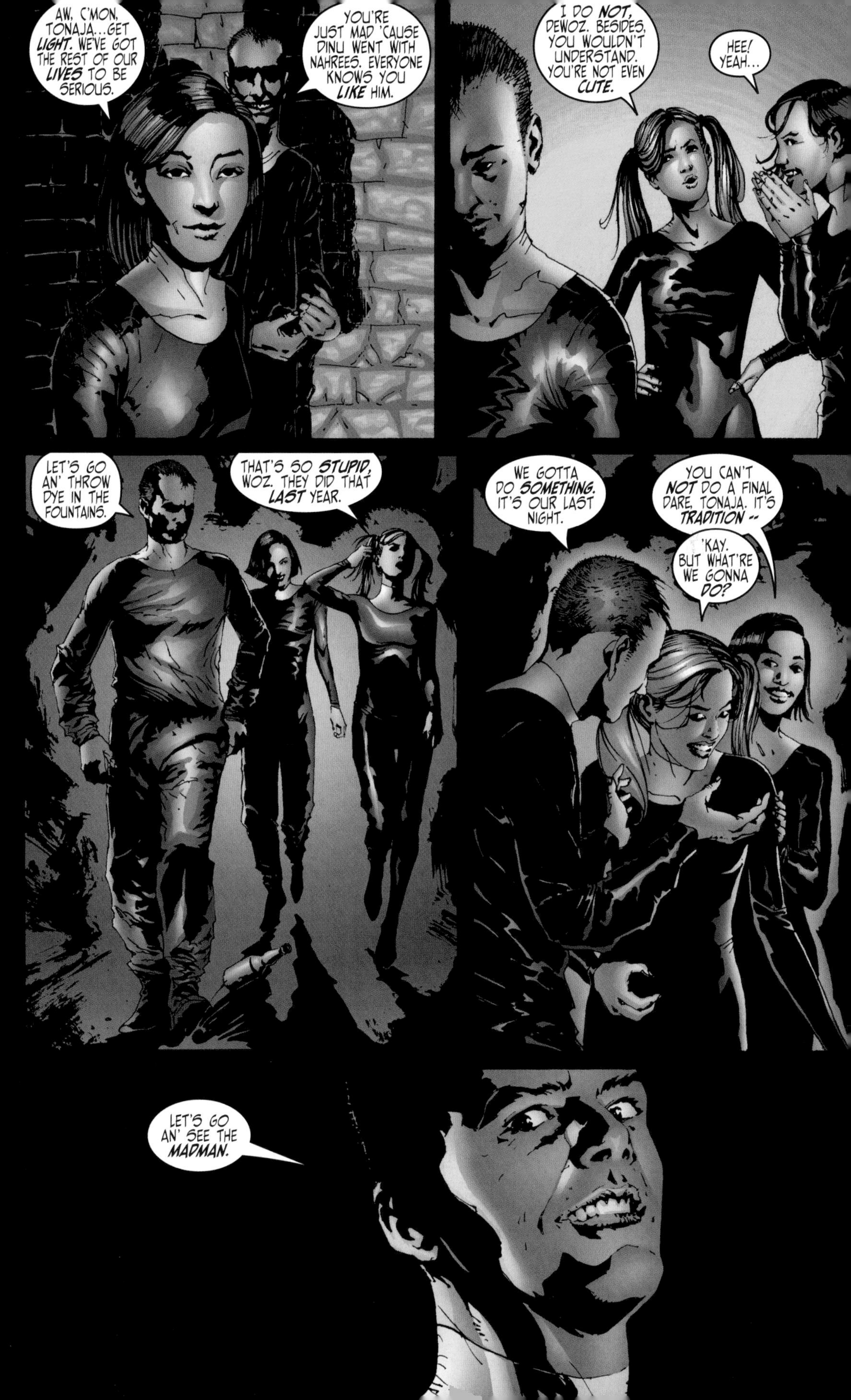
AW, C'MON, TONAJA...GET LIGHT. WE'VE GOT THE REST OF OUR LIVES TO BE SERIOUS.
YOU'RE JUST MAD 'CAUSE DINU WENT WITH NAHREES. EVERYONE KNOWS YOU LIKE HIM.
I DO NOT, DEWOZ. BESIDES, YOU WOULDN'T UNDERSTAND. YOU'RE NOT EVEN CUTE.
HEE! YEAH...
LET'S GO AN' THROW DYE IN THE FOUNTAINS.
THAT'S SO STUPID, WOZ. THEY DID THAT LAST YEAR.
WE GOTTA DO SOMETHING. IT'S OUR LAST NIGHT.
YOU CAN'T NOT DO A FINAL DARE, TONAJA. IT'S TRADITION --
'KAY. BUT WHAT'RE WE GONNA DO?
LET'S GO AN' SEE THE MADMAN.

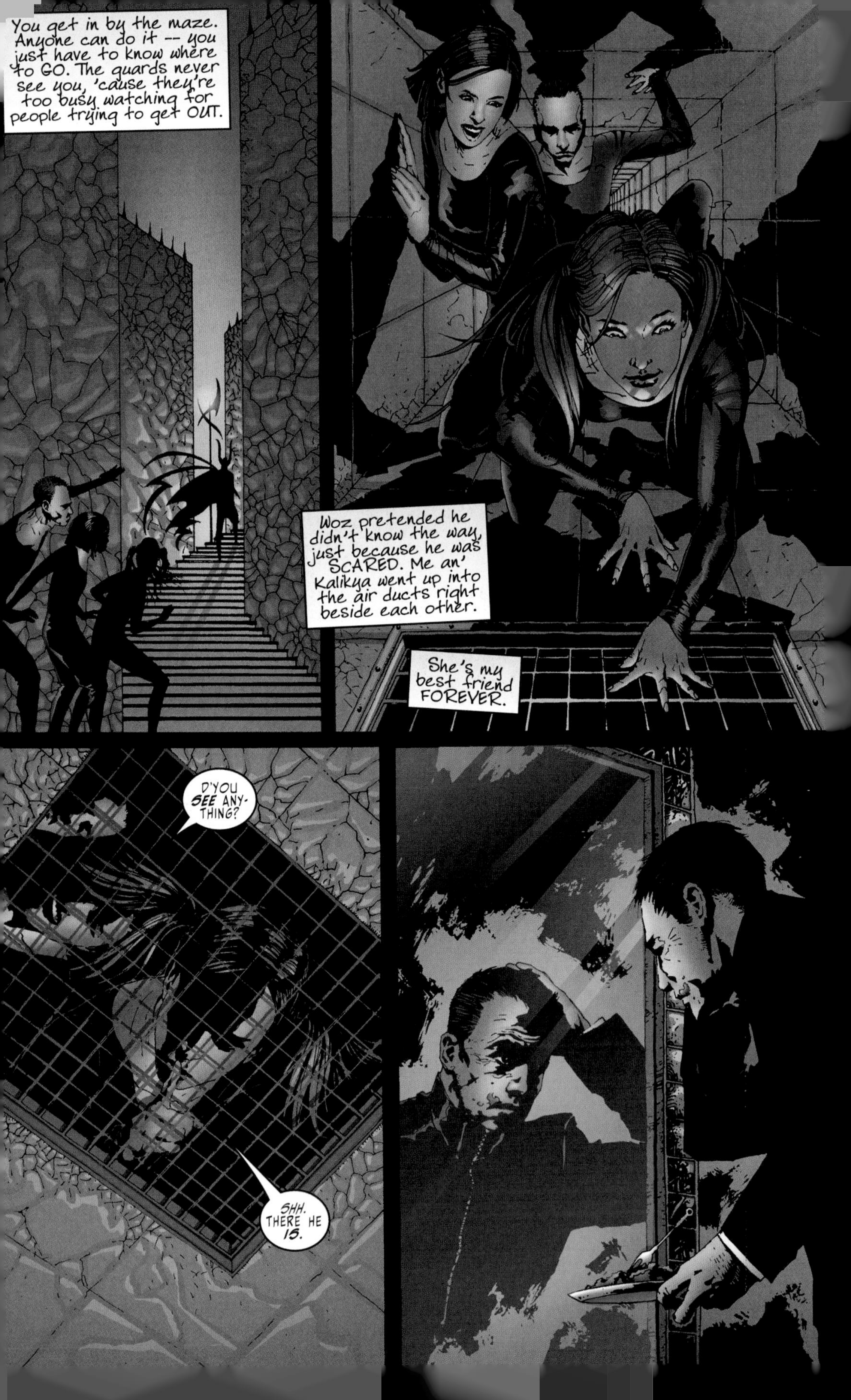
You get in by the maze. Anyone can do it -- you just have to know where to GO. The guards never see you, 'cause they're too busy watching for people trying to get OUT.
Woz pretended he didn't know the way, just because he was SCARED. Me an' Kalikya went up into the air ducts right beside each other.
She's my best friend FOREVER.
D'YOU SEE ANYTHING?
SHH. THERE HE IS.

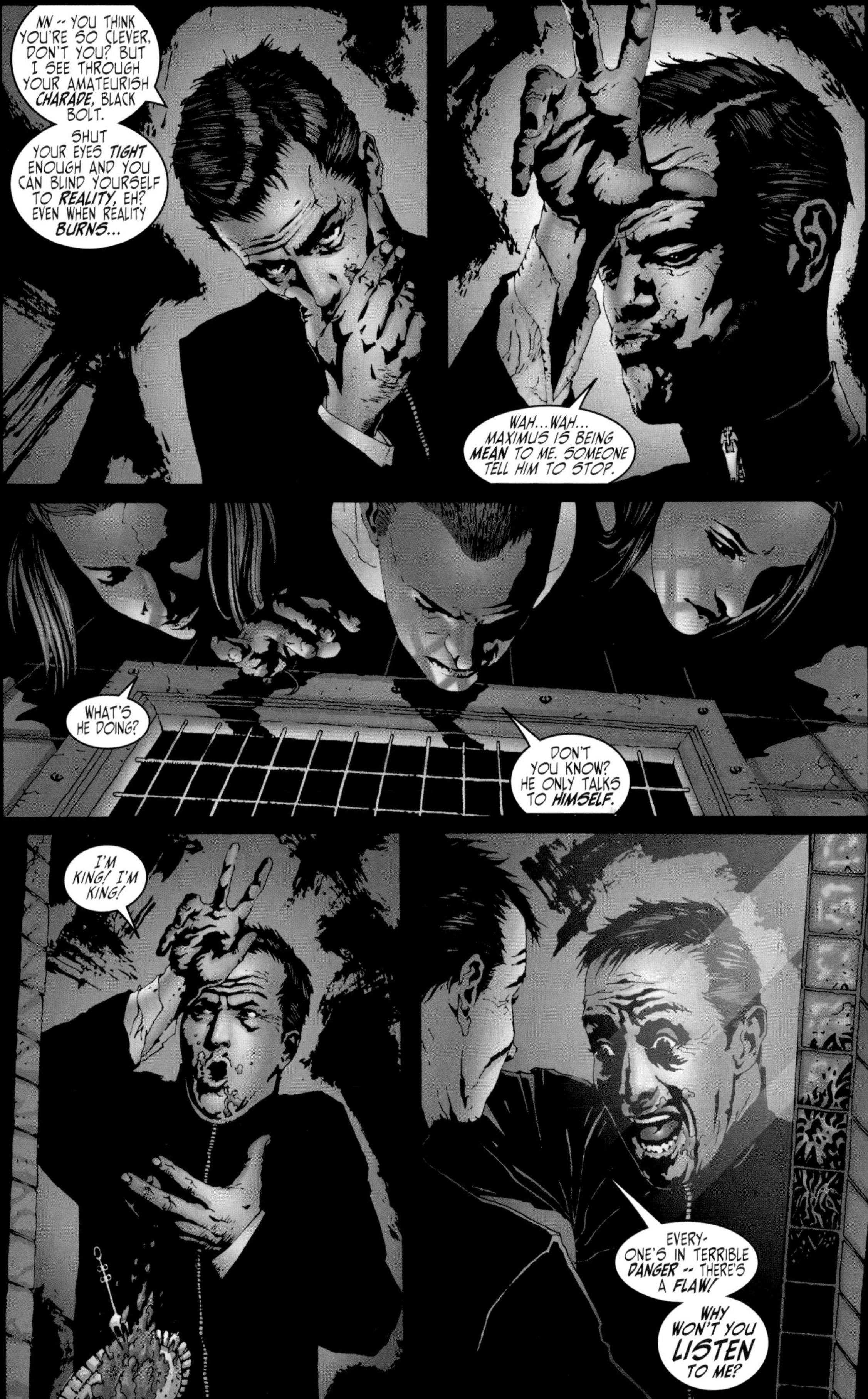
NN -- YOU THINK YOU'RE SO CLEVER, DON'T YOU? BUT I SEE THROUGH YOUR AMATEURISH CHARADE, BLACK BOLT.
SHUT YOUR EYES TIGHT ENOUGH AND YOU CAN BLIND YOURSELF TO REALITY, EH? EVEN WHEN REALITY BURNS...
WAH...WAH... MAXIMUS IS BEING MEAN TO ME. SOMEONE TELL HIM TO STOP.
WHAT'S HE DOING?
DON'T YOU KNOW? HE ONLY TALKS TO HIMSELF.
I'M KING! I'M KING!
EVERY-ONE'S IN TERRIBLE DANGER -- THERE'S A FLAW!
WHY WON'T YOU LISTEN TO ME?

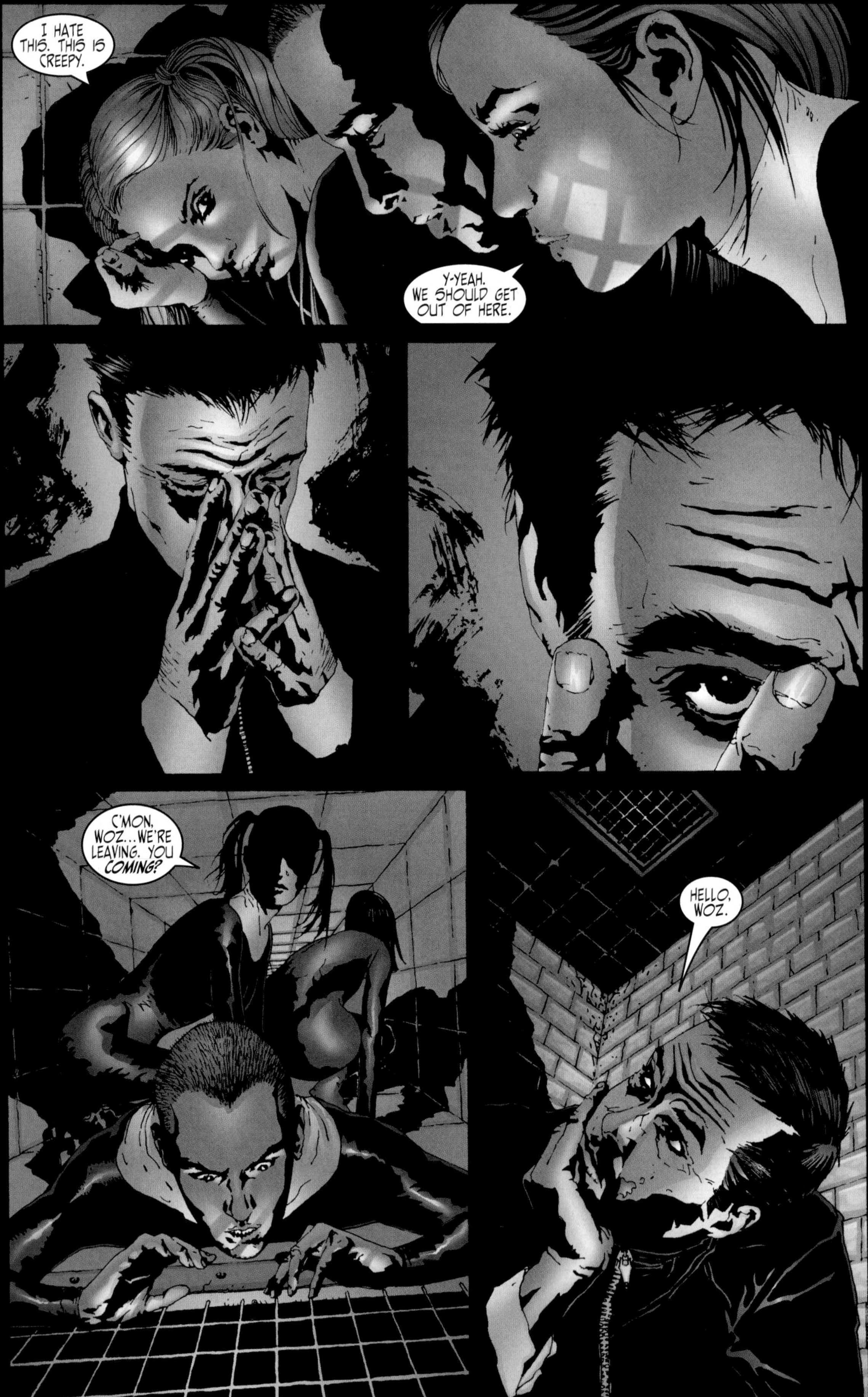
I HATE THIS. THIS IS CREEPY.
Y-YEAH. WE SHOULD GET OUT OF HERE.
C'MON, WOZ...WE'RE LEAVING. YOU *COMING?*
HELLO, WOZ.

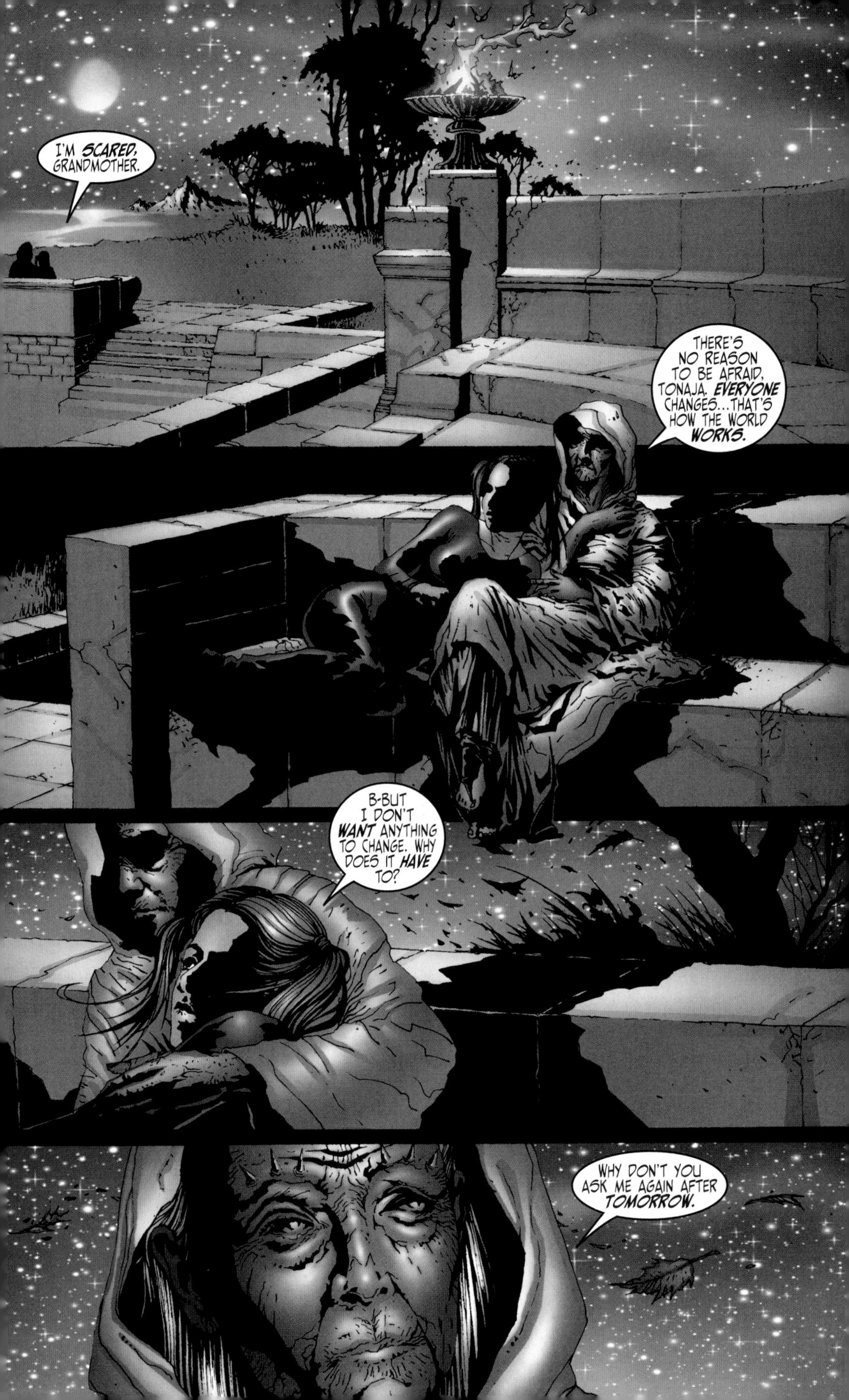
I'M SCARED, GRANDMOTHER.
THERE'S NO REASON TO BE AFRAID, TONAJA. EVERYONE CHANGES...THAT'S HOW THE WORLD WORKS.
B-BUT I DON'T WANT ANYTHING TO CHANGE. WHY DOES IT HAVE TO?
WHY DON'T YOU ASK ME AGAIN AFTER TOMORROW.

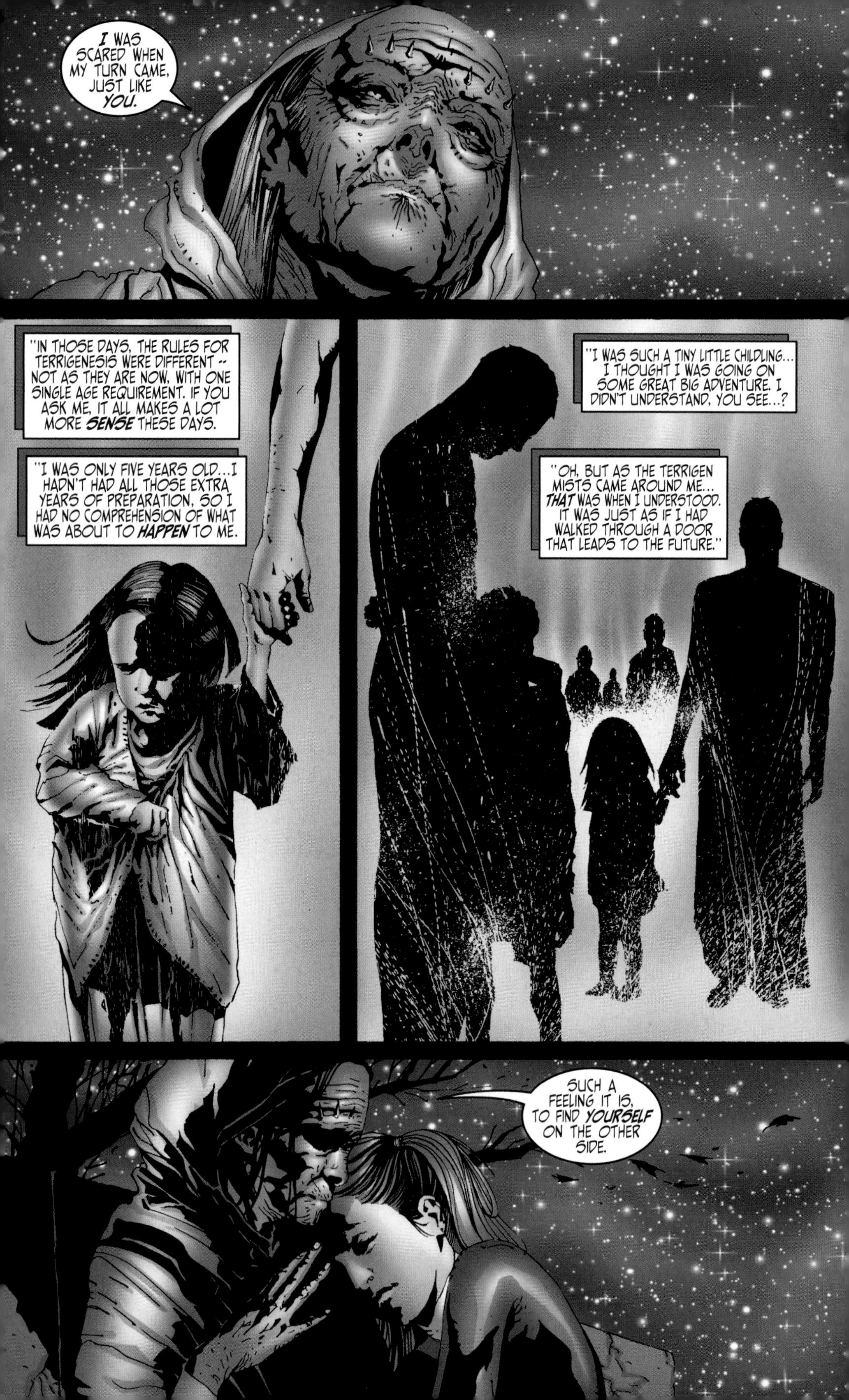
I WAS SCARED WHEN MY TURN CAME, JUST LIKE YOU.
"IN THOSE DAYS, THE RULES FOR TERRIGENESIS WERE DIFFERENT -- NOT AS THEY ARE NOW, WITH ONE SINGLE AGE REQUIREMENT. IF YOU ASK ME, IT ALL MAKES A LOT MORE SENSE THESE DAYS.
"I WAS ONLY FIVE YEARS OLD...I HADN'T HAD ALL THOSE EXTRA YEARS OF PREPARATION, SO I HAD NO COMPREHENSION OF WHAT WAS ABOUT TO HAPPEN TO ME.
"I WAS SUCH A TINY LITTLE CHILDLING... I THOUGHT I WAS GOING ON SOME GREAT BIG ADVENTURE. I DIDN'T UNDERSTAND, YOU SEE...?
"OH, BUT AS THE TERRIGEN MISTS CAME AROUND ME... THAT WAS WHEN I UNDERSTOOD. IT WAS JUST AS IF I HAD WALKED THROUGH A DOOR THAT LEADS TO THE FUTURE."
SUCH A FEELING IT IS, TO FIND YOURSELF ON THE OTHER SIDE.

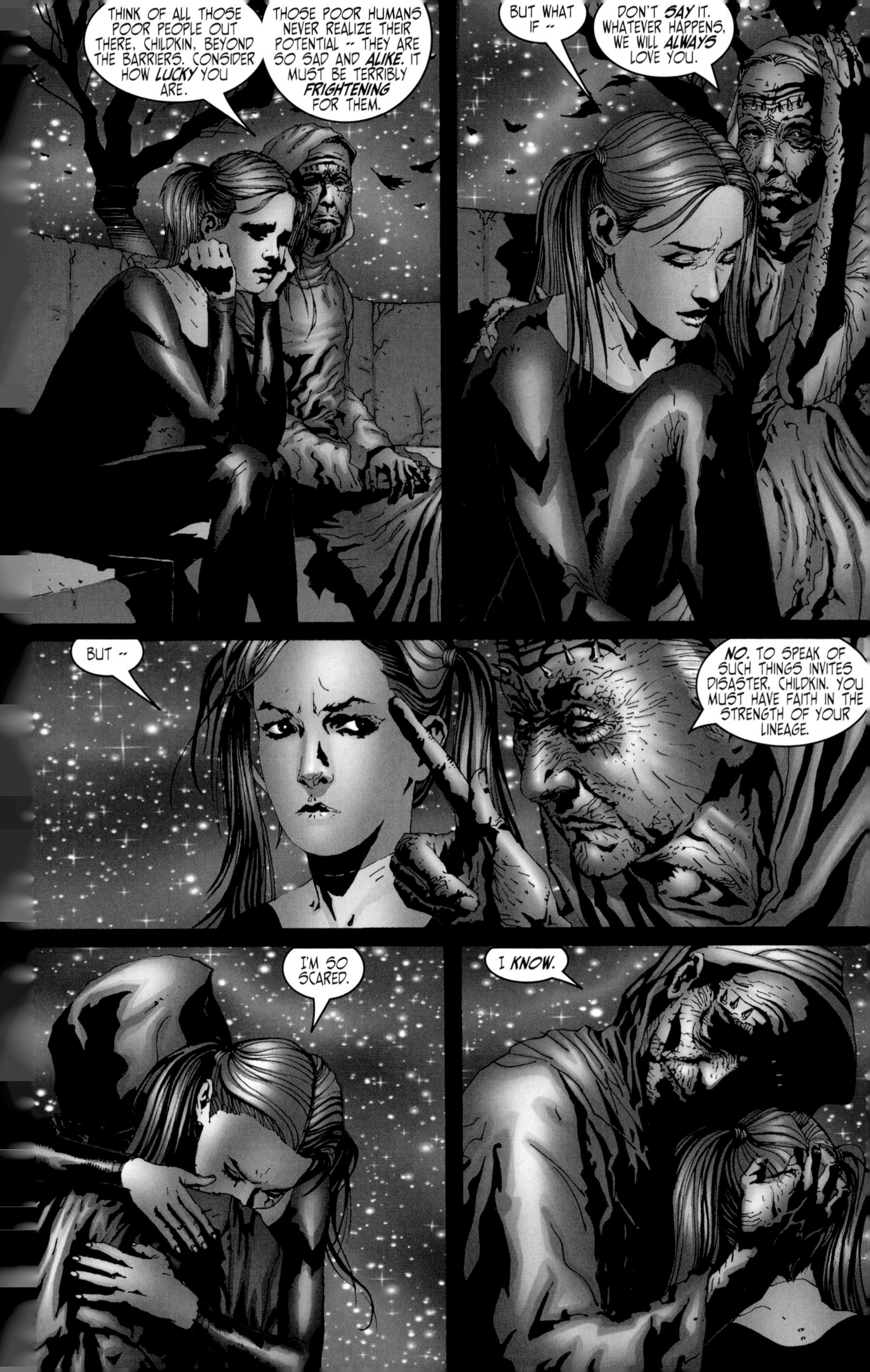
THINK OF ALL THOSE POOR PEOPLE OUT THERE, CHILDKIN, BEYOND THE BARRIERS. CONSIDER HOW LUCKY YOU ARE.
THOSE POOR HUMANS NEVER REALIZE THEIR POTENTIAL -- THEY ARE SO SAD AND ALIKE. IT MUST BE TERRIBLY FRIGHTENING FOR THEM.
BUT WHAT IF --
DON'T SAY IT. WHATEVER HAPPENS, WE WILL ALWAYS LOVE YOU.
BUT --
NO. TO SPEAK OF SUCH THINGS INVITES DISASTER, CHILDKIN. YOU MUST HAVE FAITH IN THE STRENGTH OF YOUR LINEAGE.
I'M SO SCARED.
I KNOW.

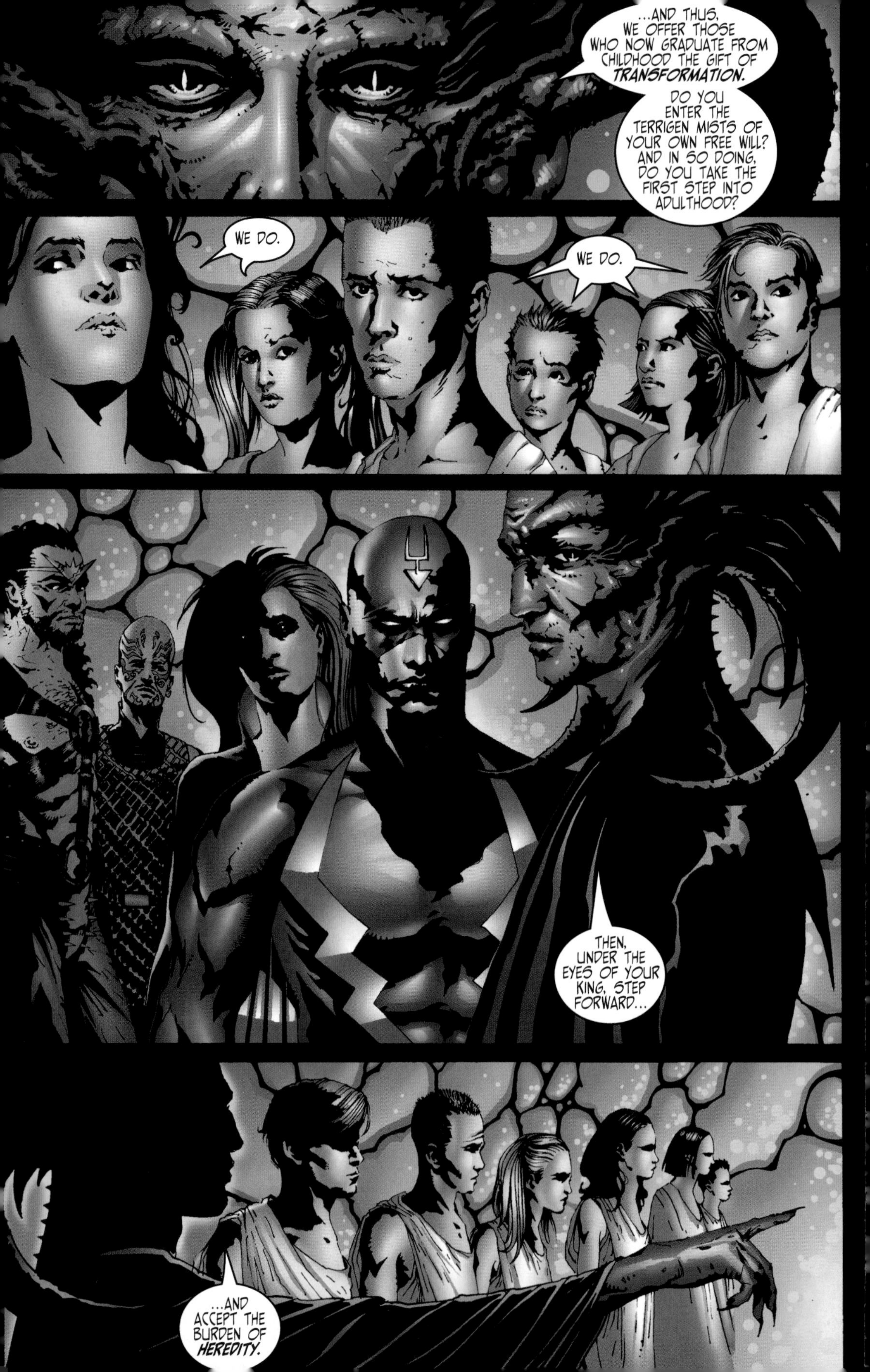
...AND THUS, WE OFFER THOSE WHO NOW GRADUATE FROM CHILDHOOD THE GIFT OF TRANSFORMATION.
DO YOU ENTER THE TERRIGEN MISTS OF YOUR OWN FREE WILL? AND IN SO DOING, DO YOU TAKE THE FIRST STEP INTO ADULTHOOD?
WE DO.
WE DO.
THEN, UNDER THE EYES OF YOUR KING, STEP FORWARD...
...AND ACCEPT THE BURDEN OF HEREDITY.

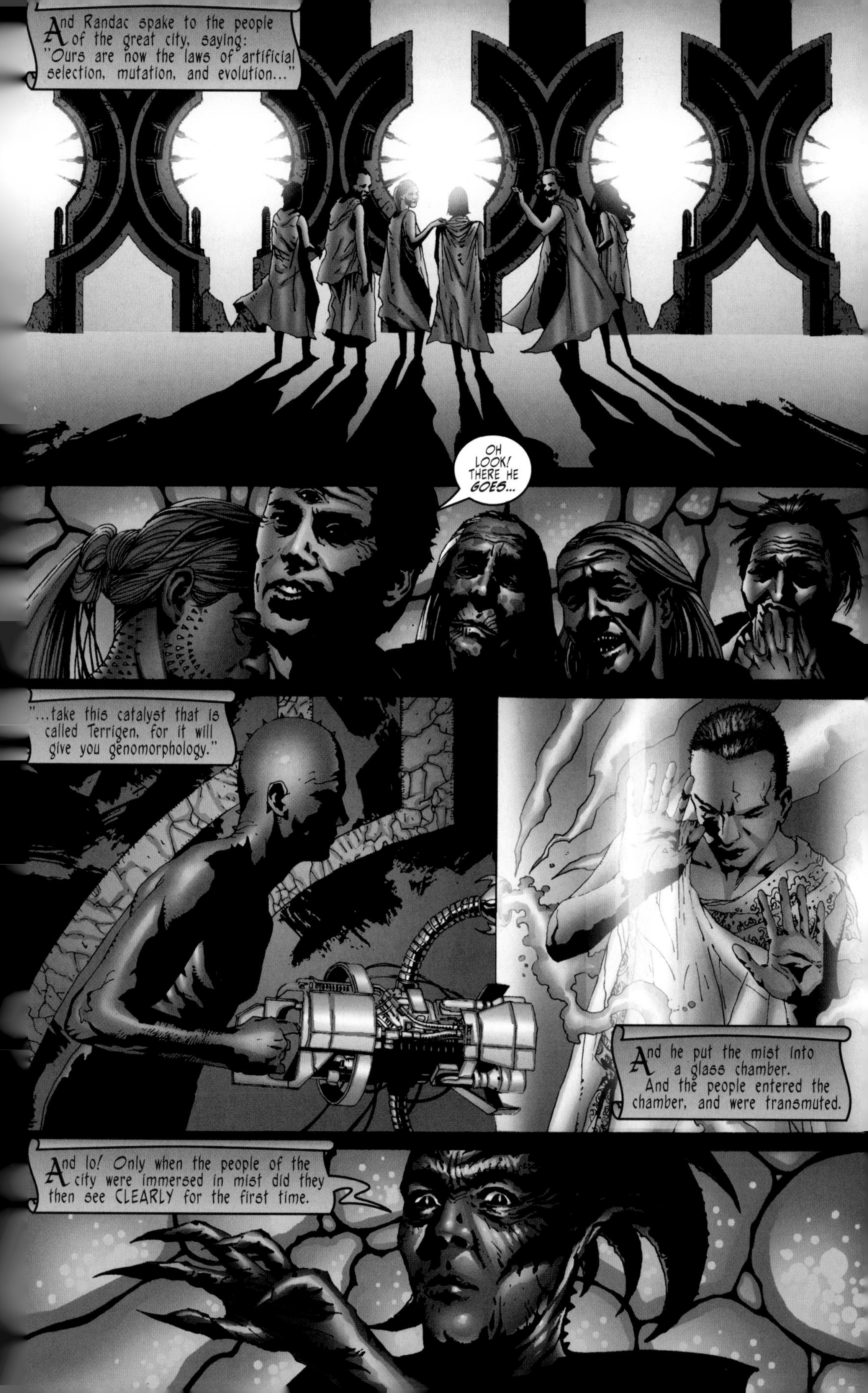
And Randac spake to the people of the great city, saying: "Ours are now the laws of artificial selection, mutation, and evolution..."
OH LOOK! THERE HE GOES...
"...take this catalyst that is called Terrigen, for it will give you genomorphology."
And he put the mist into a glass chamber. And the people entered the chamber, and were transmuted.
And lo! Only when the people of the city were immersed in mist did they then see CLEARLY for the first time.

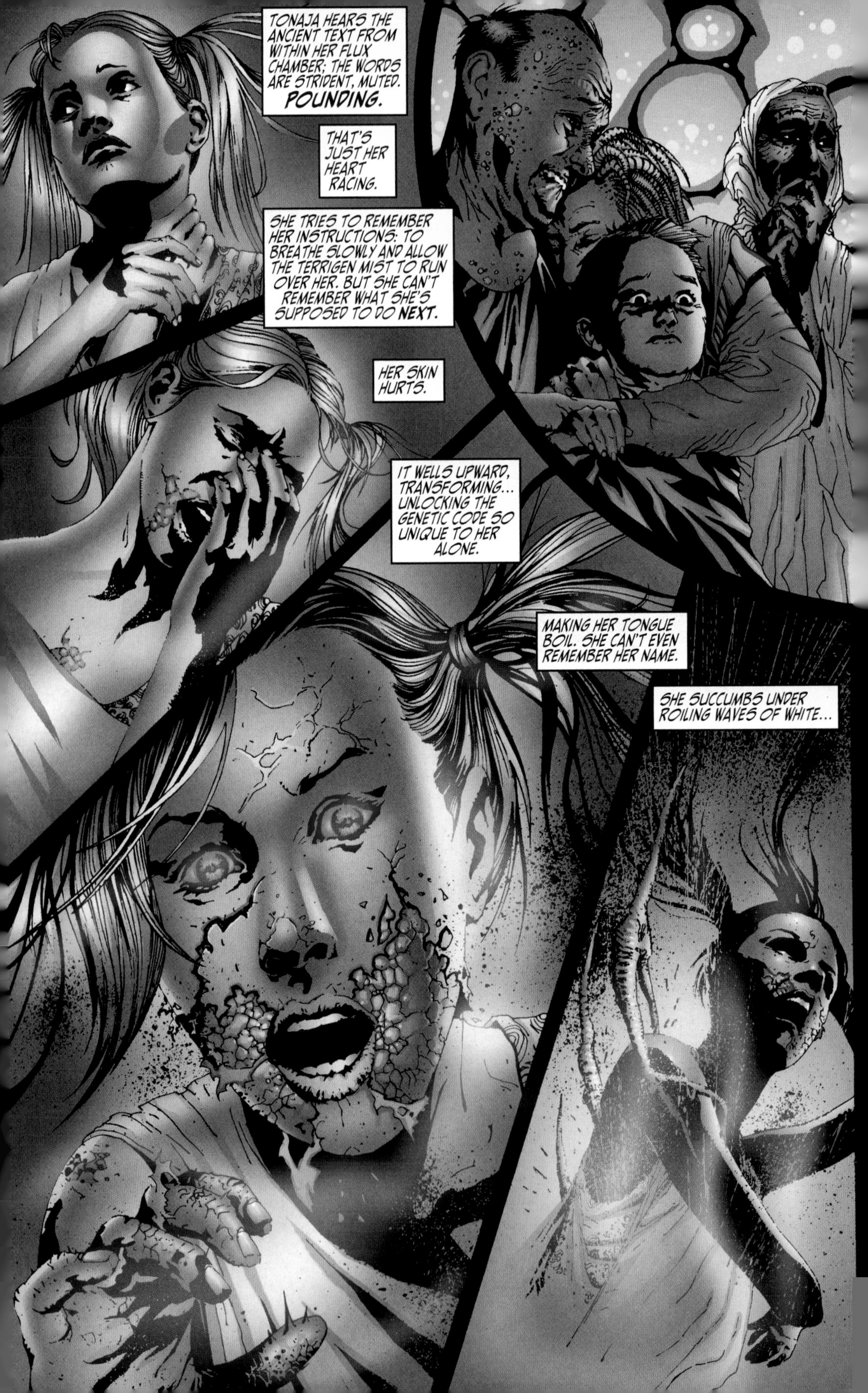
TONAJA HEARS THE ANCIENT TEXT FROM WITHIN HER FLUX CHAMBER; THE WORDS ARE STRIDENT, MUTED. POUNDING.
THAT'S JUST HER HEART RACING.
SHE TRIES TO REMEMBER HER INSTRUCTIONS: TO BREATHE SLOWLY AND ALLOW THE TERRIGEN MIST TO RUN OVER HER. BUT SHE CAN'T REMEMBER WHAT SHE'S SUPPOSED TO DO NEXT.
HER SKIN HURTS.
IT WELLS UPWARD, TRANSFORMING... UNLOCKING THE GENETIC CODE SO UNIQUE TO HER ALONE.
MAKING HER TONGUE BOIL. SHE CAN'T EVEN REMEMBER HER NAME.
SHE SUCCUMBS UNDER ROILING WAVES OF WHITE...

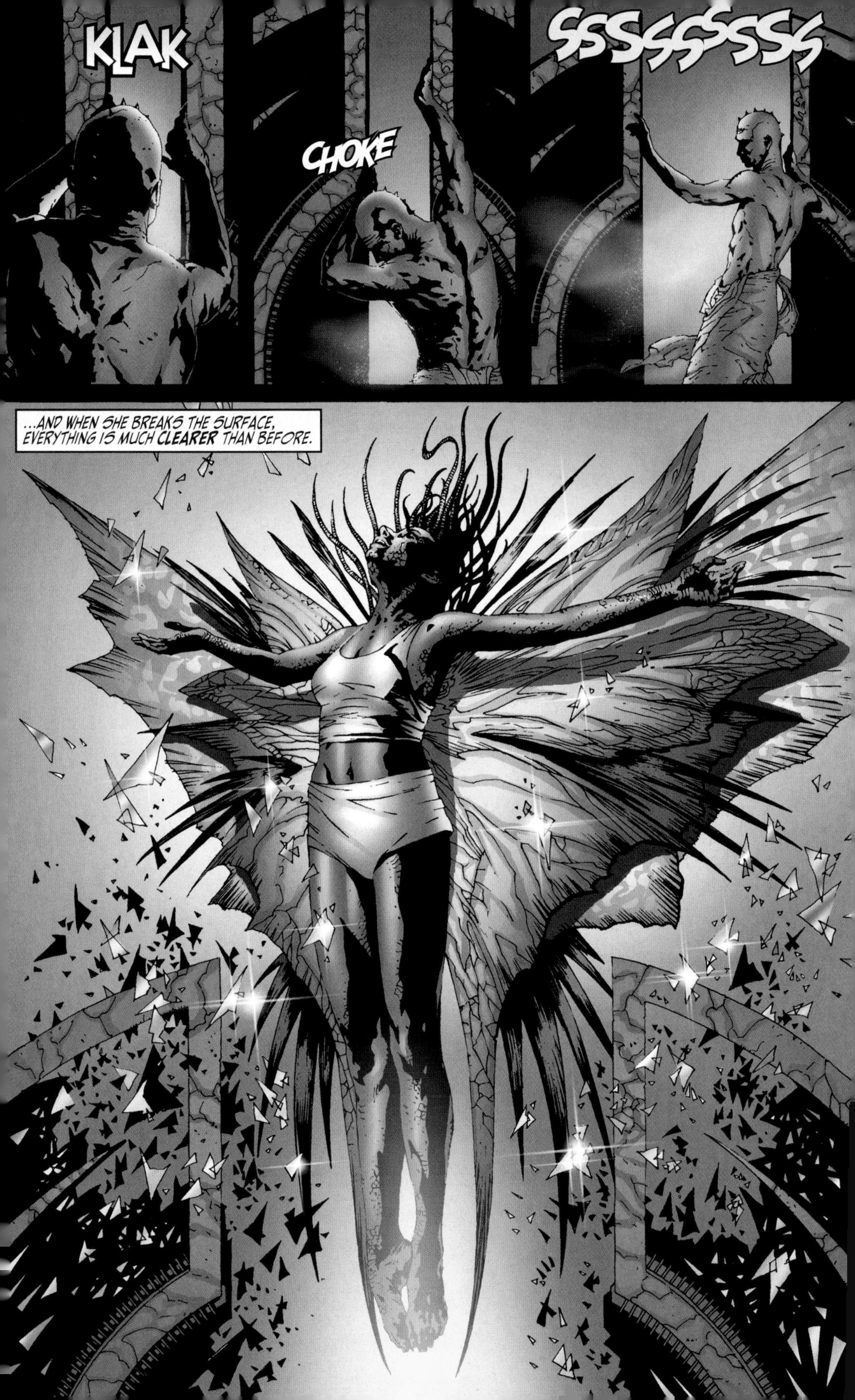
KLAK
CHOKE
SSSSSSSSS
...AND WHEN SHE BREAKS THE SURFACE, EVERYTHING IS MUCH CLEARER THAN BEFORE.

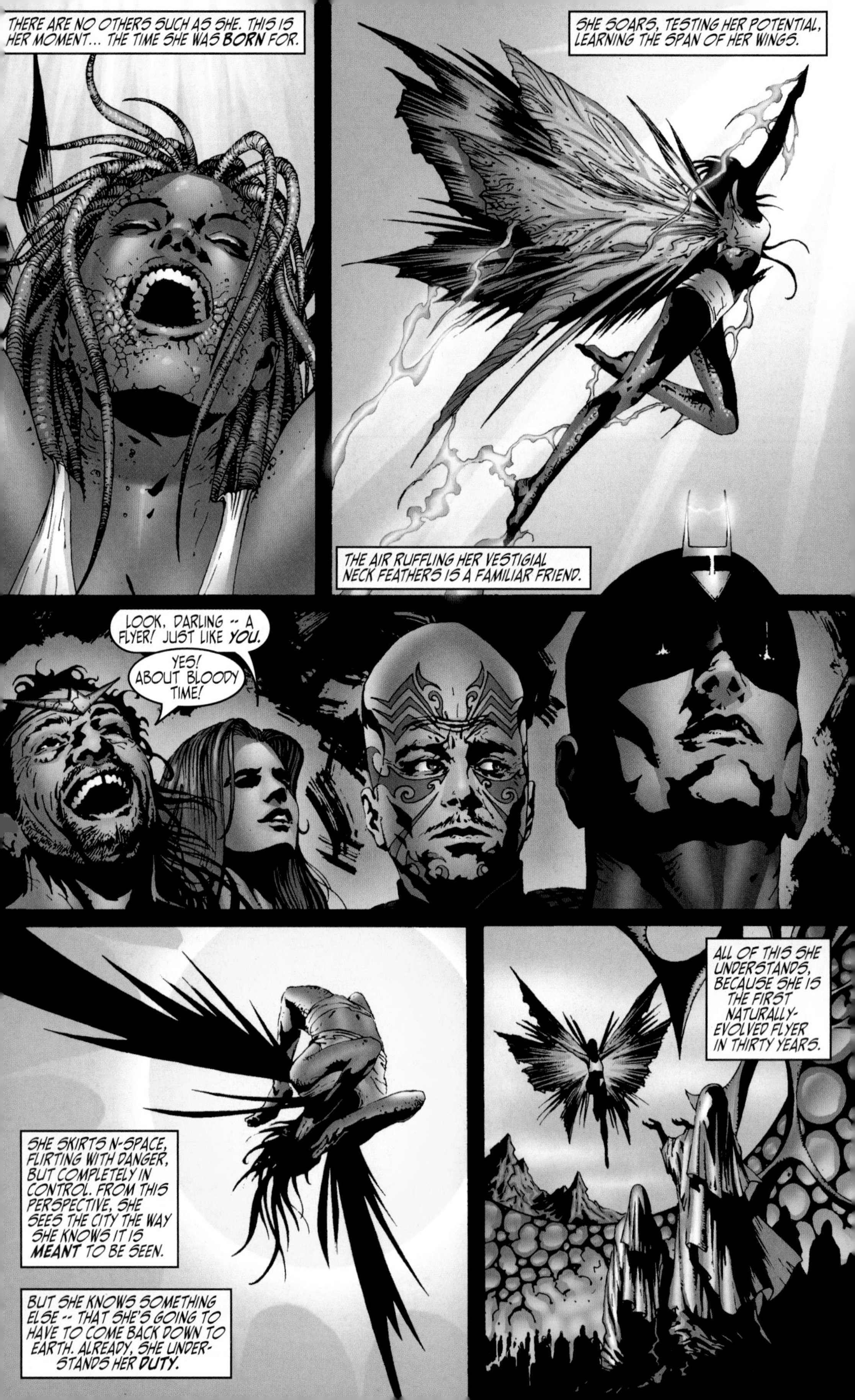
THERE ARE NO OTHERS SUCH AS SHE. THIS IS HER MOMENT... THE TIME SHE WAS BORN FOR.
SHE SOARS, TESTING HER POTENTIAL, LEARNING THE SPAN OF HER WINGS.
THE AIR RUFFLING HER VESTIGIAL NECK FEATHERS IS A FAMILIAR FRIEND.
LOOK, DARLING -- A FLYER! JUST LIKE YOU.
YES! ABOUT BLOODY TIME!
SHE SKIRTS N-SPACE, FLIRTING WITH DANGER, BUT COMPLETELY IN CONTROL. FROM THIS PERSPECTIVE, SHE SEES THE CITY THE WAY SHE KNOWS IT IS MEANT TO BE SEEN.
BUT SHE KNOWS SOMETHING ELSE -- THAT SHE'S GOING TO HAVE TO COME BACK DOWN TO EARTH. ALREADY, SHE UNDERSTANDS HER DUTY.
ALL OF THIS SHE UNDERSTANDS, BECAUSE SHE IS THE FIRST NATURALLY-EVOLVED FLYER IN THIRTY YEARS.

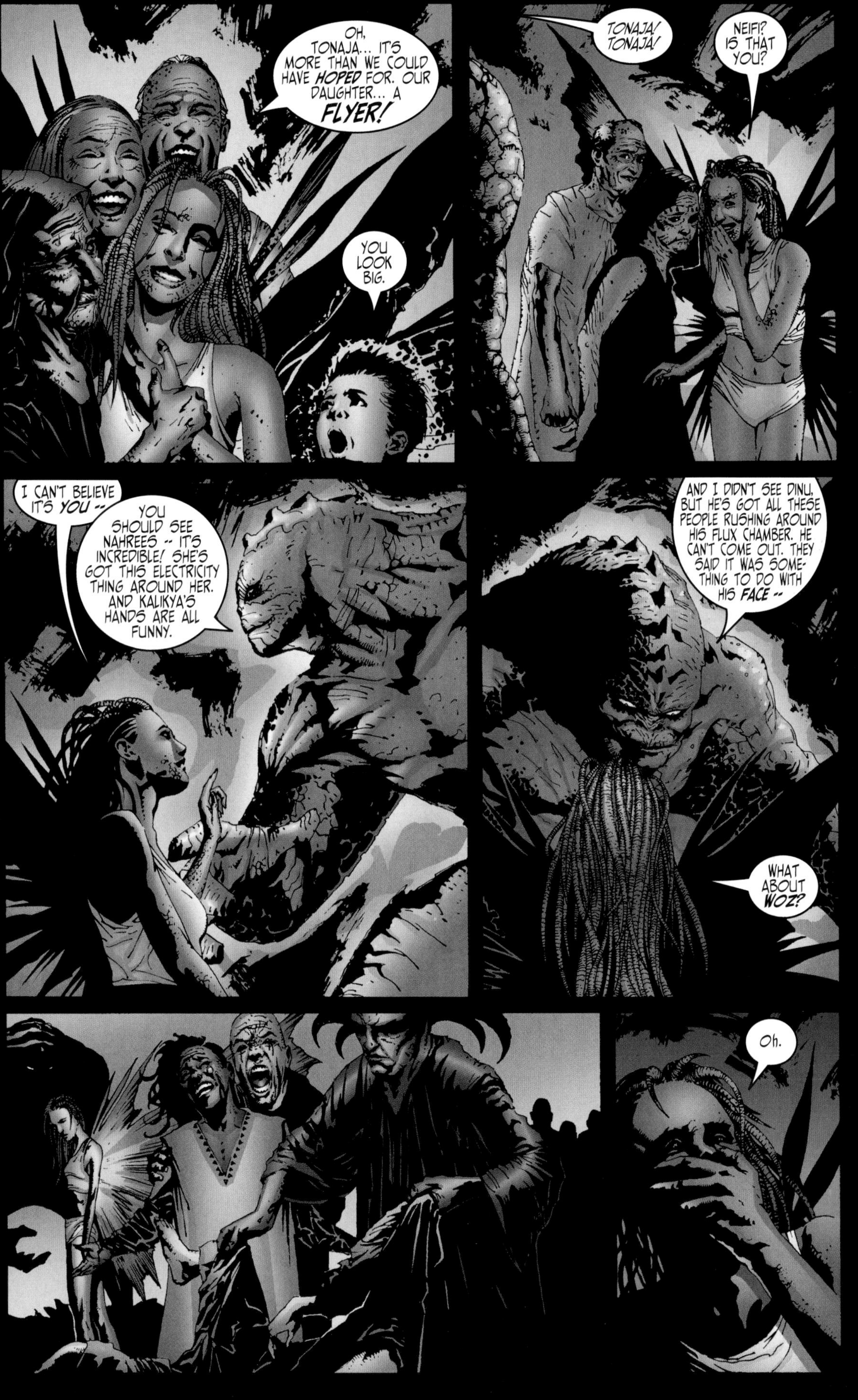

OH, TONAJA... IT'S MORE THAN WE COULD HAVE HOPED FOR. OUR DAUGHTER... A FLYER!
YOU LOOK BIG.
TONAJA! TONAJA!
NEIFI? IS THAT YOU?
I CAN'T BELIEVE IT'S YOU --
YOU SHOULD SEE NAHREES -- IT'S INCREDIBLE! SHE'S GOT THIS ELECTRICITY THING AROUND HER. AND KALIKYA'S HANDS ARE ALL FUNNY.
AND I DIDN'T SEE DINU, BUT HE'S GOT ALL THESE PEOPLE RUSHING AROUND HIS FLUX CHAMBER. HE CAN'T COME OUT. THEY SAID IT WAS SOMETHING TO DO WITH HIS FACE --
WHAT ABOUT WOZ?
Oh.

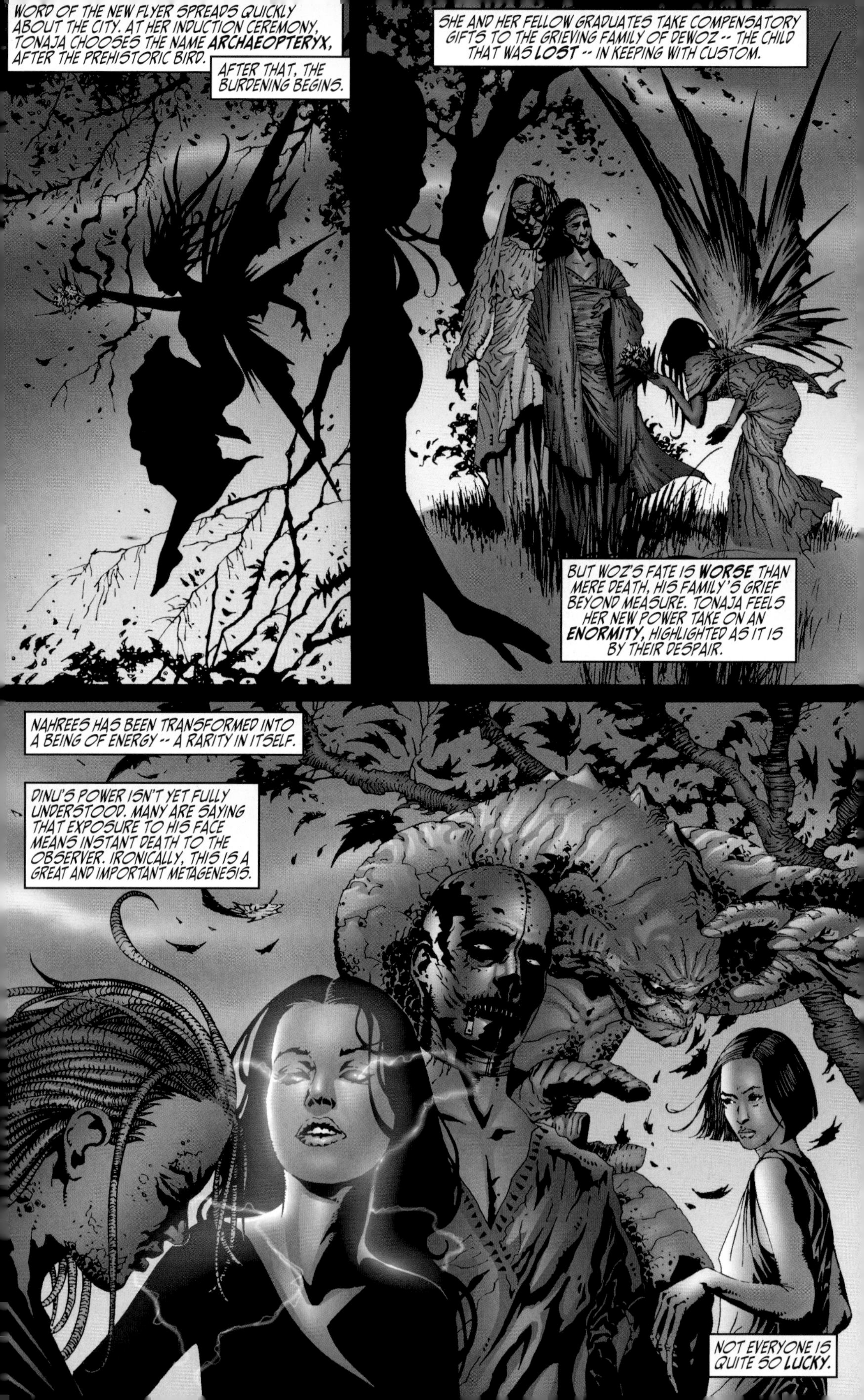
WORD OF THE NEW FLYER SPREADS QUICKLY ABOUT THE CITY. AT HER INDUCTION CEREMONY, TONAJA CHOOSES THE NAME ARCHAEOPTERYX, AFTER THE PREHISTORIC BIRD.
AFTER THAT, THE BURDENING BEGINS.
SHE AND HER FELLOW GRADUATES TAKE COMPENSATORY GIFTS TO THE GRIEVING FAMILY OF DEWOZ -- THE CHILD THAT WAS LOST -- IN KEEPING WITH CUSTOM.
BUT WOZ'S FATE IS WORSE THAN MERE DEATH, HIS FAMILY'S GRIEF BEYOND MEASURE. TONAJA FEELS HER NEW POWER TAKE ON AN ENORMITY, HIGHLIGHTED AS IT IS BY THEIR DESPAIR.
NAHREES HAS BEEN TRANSFORMED INTO A BEING OF ENERGY -- A RARITY IN ITSELF.
DINU'S POWER ISN'T YET FULLY UNDERSTOOD. MANY ARE SAYING THAT EXPOSURE TO HIS FACE MEANS INSTANT DEATH TO THE OBSERVER. IRONICALLY, THIS IS A GREAT AND IMPORTANT METAGENESIS.
NOT EVERYONE IS QUITE SO LUCKY.

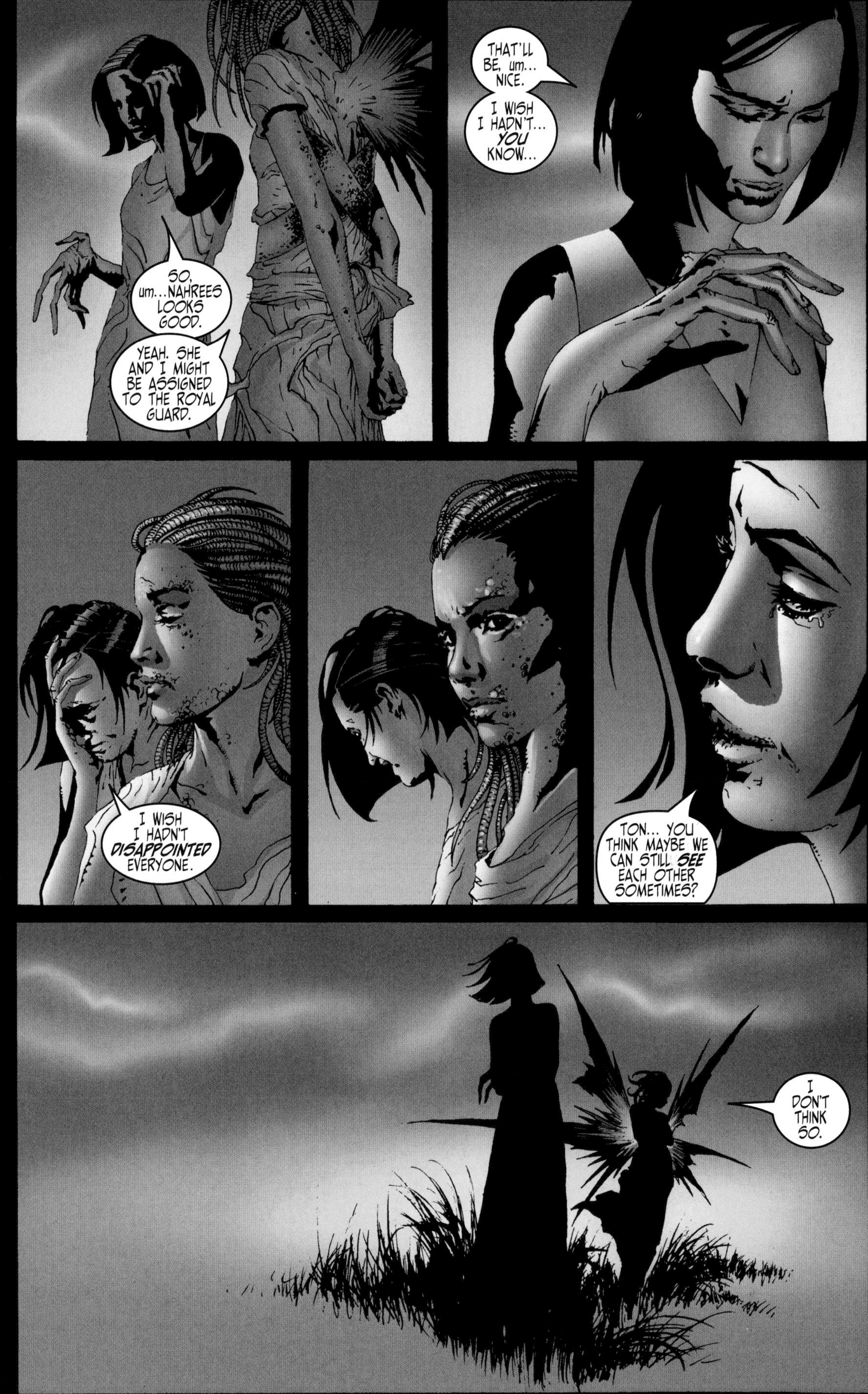
SO, um...NAHREES LOOKS GOOD.
YEAH. SHE AND I MIGHT BE ASSIGNED TO THE ROYAL GUARD.
THAT'LL BE, um... NICE.
I WISH I HADN'T... *YOU* KNOW...
I WISH I HADN'T *DISAPPOINTED* EVERYONE.
TON... YOU THINK MAYBE WE CAN STILL *SEE* EACH OTHER SOMETIMES?
I DON'T THINK SO.

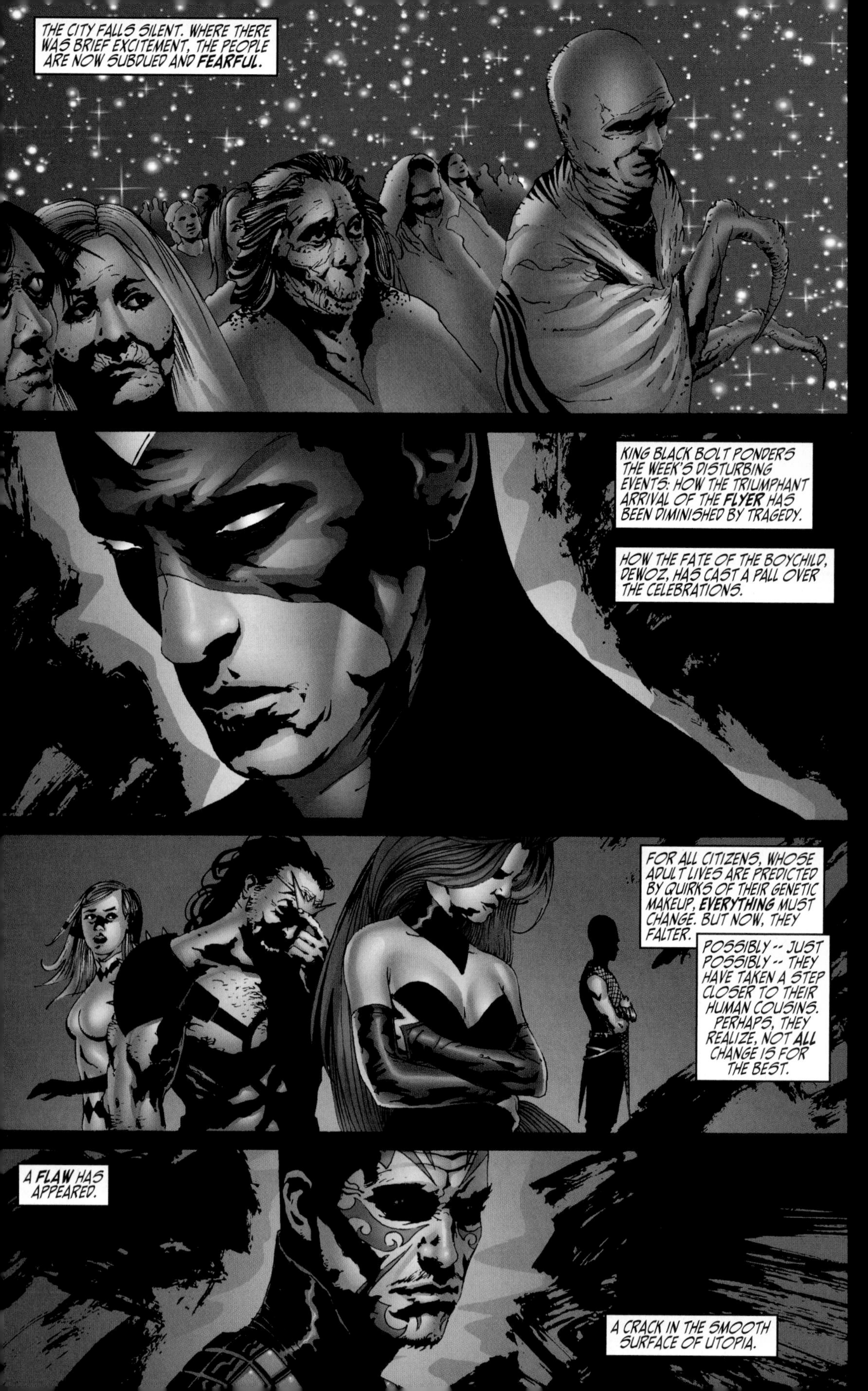
THE CITY FALLS SILENT. WHERE THERE WAS BRIEF EXCITEMENT, THE PEOPLE ARE NOW SUBDUED AND FEARFUL.
KING BLACK BOLT PONDERS THE WEEK'S DISTURBING EVENTS: HOW THE TRIUMPHANT ARRIVAL OF THE FLYER HAS BEEN DIMINISHED BY TRAGEDY.
HOW THE FATE OF THE BOYCHILD, DEWOZ, HAS CAST A PALL OVER THE CELEBRATIONS.
FOR ALL CITIZENS, WHOSE ADULT LIVES ARE PREDICTED BY QUIRKS OF THEIR GENETIC MAKEUP, EVERYTHING MUST CHANGE. BUT NOW, THEY FALTER.
POSSIBLY -- JUST POSSIBLY -- THEY HAVE TAKEN A STEP CLOSER TO THEIR HUMAN COUSINS. PERHAPS, THEY REALIZE, NOT ALL CHANGE IS FOR THE BEST.
A FLAW HAS APPEARED.
A CRACK IN THE SMOOTH SURFACE OF UTOPIA.

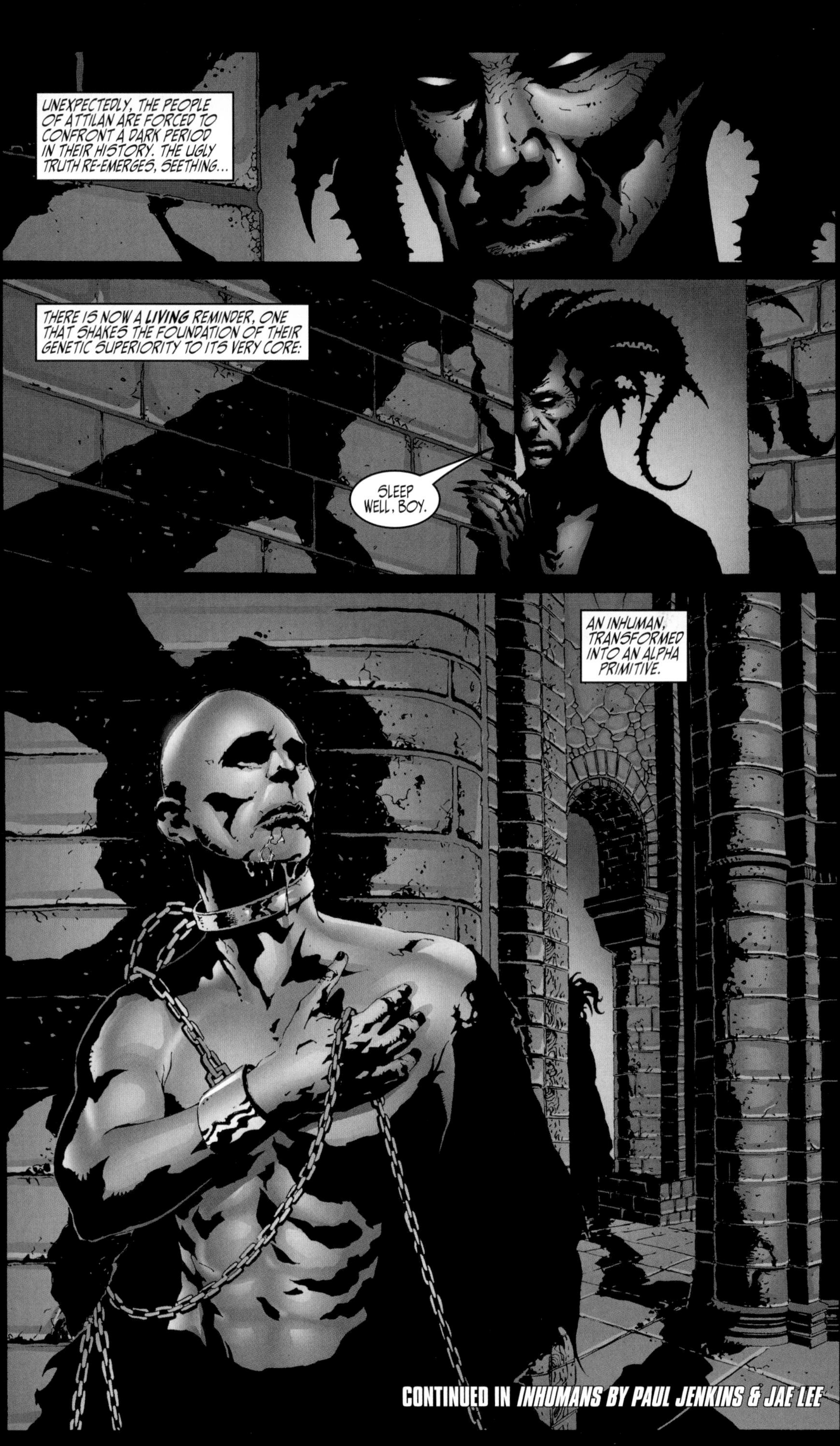
UNEXPECTEDLY, THE PEOPLE OF ATTILAN ARE FORCED TO CONFRONT A DARK PERIOD IN THEIR HISTORY. THE UGLY TRUTH RE-EMERGES, SEETHING...
THERE IS NOW A LIVING REMINDER, ONE THAT SHAKES THE FOUNDATION OF THEIR GENETIC SUPERIORITY TO ITS VERY CORE:
SLEEP WELL, BOY.
AN INHUMAN, TRANSFORMED INTO AN ALPHA PRIMITIVE.
CONTINUED IN INHUMANS BY PAUL JENKINS & JAE LEE

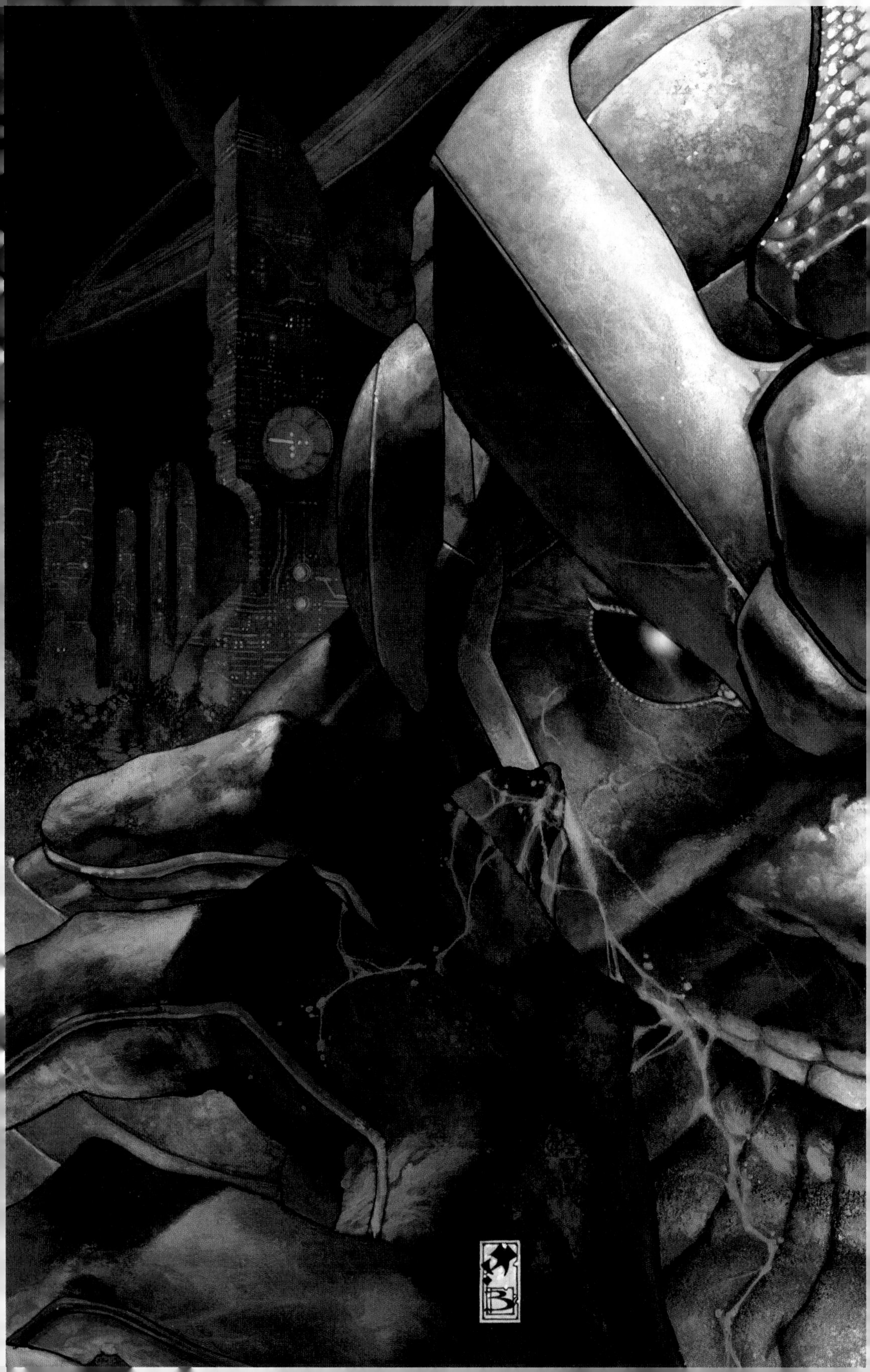

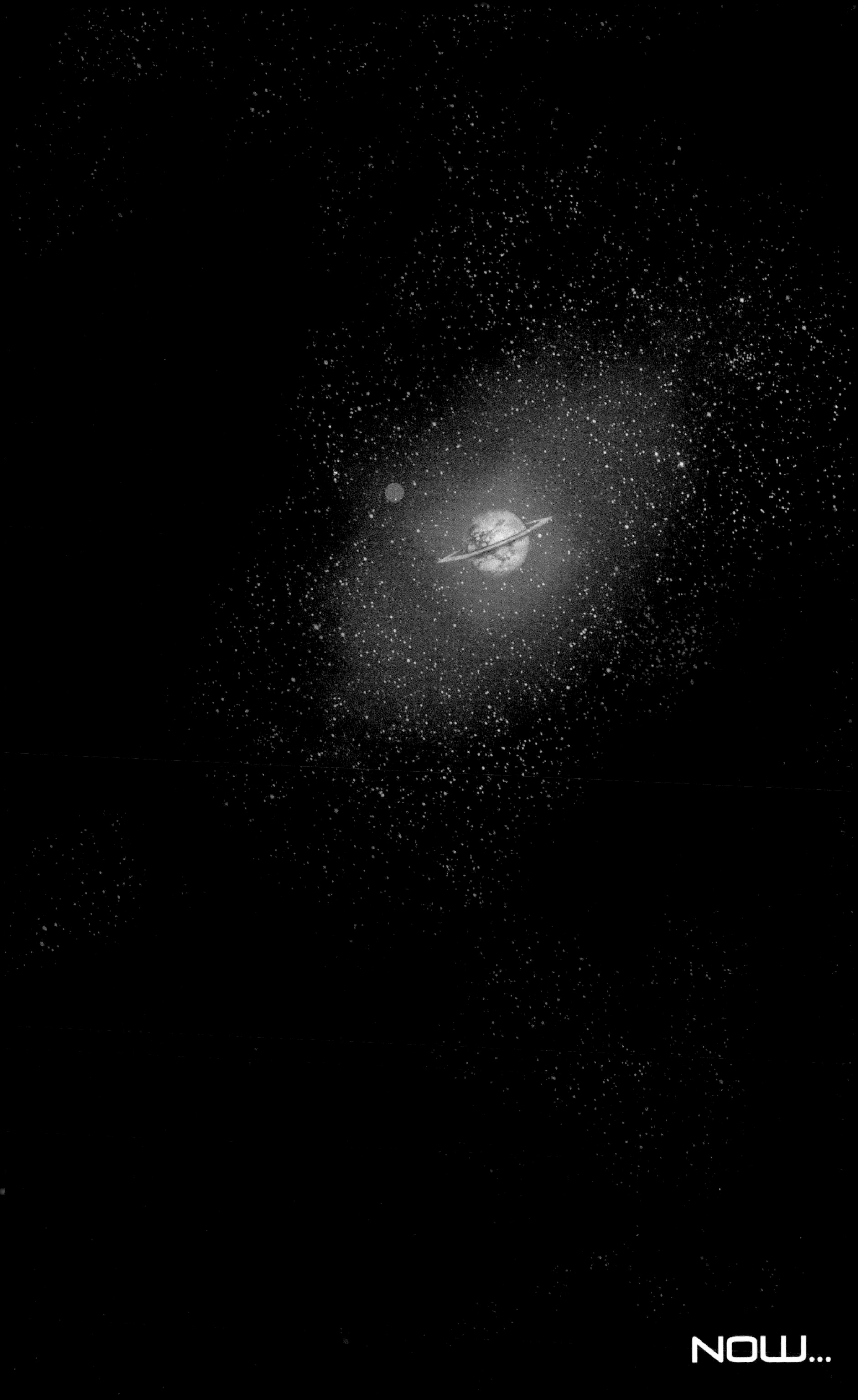
NOW...

THANOS RISING

WRITER **JASON AARON**

COLORS **SIMONE PERUZZI** LETTERER **VC'S CLAY**

COVER BY **SIMONE BIANCHI**

NOS
ING

ART **SIMONE BIANCHI**

TON COWLES PRODUCTION **MANNY MEDEROS**

VARIANT COVERS BY **MARKO DJURDJEVIC** AND **SKOTTIE YOUNG**

ASSISTANT EDITOR **ELLIE PYLE** ASSOCIATE EDITOR **SANA AMANAT** EDITOR **STEPHEN WACKER**

EDITOR IN CHIEF **AXEL ALONSO** CHIEF CREATIVE OFFICER **JOE QUESADA**

PUBLISHER **DAN BUCKLEY** EXECUTIVE PRODUCER **ALAN FINE**

DEDICATED TO JIM STARLIN

When you see this: AR , open up the MARVEL AR APP (available on applicable Apple ® iOS or Android TM devices) and use your camera-enabled device to unlock extra-special exclusive features!

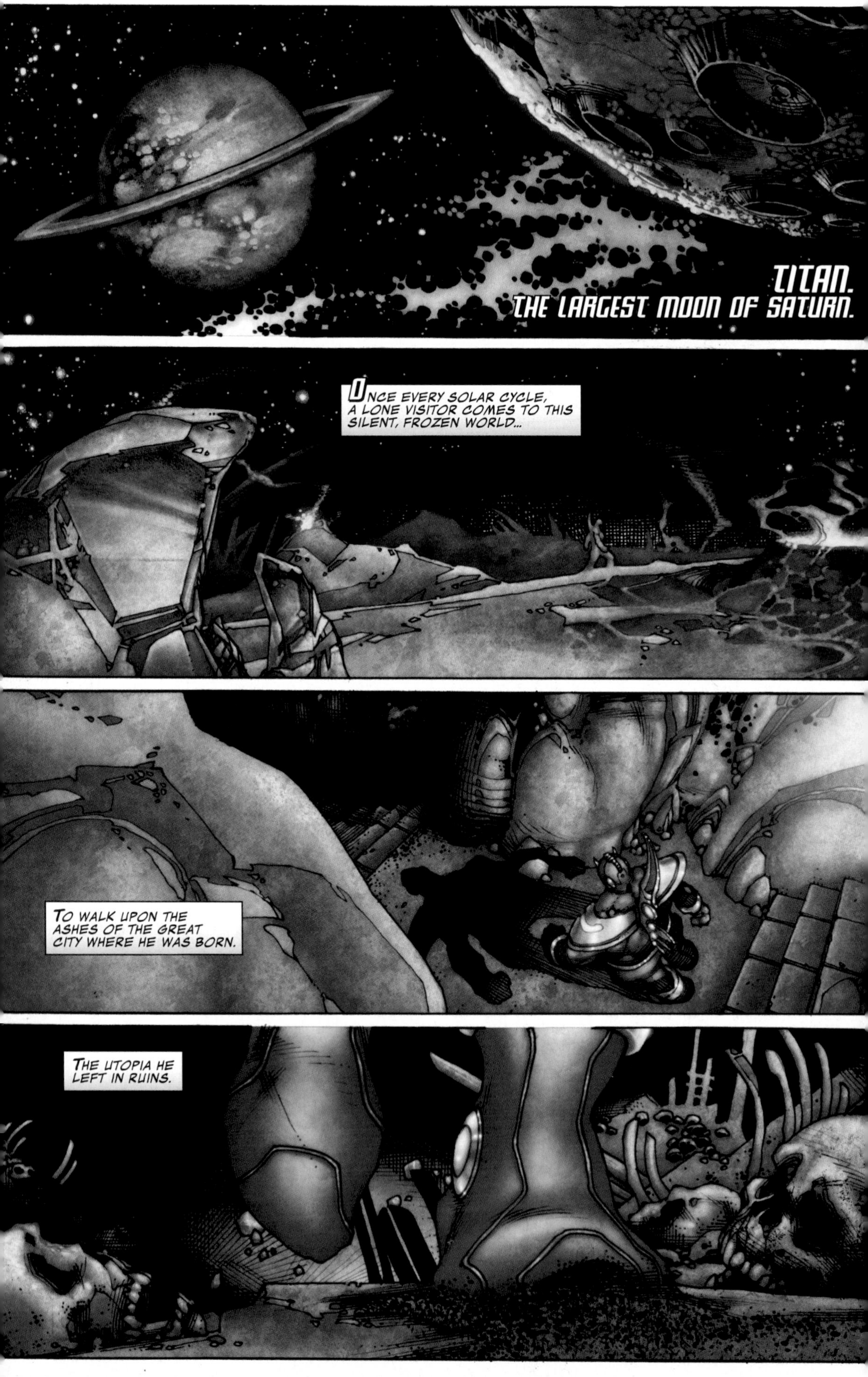
TITAN.
THE LARGEST MOON OF SATURN.
ONCE EVERY SOLAR CYCLE, A LONE VISITOR COMES TO THIS SILENT, FROZEN WORLD...
TO WALK UPON THE ASHES OF THE GREAT CITY WHERE HE WAS BORN.
THE UTOPIA HE LEFT IN RUINS.

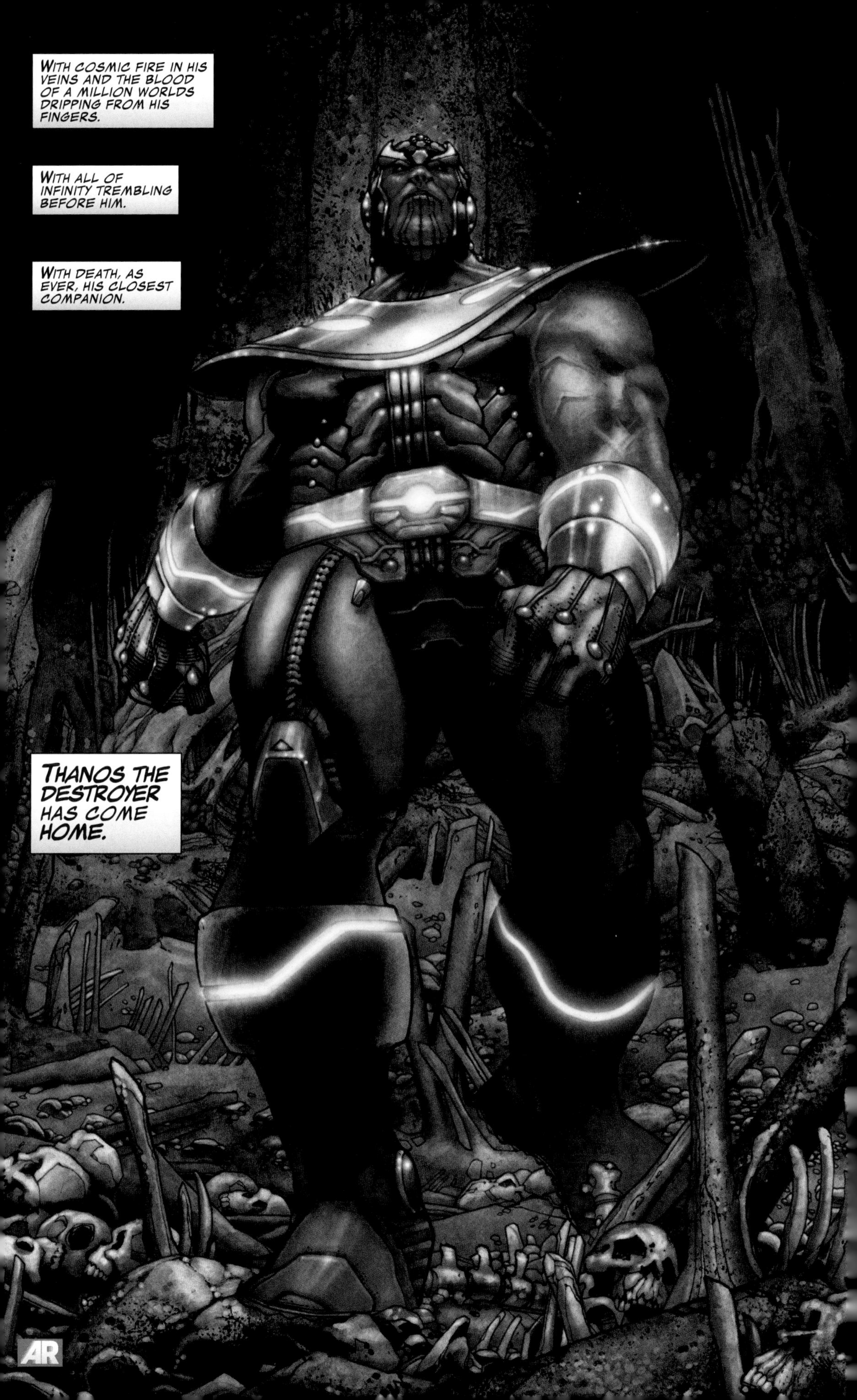
WITH COSMIC FIRE IN HIS VEINS AND THE BLOOD OF A MILLION WORLDS DRIPPING FROM HIS FINGERS.
WITH ALL OF INFINITY TREMBLING BEFORE HIM.
WITH DEATH, AS EVER, HIS CLOSEST COMPANION.
THANOS THE DESTROYER HAS COME HOME.

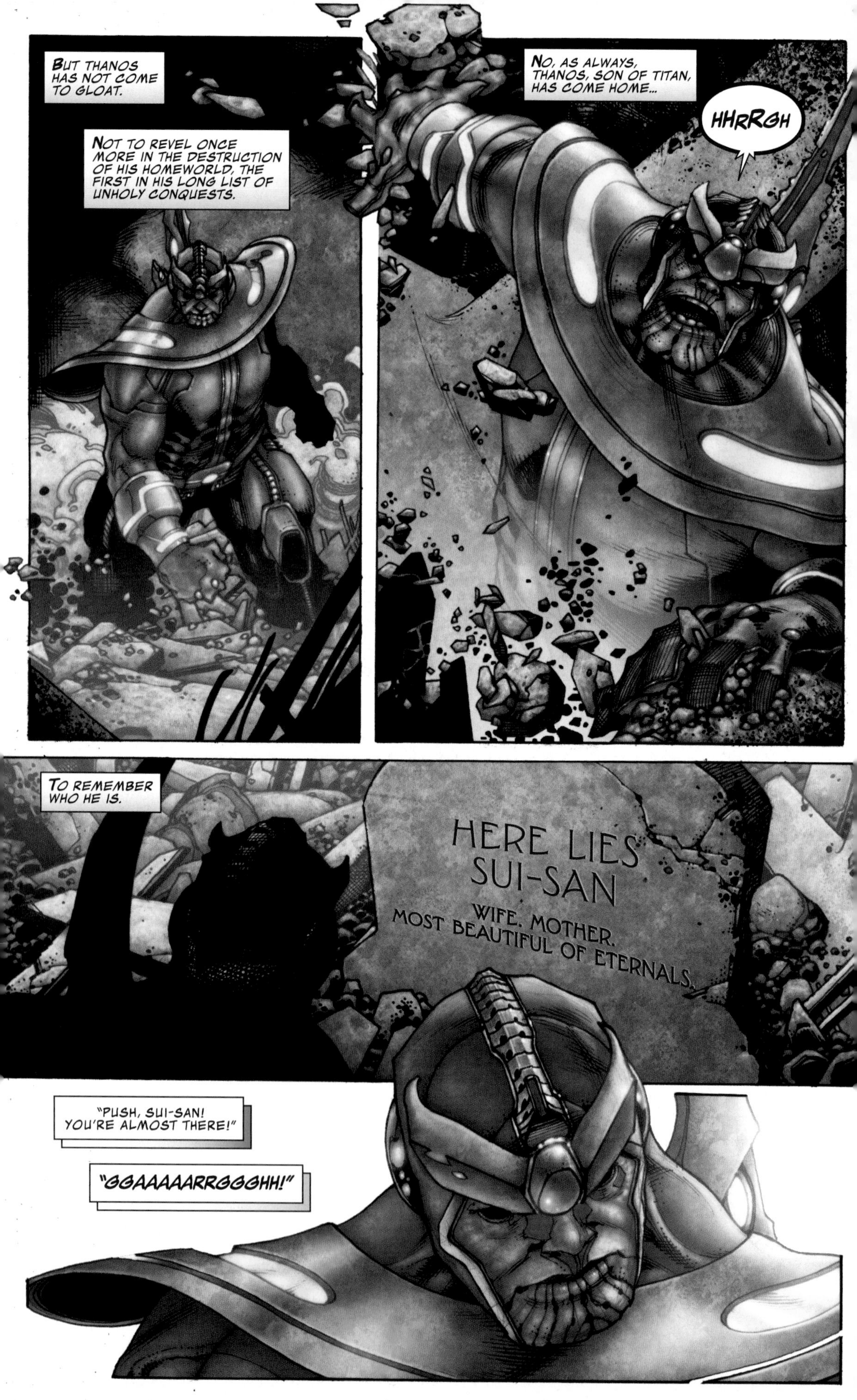

BUT THANOS HAS NOT COME TO GLOAT.
NOT TO REVEL ONCE MORE IN THE DESTRUCTION OF HIS HOMEWORLD, THE FIRST IN HIS LONG LIST OF UNHOLY CONQUESTS.
NO, AS ALWAYS, THANOS, SON OF TITAN, HAS COME HOME...
HHRRGH
TO REMEMBER WHO HE IS.
HERE LIES SUI-SAN
WIFE. MOTHER. MOST BEAUTIFUL OF ETERNALS.
"PUSH, SUI-SAN! YOU'RE ALMOST THERE!"
"GGAAAAARRGGGHH!"

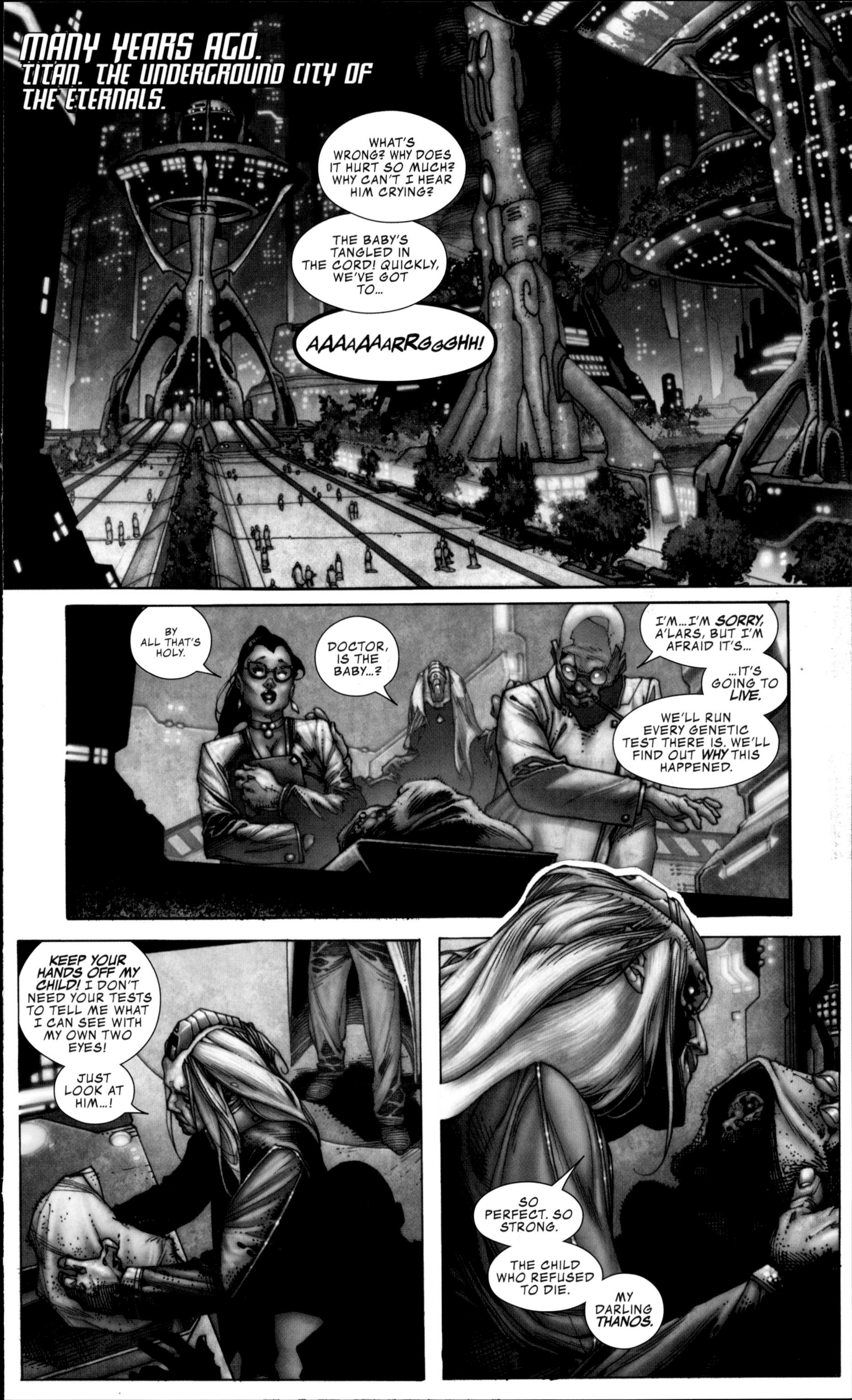
MANY YEARS AGO.
TITAN. THE UNDERGROUND CITY OF THE ETERNALS.
WHAT'S WRONG? WHY DOES IT HURT SO MUCH? WHY CAN'T I HEAR HIM CRYING?
THE BABY'S TANGLED IN THE CORD! QUICKLY, WE'VE GOT TO...
AAAAAAARRGGGHH!
BY ALL THAT'S HOLY.
DOCTOR, IS THE BABY...?
I'M...I'M SORRY, A'LARS, BUT I'M AFRAID IT'S...
...IT'S GOING TO LIVE.
WE'LL RUN EVERY GENETIC TEST THERE IS. WE'LL FIND OUT WHY THIS HAPPENED.
KEEP YOUR HANDS OFF MY CHILD! I DON'T NEED YOUR TESTS TO TELL ME WHAT I CAN SEE WITH MY OWN TWO EYES!
JUST LOOK AT HIM...!
SO PERFECT. SO STRONG.
THE CHILD WHO REFUSED TO DIE.
MY DARLING THANOS.

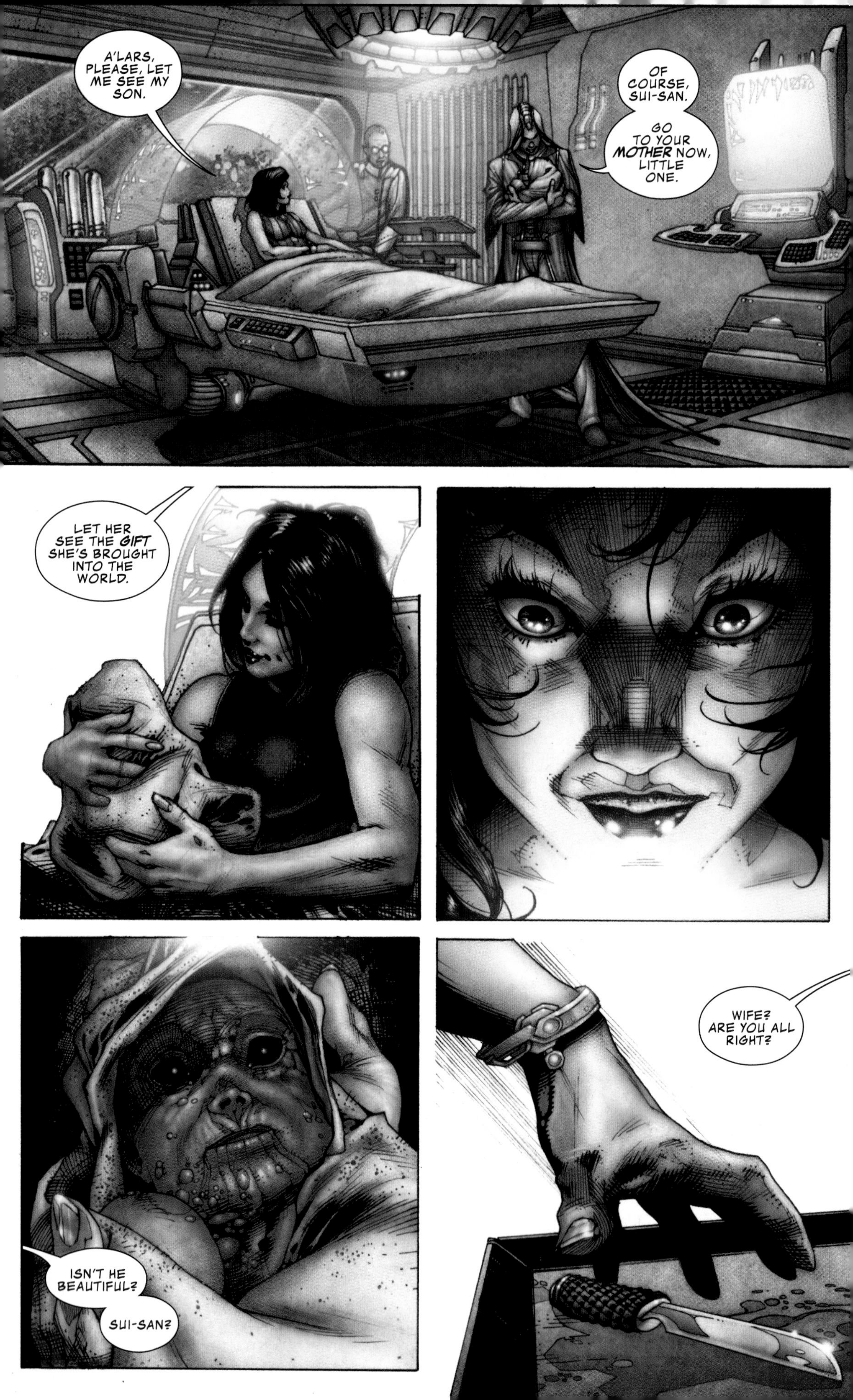
A'LARS, PLEASE, LET ME SEE MY SON.
OF COURSE, SUI-SAN.
GO TO YOUR MOTHER NOW, LITTLE ONE.
LET HER SEE THE GIFT SHE'S BROUGHT INTO THE WORLD.
ISN'T HE BEAUTIFUL?
SUI-SAN?
WIFE? ARE YOU ALL RIGHT?

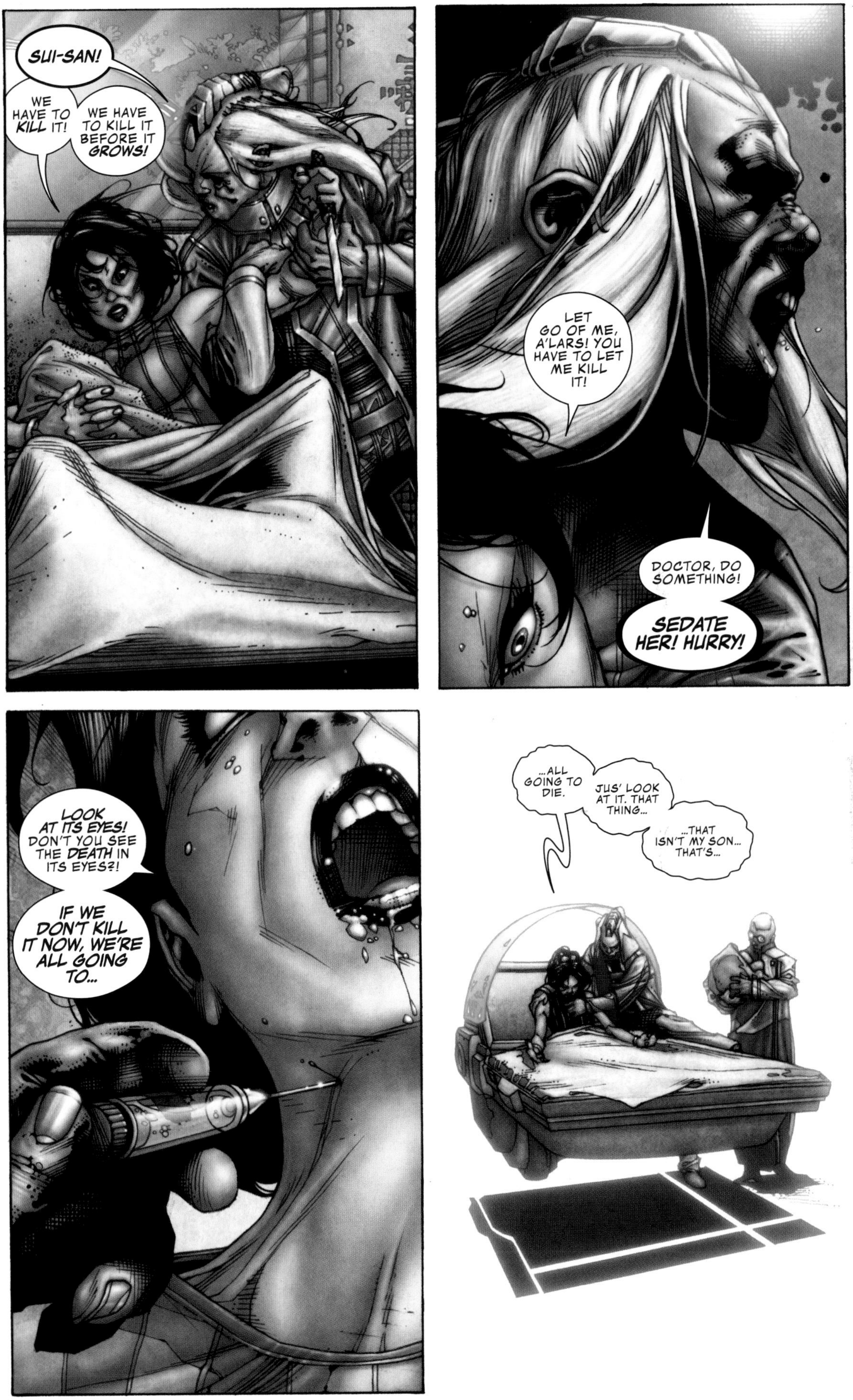
SUI-SAN!
WE HAVE TO KILL IT!
WE HAVE TO KILL IT BEFORE IT GROWS!
LET GO OF ME, A'LARS! YOU HAVE TO LET ME KILL IT!
DOCTOR, DO SOMETHING!
SEDATE HER! HURRY!
LOOK AT ITS EYES! DON'T YOU SEE THE DEATH IN ITS EYES?!
IF WE DON'T KILL IT NOW, WE'RE ALL GOING TO...
...ALL GOING TO DIE.
JUS' LOOK AT IT. THAT THING...
...THAT ISN'T MY SON... THAT'S...

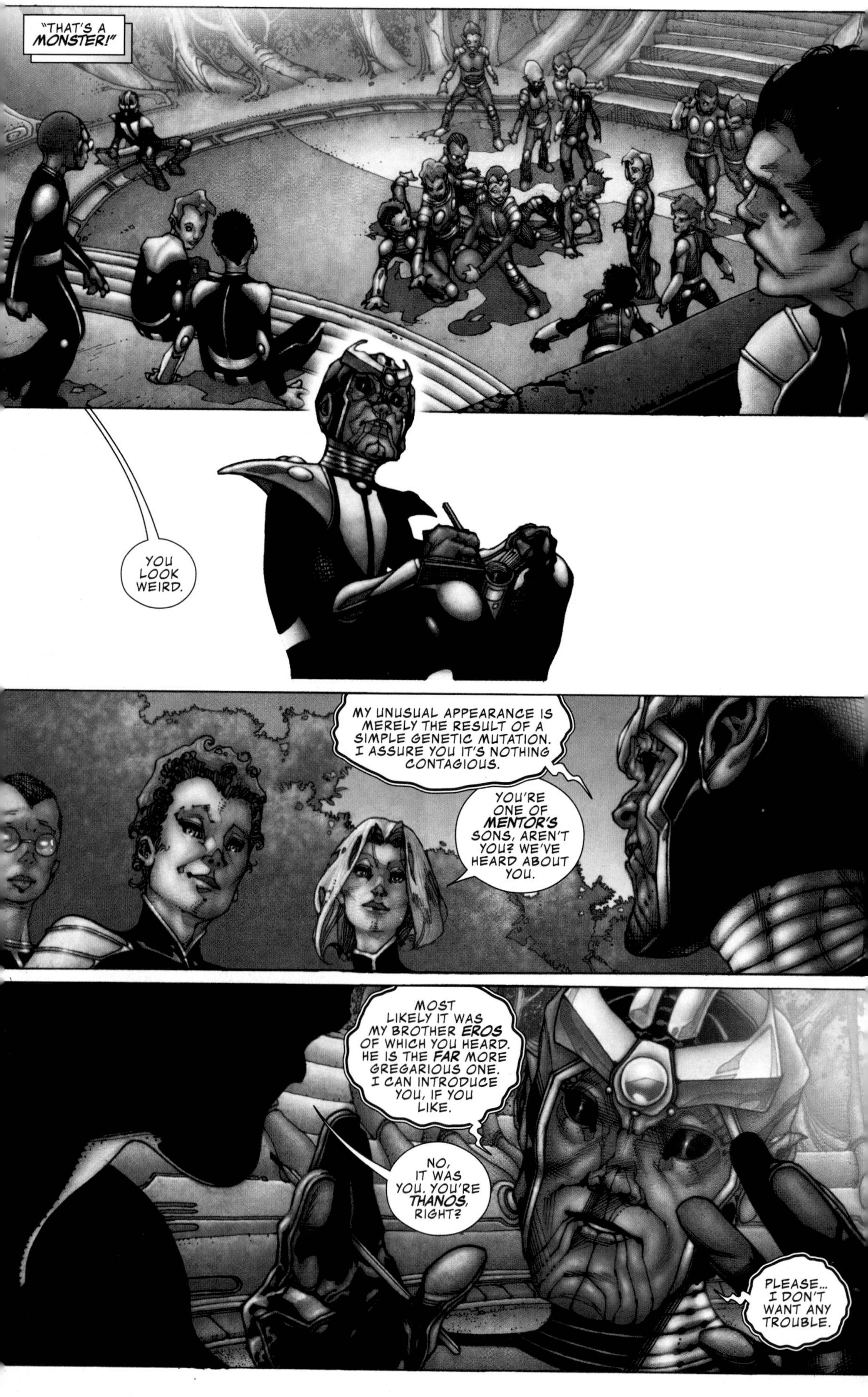
"THAT'S A MONSTER!"
YOU LOOK WEIRD.
MY UNUSUAL APPEARANCE IS MERELY THE RESULT OF A SIMPLE GENETIC MUTATION. I ASSURE YOU IT'S NOTHING CONTAGIOUS.
YOU'RE ONE OF MENTOR'S SONS, AREN'T YOU? WE'VE HEARD ABOUT YOU.
MOST LIKELY IT WAS MY BROTHER EROS OF WHICH YOU HEARD. HE IS THE FAR MORE GREGARIOUS ONE. I CAN INTRODUCE YOU, IF YOU LIKE.
NO, IT WAS YOU. YOU'RE THANOS, RIGHT?
PLEASE... I DON'T WANT ANY TROUBLE.

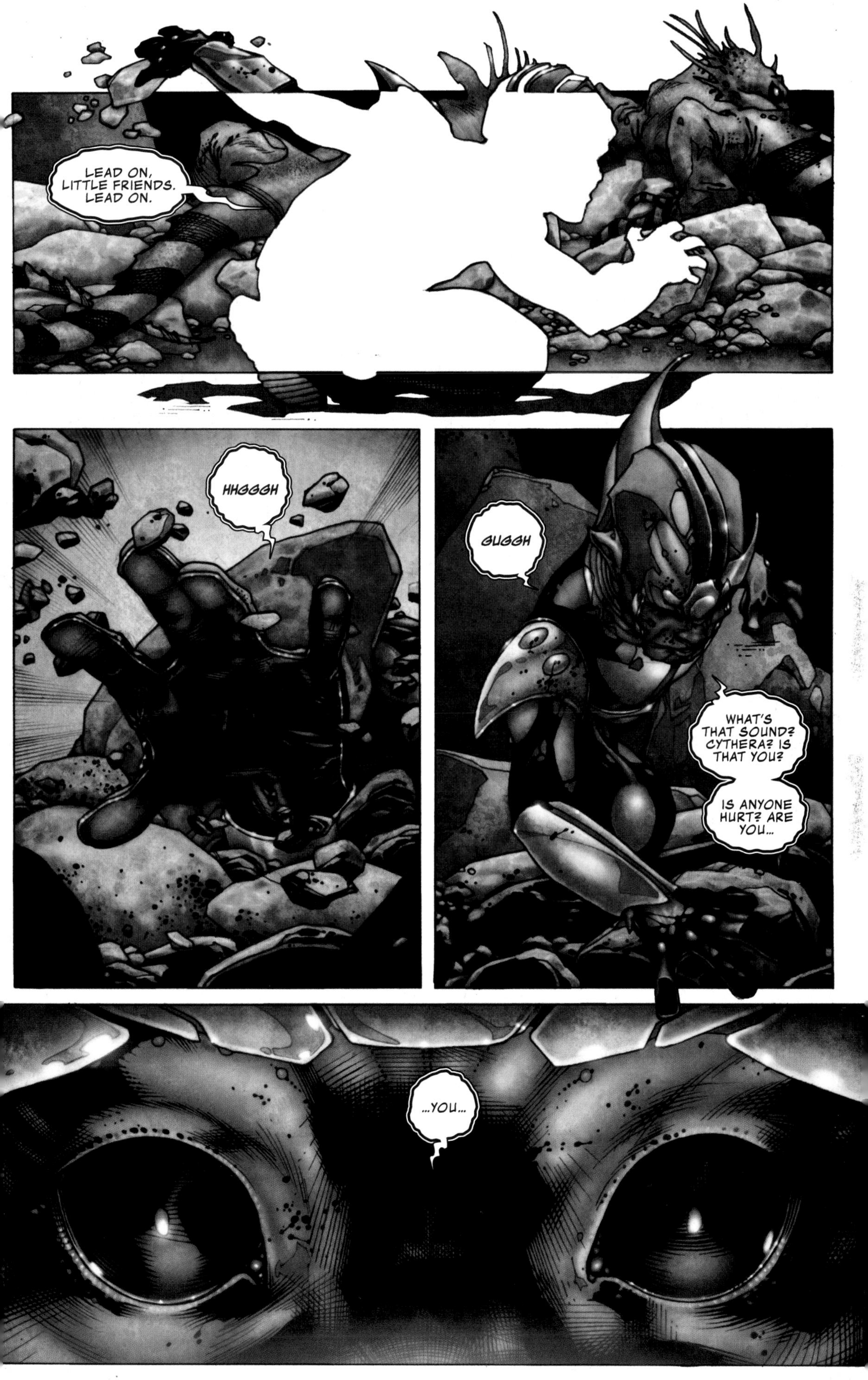
LEAD ON, LITTLE FRIENDS. LEAD ON.
HHGGGH
GUGGH
WHAT'S THAT SOUND? CYTHERA? IS THAT YOU?
IS ANYONE HURT? ARE YOU...
...YOU...

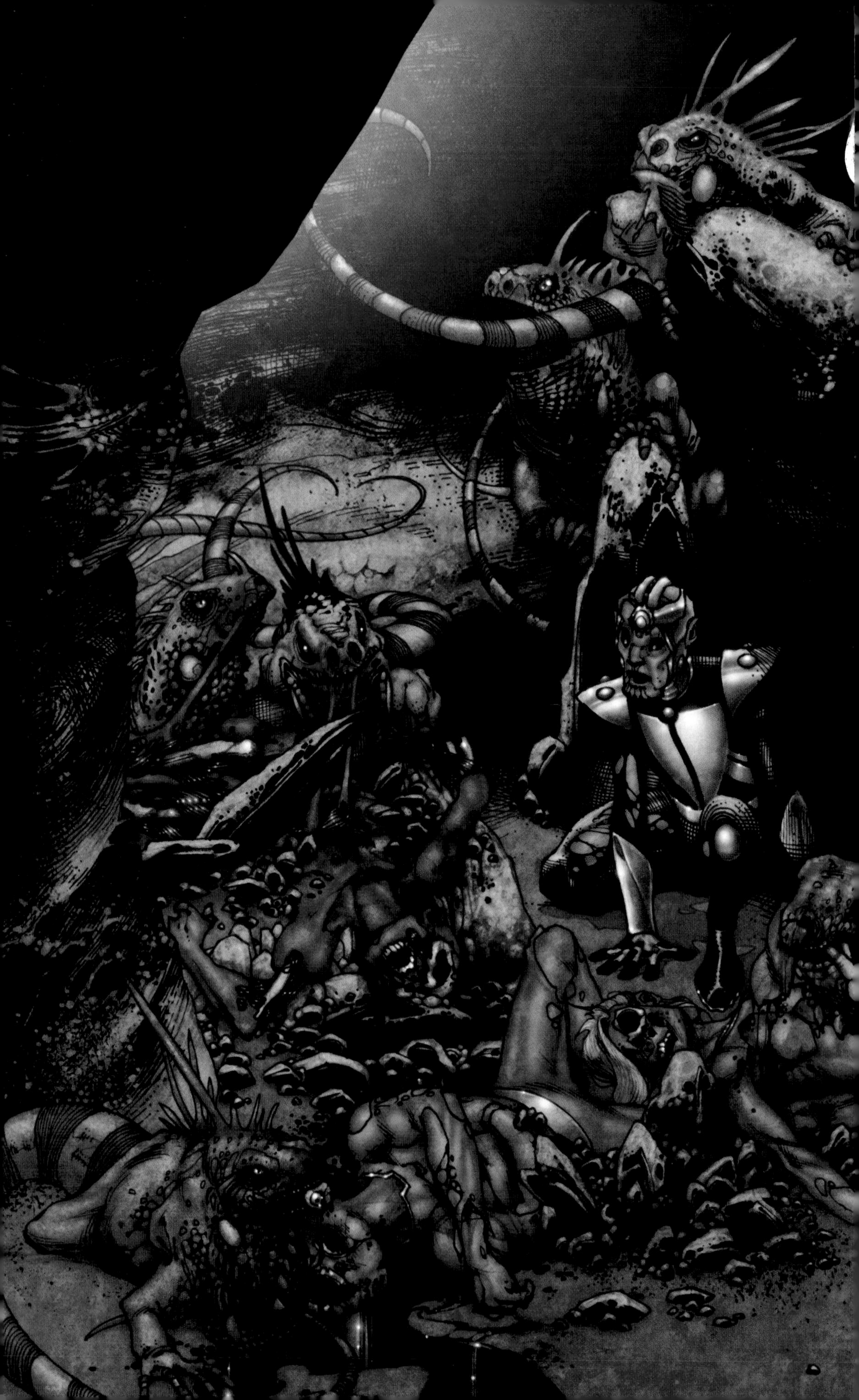

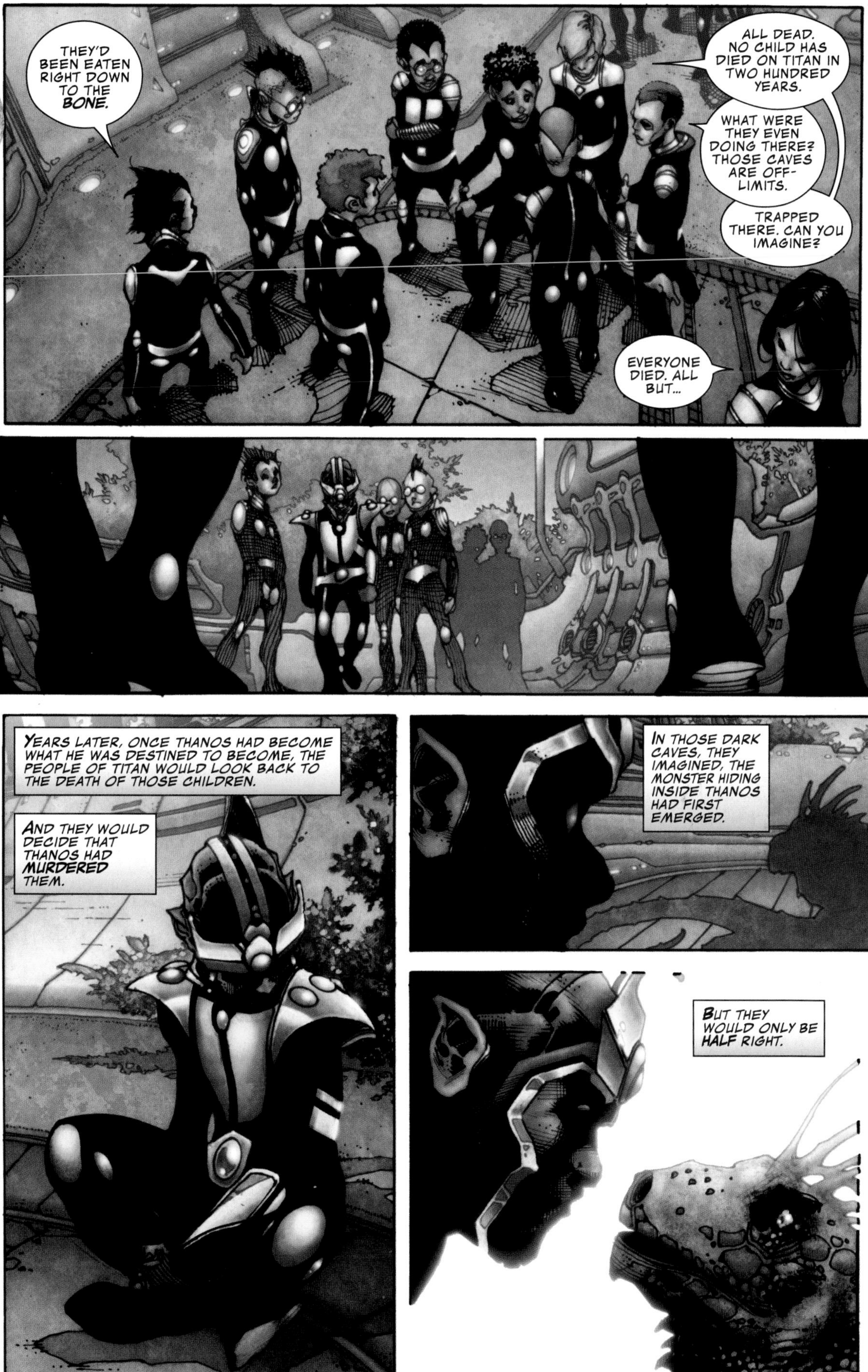
THEY'D BEEN EATEN RIGHT DOWN TO THE BONE.
ALL DEAD. NO CHILD HAS DIED ON TITAN IN TWO HUNDRED YEARS.
WHAT WERE THEY EVEN DOING THERE? THOSE CAVES ARE OFF-LIMITS.
TRAPPED THERE. CAN YOU IMAGINE?
EVERYONE DIED. ALL BUT...
YEARS LATER, ONCE THANOS HAD BECOME WHAT HE WAS DESTINED TO BECOME, THE PEOPLE OF TITAN WOULD LOOK BACK TO THE DEATH OF THOSE CHILDREN.
AND THEY WOULD DECIDE THAT THANOS HAD MURDERED THEM.
IN THOSE DARK CAVES, THEY IMAGINED, THE MONSTER HIDING INSIDE THANOS HAD FIRST EMERGED.
BUT THEY WOULD ONLY BE HALF RIGHT.

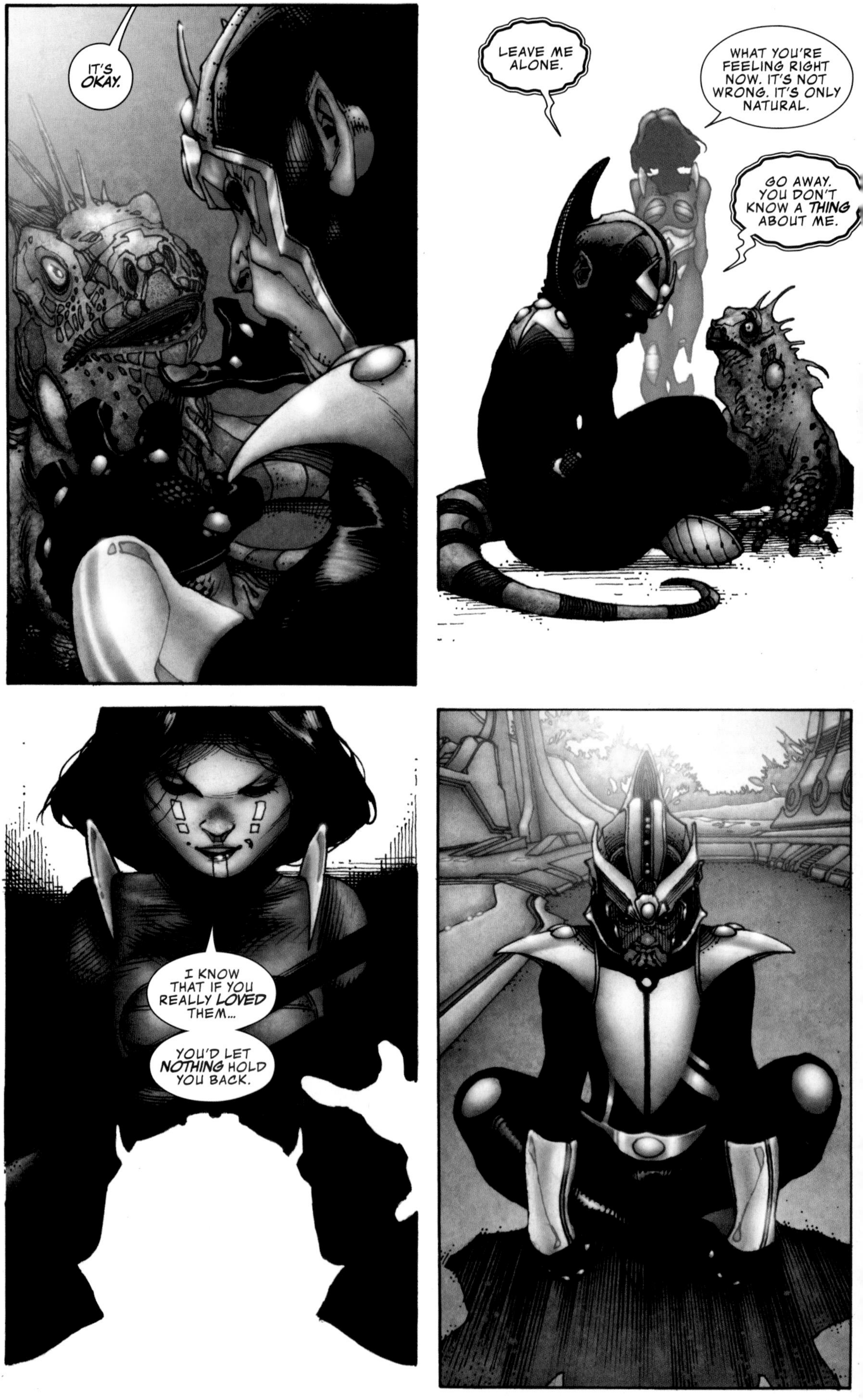

IT'S OKAY.
LEAVE ME ALONE.
WHAT YOU'RE FEELING RIGHT NOW. IT'S NOT WRONG. IT'S ONLY NATURAL.
GO AWAY. YOU DON'T KNOW A THING ABOUT ME.
I KNOW THAT IF YOU REALLY LOVED THEM...
YOU'D LET NOTHING HOLD YOU BACK.

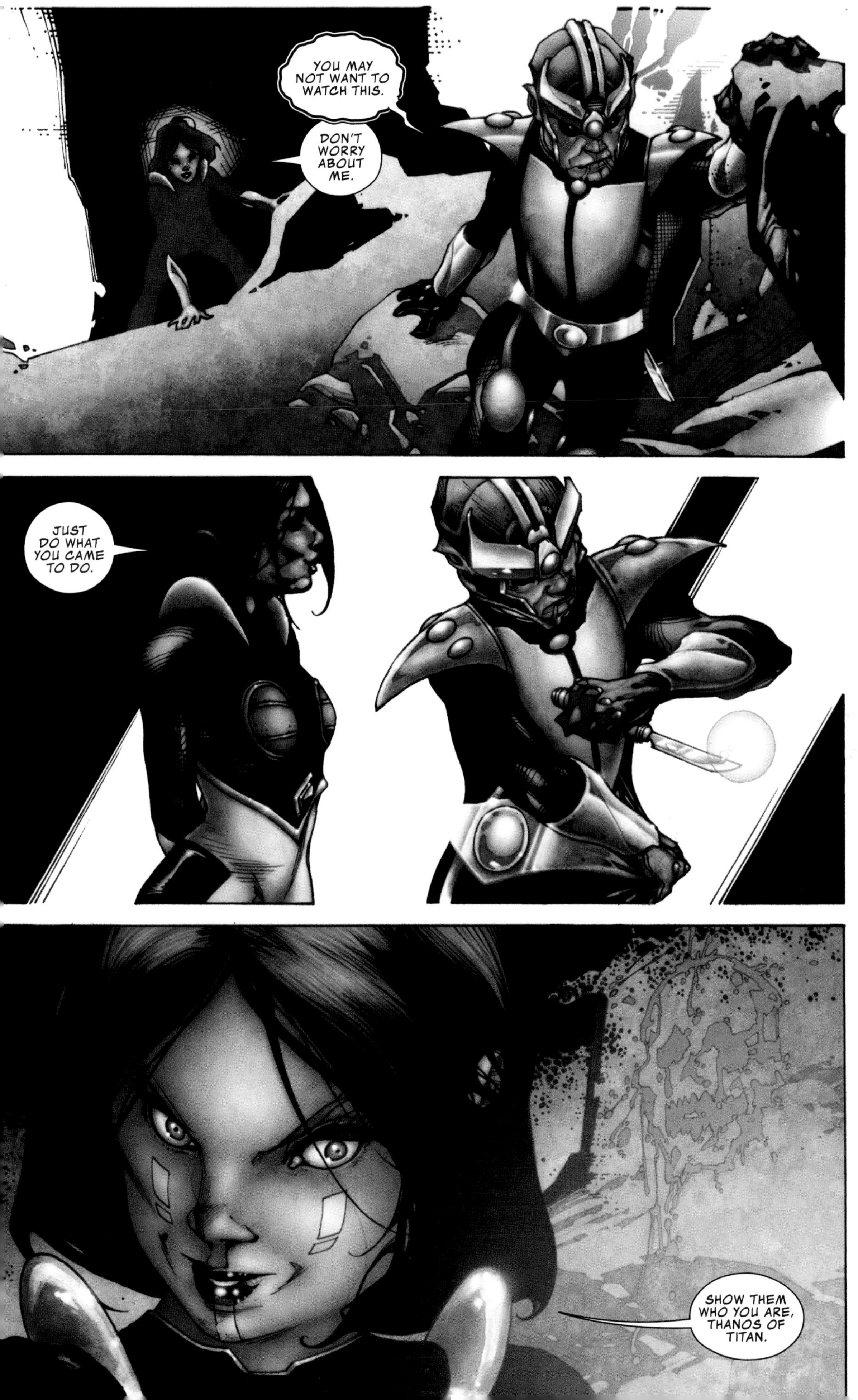
YOU MAY NOT WANT TO WATCH THIS.
DON'T WORRY ABOUT ME.
JUST DO WHAT YOU CAME TO DO.
SHOW THEM WHO YOU ARE, THANOS OF TITAN.

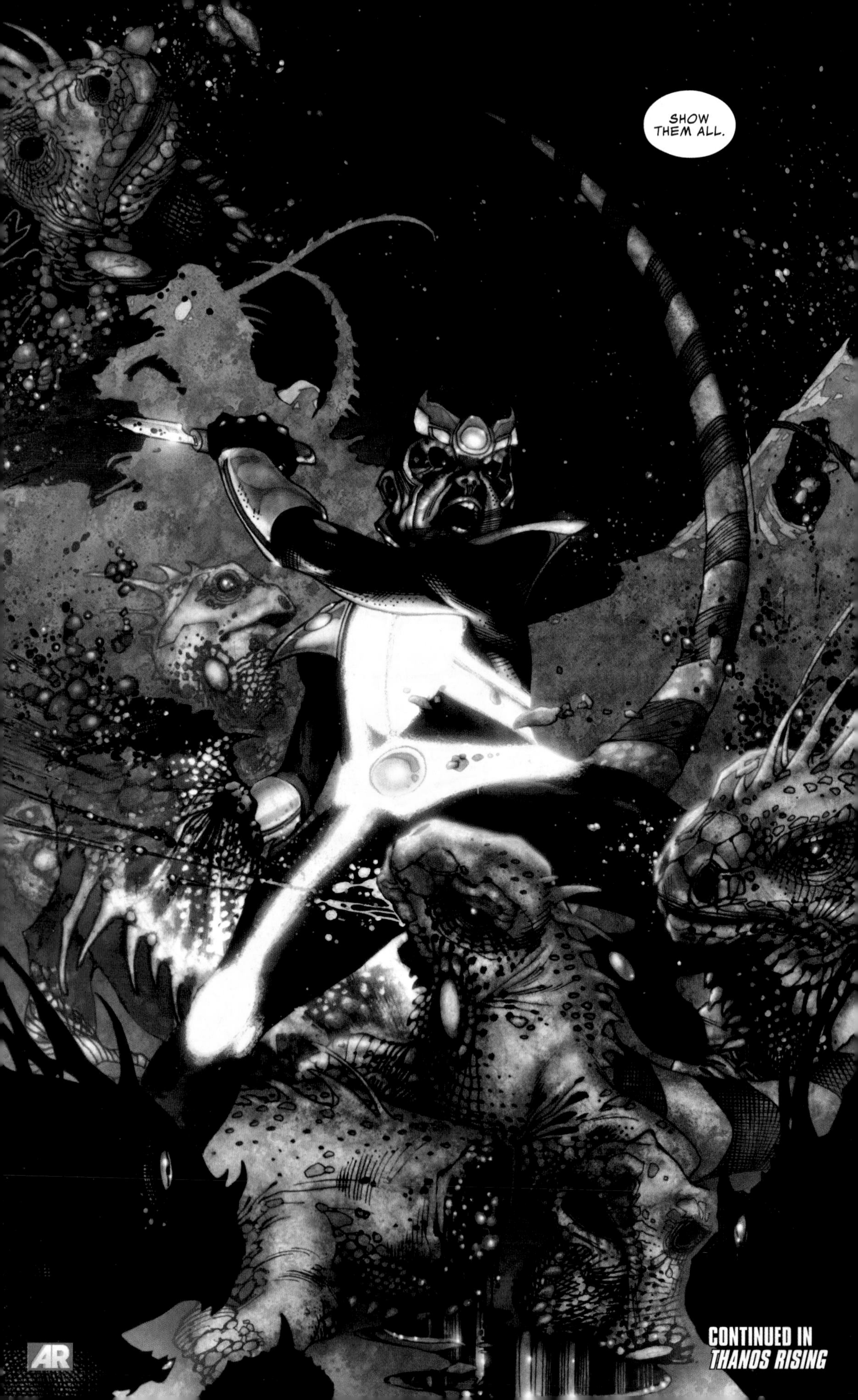
SHOW THEM ALL.

CONTINUED IN *THANOS RISING*

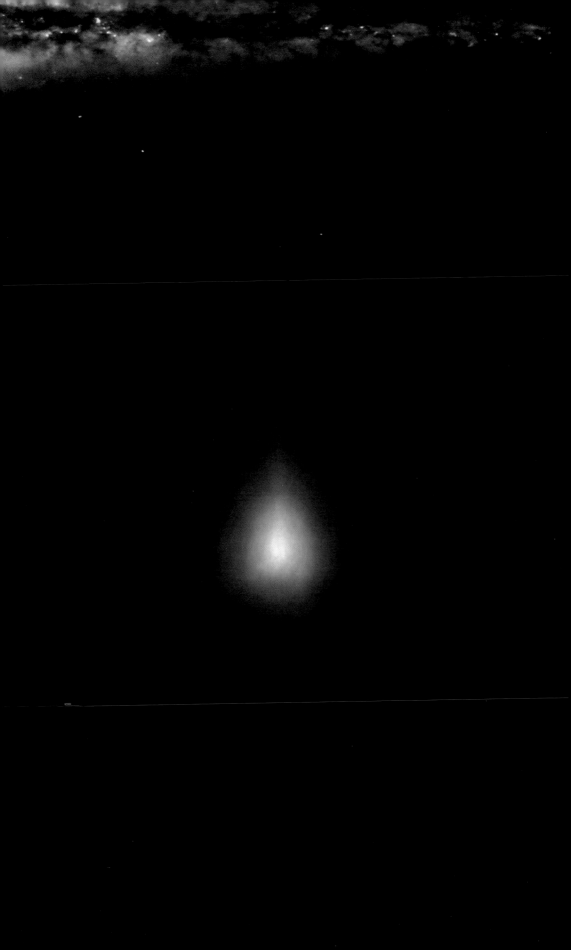

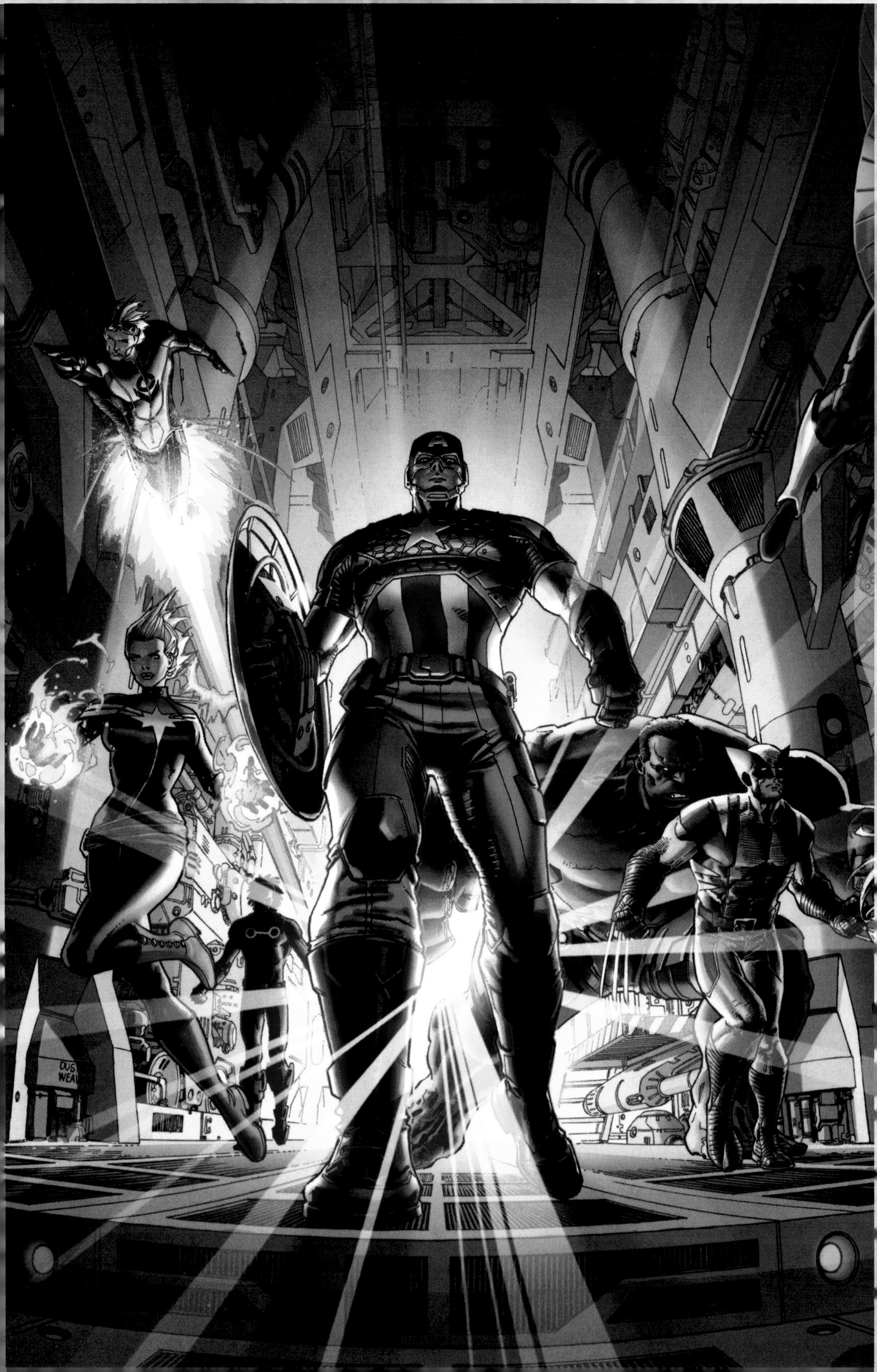

PREVIOUSLY IN AVENGERS

THERE WAS *NOTHING.*

FOLLOWED BY *EVERYTHING.*

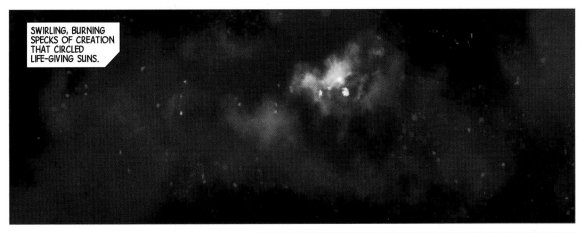

SWIRLING, BURNING SPECKS OF CREATION THAT CIRCLED LIFE-GIVING SUNS.

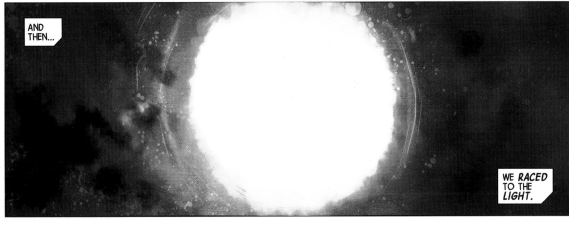

AND THEN...

WE *RACED* TO THE *LIGHT.*

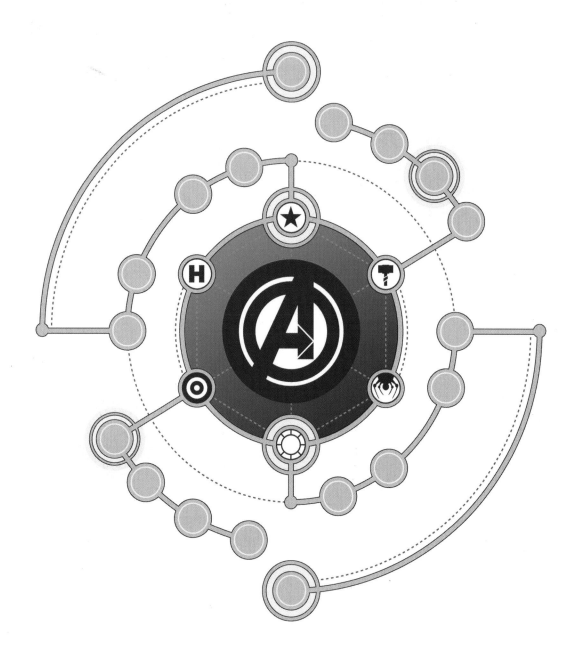

EARTH'S MIGHTIEST HEROES

CAPTAIN AMERICA
(Steve Rogers)

IRON MAN
(Tony Stark)

HAWKEYE
(Clint Barton)

BLACK WIDOW
(Natasha Romanova)

THE HULK
(Dr. Bruce Banner)

THOR
(Odinson)

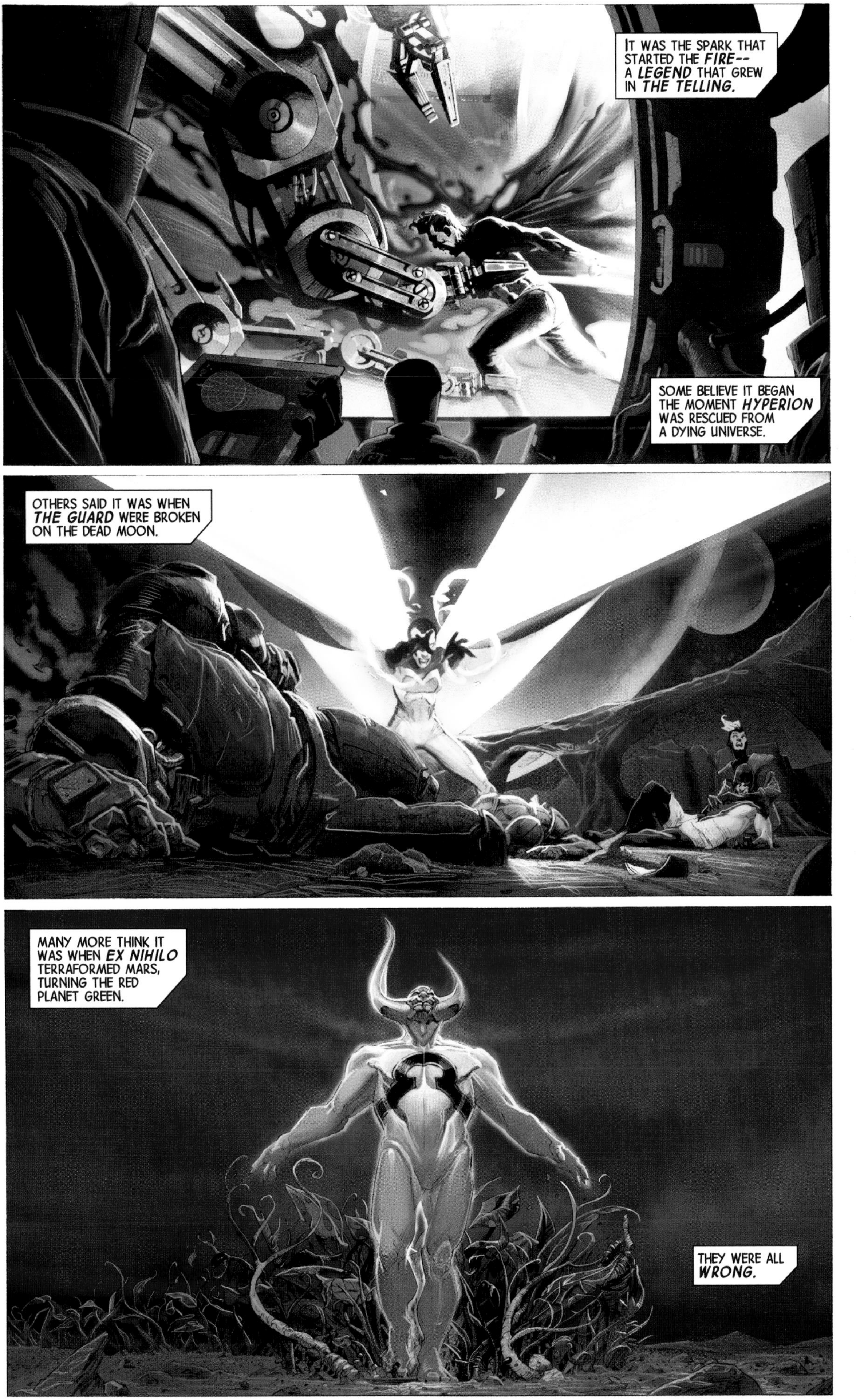
IT WAS THE SPARK THAT STARTED THE FIRE-- A LEGEND THAT GREW IN THE TELLING.
SOME BELIEVE IT BEGAN THE MOMENT HYPERION WAS RESCUED FROM A DYING UNIVERSE.
OTHERS SAID IT WAS WHEN THE GUARD WERE BROKEN ON THE DEAD MOON.
MANY MORE THINK IT WAS WHEN EX NIHILO TERRAFORMED MARS, TURNING THE RED PLANET GREEN.
THEY WERE ALL WRONG.

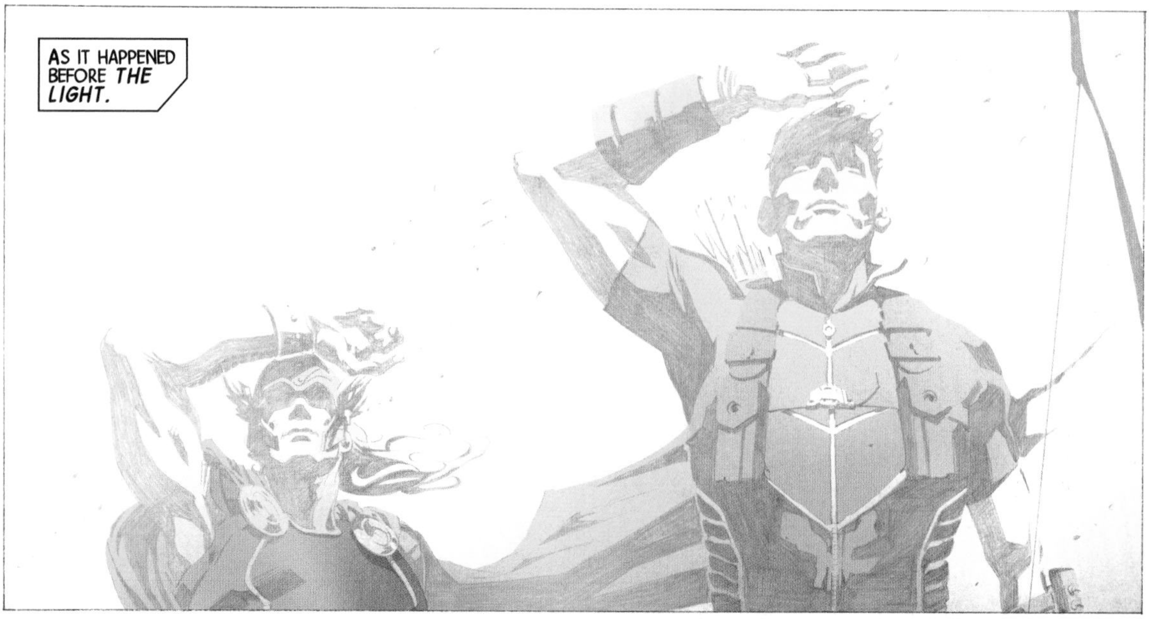
AS IT HAPPENED BEFORE THE LIGHT.

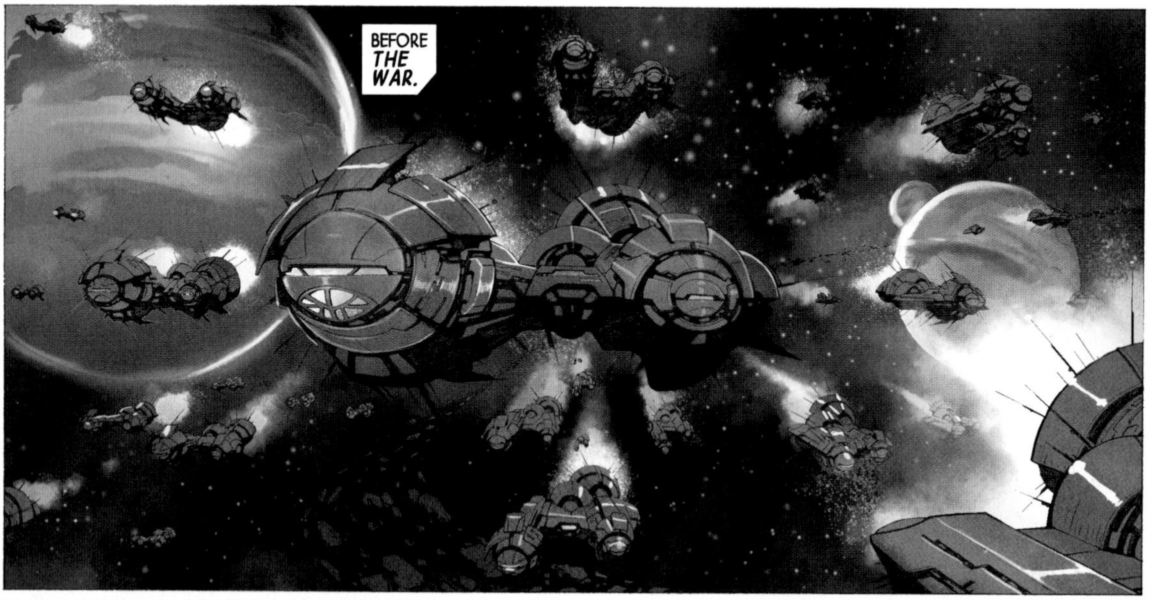
BEFORE THE WAR.

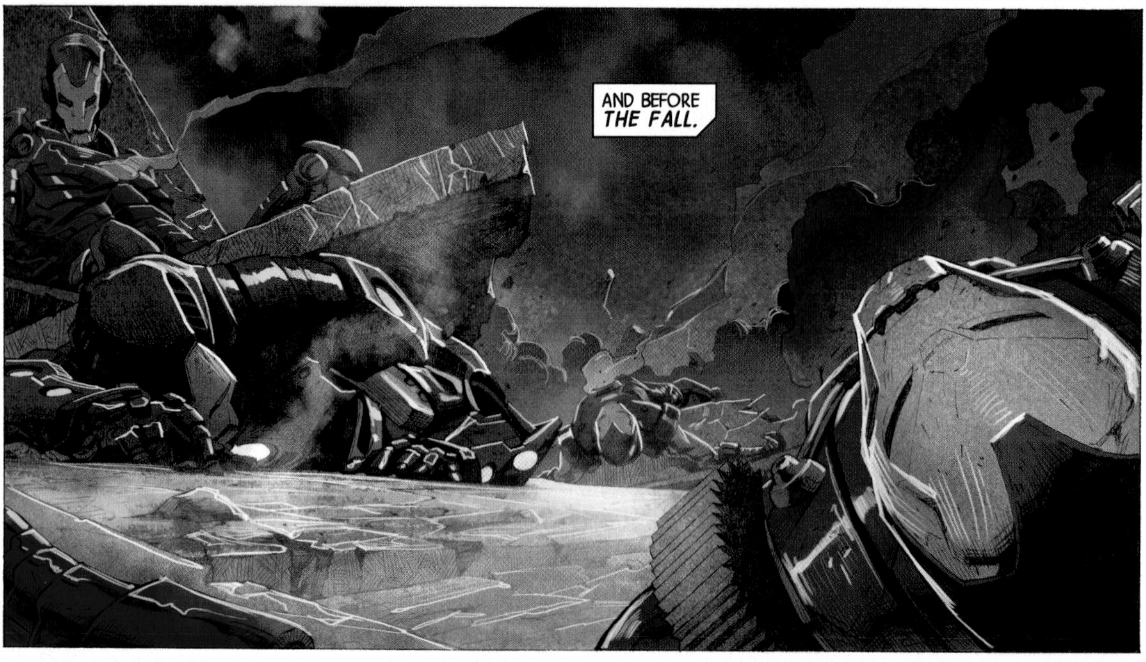
AND BEFORE THE FALL.

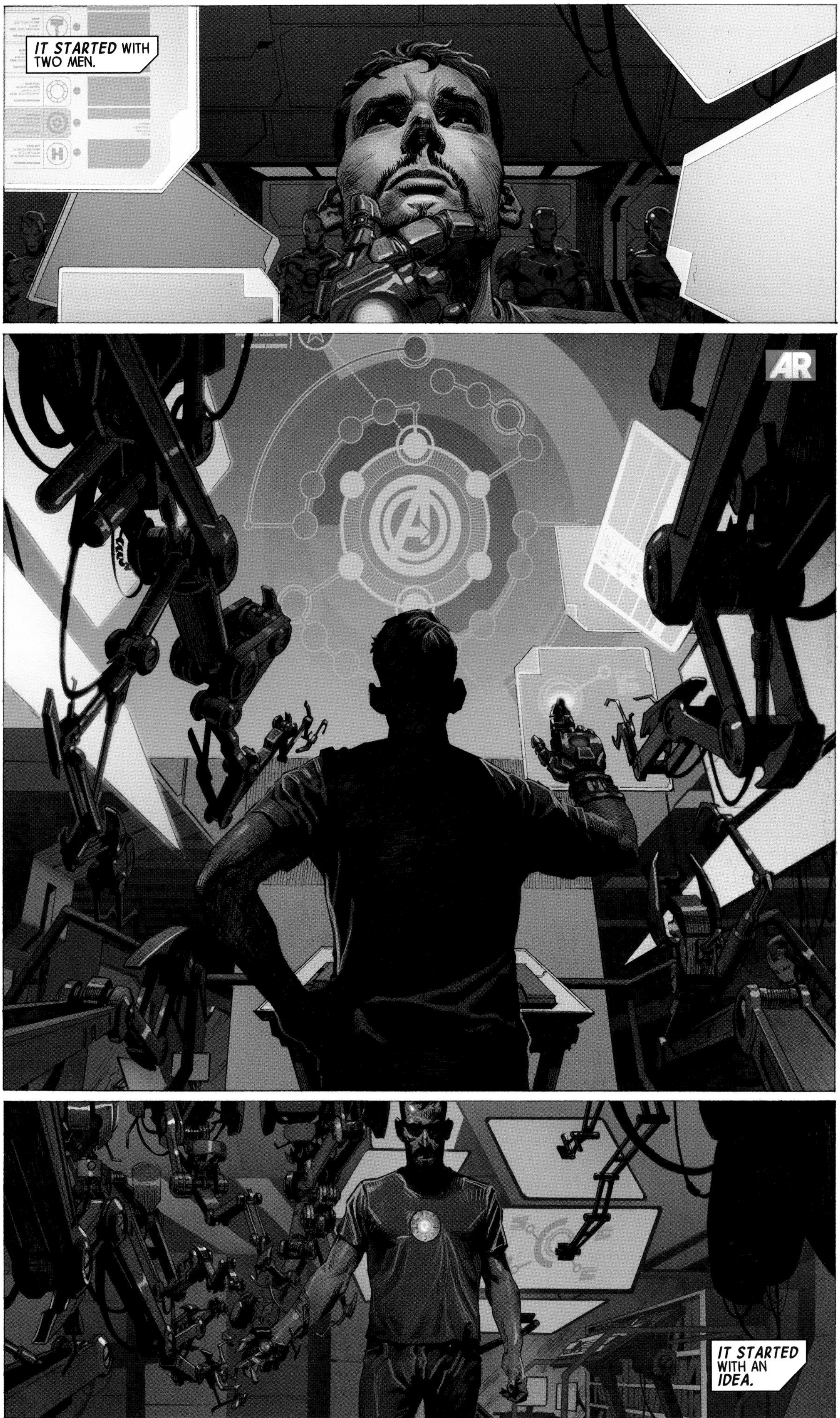
IT STARTED WITH TWO MEN.
AR
IT STARTED WITH AN IDEA.

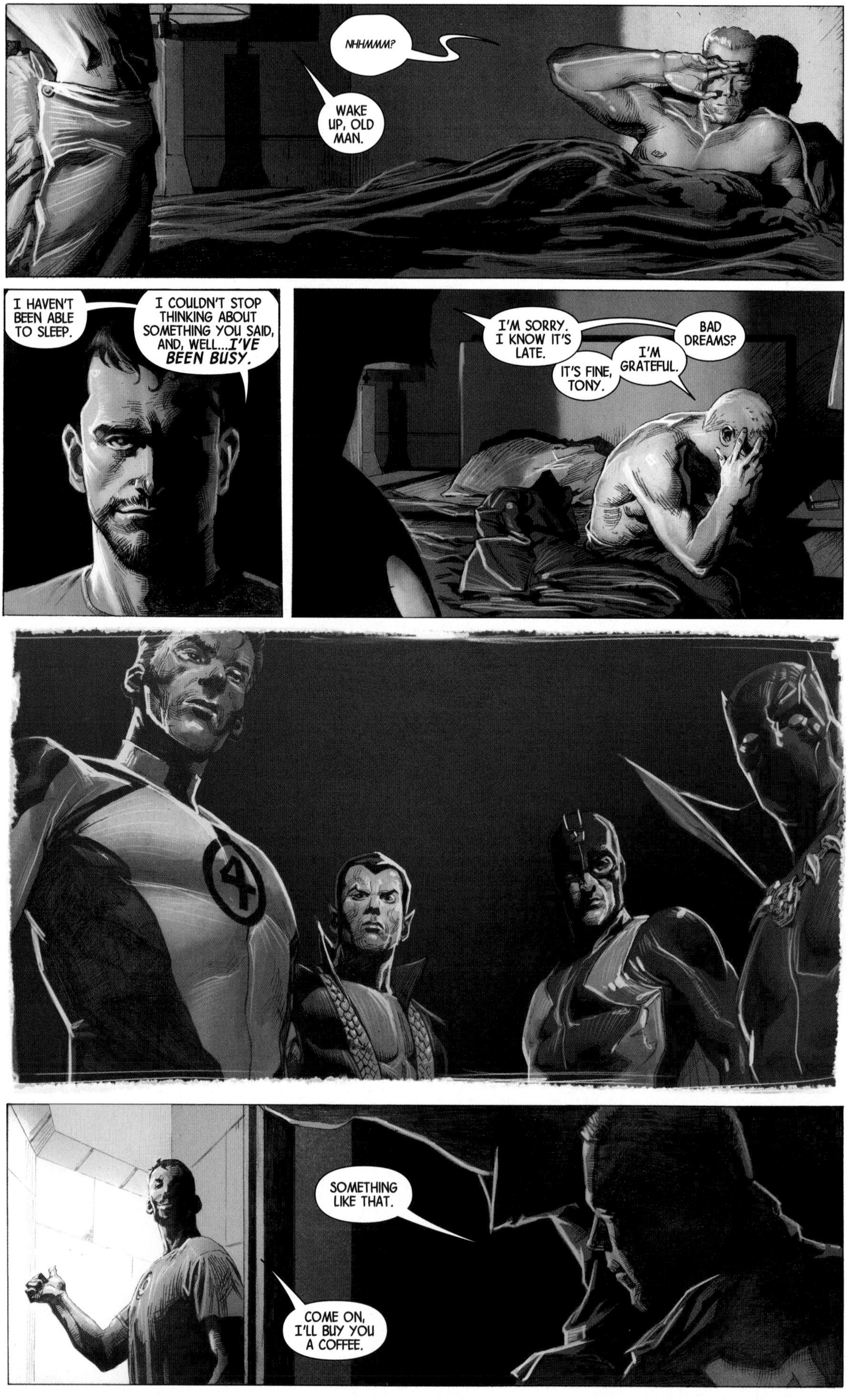
NHHMMM?
WAKE UP, OLD MAN.
I HAVEN'T BEEN ABLE TO SLEEP.
I COULDN'T STOP THINKING ABOUT SOMETHING YOU SAID, AND, WELL...I'VE BEEN BUSY.
I'M SORRY. I KNOW IT'S LATE.
BAD DREAMS?
IT'S FINE, TONY.
I'M GRATEFUL.
SOMETHING LIKE THAT.
COME ON, I'LL BUY YOU A COFFEE.

SO...THIS IDEA HAS BEEN RUNNING THROUGH MY MIND. IT'S OVERWHELMING--*ALL-CONSUMING*-- AND I CAN'T SH!T IT OFF.

THE EXACT SAME THING HAPPENED THE DAY WE FOUND YOU.

YOU REMEMBER THAT?

OH...I REMEMBER *EVERYTHING* ABOUT THAT DAY.

WE STARTED SOMETHING THAT *MATTERED.* BECAUSE OF YOU, THE WORLD CHANGED.

I CHANGED.

SEE, THE *BEST* IDEAS ARE ALWAYS THE *SIMPLEST.* AND THE LAST WEEK WHEN WE WERE TALKING ABOUT HOW THINGS KEEP *ESCALATING...*

HOW THE WORLD IS EVER MORE DANGEROUS, HOW THREATS ARE MORE FREQUENT... HOW OUR ENEMIES ARE SEEMINGLY ENDLESS...

WELL, STEVE, THAT'S A COMPLEX PROBLEM, BUT YOU HAD A PRETTY SIMPLE ANSWER...

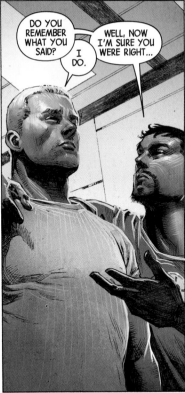

DO YOU REMEMBER WHAT YOU SAID?

I DO.

WELL, NOW I'M SURE YOU WERE RIGHT...

"WE HAVE TO GET *BIGGER.*"

THE AVENGERS:

AVENGER

S WORLD

WRITER: **JONATHAN HICKMAN**

ARTIST: **JEROME OPEÑA**

COLOR ARTIST: **DEAN WHITE**
LETTERER: **VC's CORY PETIT**
COVER ART: **DUSTIN WEAVER & JUSTIN PONSOR**
VARIANT COVER ART: **STEVE MCNIVEN & JUSTIN PONSOR; ESAD RIBIC; SKOTTIE YOUNG; AND MARK BROOKS**
ASSISTANT EDITOR: **JAKE THOMAS**
EDITORS: **TOM BREVOORT with LAUREN SANKOVITCH**
EDITOR IN CHIEF: **AXEL ALONSO**
CHIEF CREATIVE OFFICER: **JOE QUESADA**
PUBLISHER: **DAN BUCKLEY**
EXECUTIVE PRODUCER: **ALAN FINE**

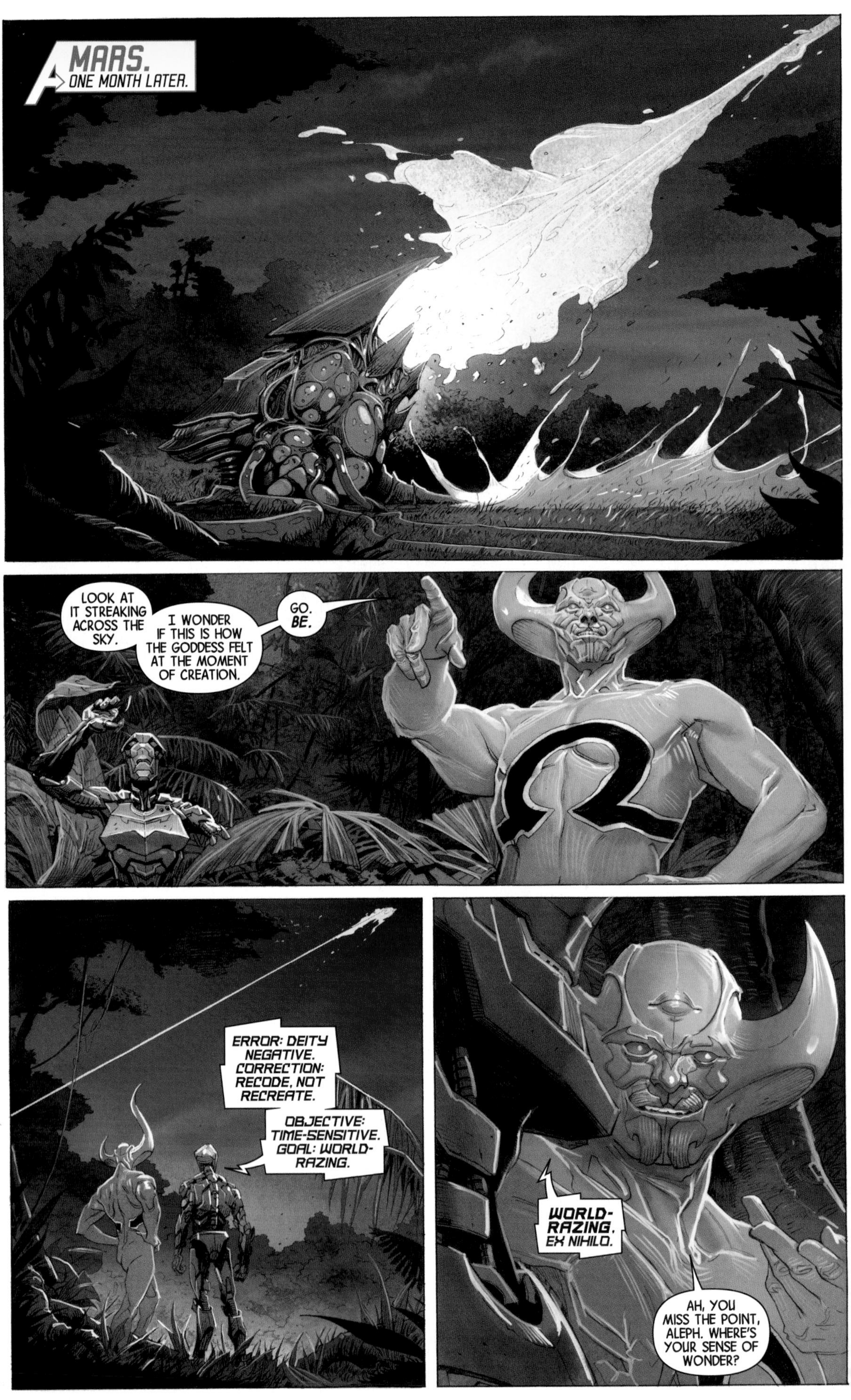
MARS.
ONE MONTH LATER.
LOOK AT IT STREAKING ACROSS THE SKY.
I WONDER IF THIS IS HOW THE GODDESS FELT AT THE MOMENT OF CREATION.
GO. BE.
ERROR: DEITY NEGATIVE. CORRECTION: RECODE, NOT RECREATE.
OBJECTIVE: TIME-SENSITIVE. GOAL: WORLD-RAZING.
WORLD-RAZING, EX NIHILO.
AH, YOU MISS THE POINT, ALEPH. WHERE'S YOUR SENSE OF WONDER?

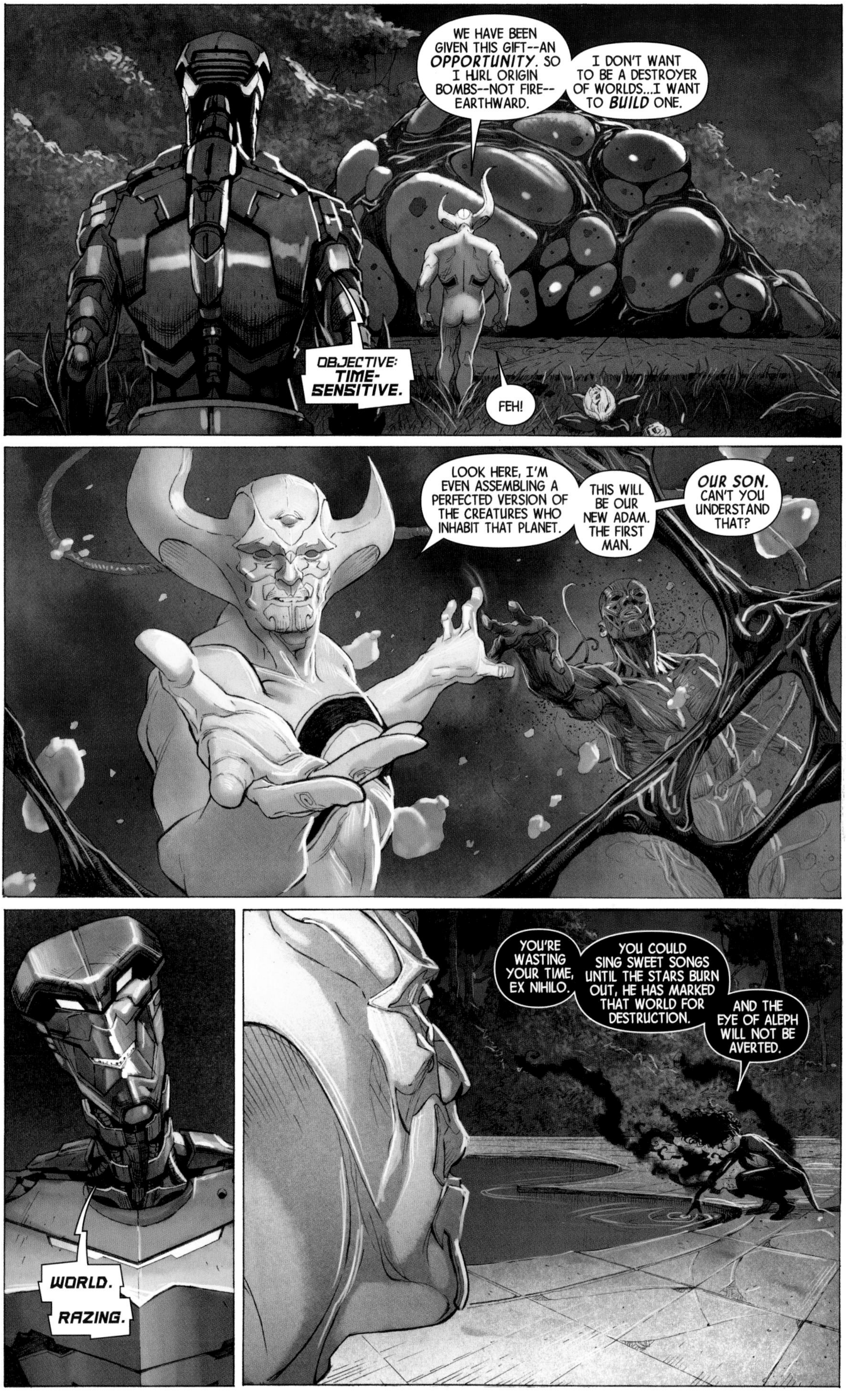
WE HAVE BEEN GIVEN THIS GIFT--AN OPPORTUNITY. SO I HURL ORIGIN BOMBS--NOT FIRE--EARTHWARD.
I DON'T WANT TO BE A DESTROYER OF WORLDS...I WANT TO BUILD ONE.
OBJECTIVE: TIME-SENSITIVE.
FEH!
LOOK HERE, I'M EVEN ASSEMBLING A PERFECTED VERSION OF THE CREATURES WHO INHABIT THAT PLANET.
THIS WILL BE OUR NEW ADAM. THE FIRST MAN.
OUR SON. CAN'T YOU UNDERSTAND THAT?
WORLD.
RAZING.
YOU'RE WASTING YOUR TIME, EX NIHILO.
YOU COULD SING SWEET SONGS UNTIL THE STARS BURN OUT, HE HAS MARKED THAT WORLD FOR DESTRUCTION.
AND THE EYE OF ALEPH WILL NOT BE AVERTED.

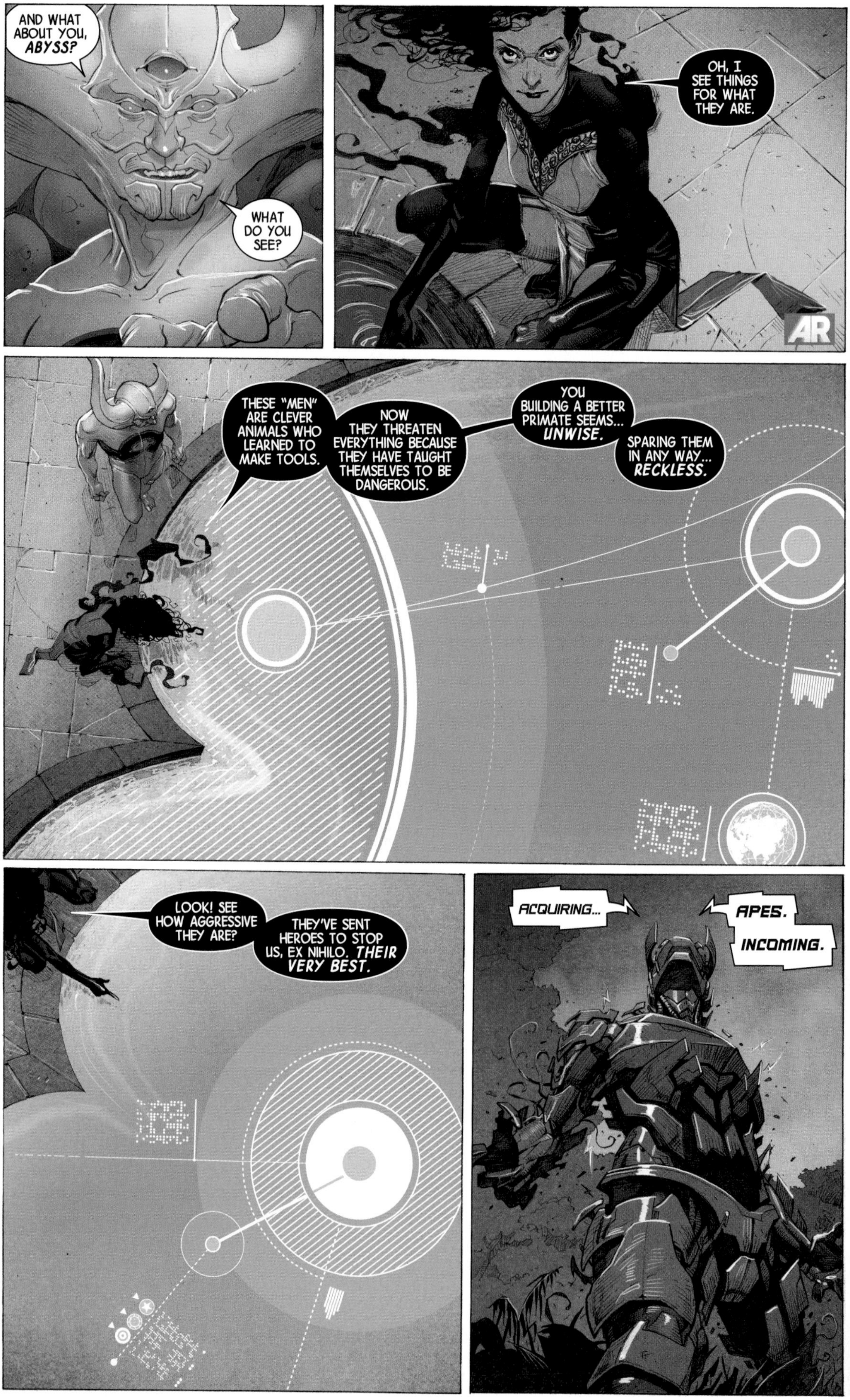
AND WHAT ABOUT YOU, ABYSS?
WHAT DO YOU SEE?
OH, I SEE THINGS FOR WHAT THEY ARE.
AR
THESE "MEN" ARE CLEVER ANIMALS WHO LEARNED TO MAKE TOOLS.
NOW THEY THREATEN EVERYTHING BECAUSE THEY HAVE TAUGHT THEMSELVES TO BE DANGEROUS.
YOU BUILDING A BETTER PRIMATE SEEMS... UNWISE.
SPARING THEM IN ANY WAY... RECKLESS.
LOOK! SEE HOW AGGRESSIVE THEY ARE?
THEY'VE SENT HEROES TO STOP US, EX NIHILO. THEIR VERY BEST.
ACQUIRING...
APES.
INCOMING.

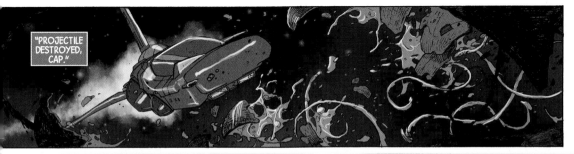

"PROJECTILE DESTROYED, CAP."

NICELY DONE, CLINT.

I MARKED, AND RECORDED, THE TRAJECTORY. BLACK WIDOW SHOULD BE ABLE TO FOLLOW--

GOT IT. PLOTTED, AND WE'RE LOCKED ON. SETTING A COURSE TO SLIP US IN ALONG THE HORIZON.

THEY WON'T SEE US COMING.

VEGETATION? IS THAT EVEN POSSIBLE.

I DON'T KNOW WHY IT WOULDN'T BE...

THERE IT IS!

IT'S...IT'S GREEN.

PREPARE FOR LANDING.

"THE FIRST TWO BOMBS THAT HIT EARTH COMPLETELY CHANGED THE BIOSPHERES OF THE IMPACT ZONES.

"WHOEVER THESE PEOPLE ARE, THEY'VE ALTERED BILLIONS OF YEARS OF EVOLUTION IN MINUTES."

AND THEY DID IT BY REMOTE, FROM OVER TWO HUNDRED MILLION KILOMETERS AWAY. AN IMPRESSIVE FEAT...

GODLIKE EVEN.

PFFT!

BRUCE, YOU'RE BETTER AT THIS STUFF THAN I AM. ANYTHING ELSE THAT NEEDS TO BE SAID?

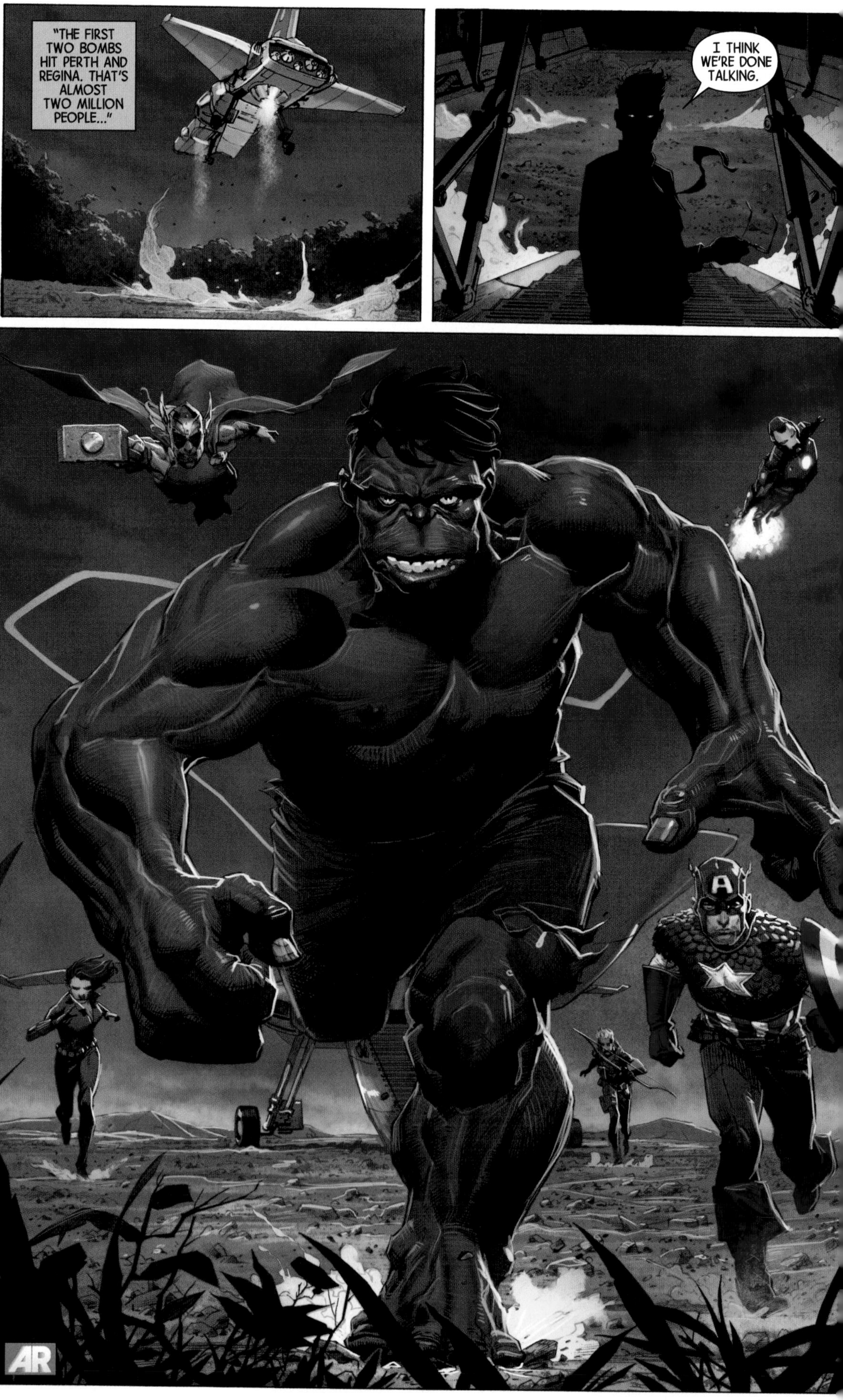
"THE FIRST TWO BOMBS HIT PERTH AND REGINA. THAT'S ALMOST TWO MILLION PEOPLE..."
I THINK WE'RE DONE TALKING.

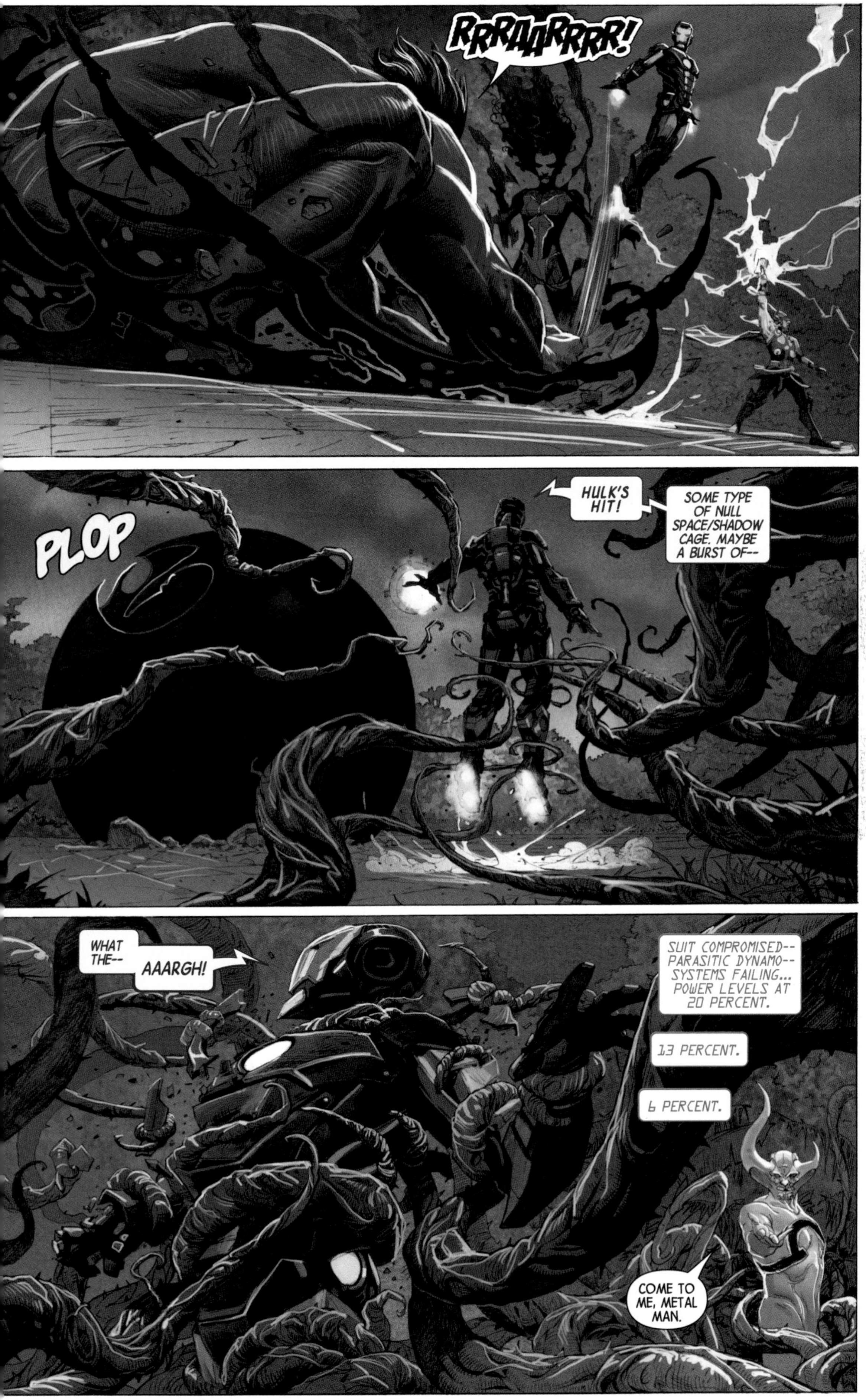
RRRAAARRRR!
PLOP
HULK'S HIT!
SOME TYPE OF NULL SPACE/SHADOW CAGE. MAYBE A BURST OF--
WHAT THE--
AAARGH!
SUIT COMPROMISED--PARASITIC DYNAMO--SYSTEMS FAILING... POWER LEVELS AT 20 PERCENT.
13 PERCENT.
6 PERCENT.
COME TO ME, METAL MAN.

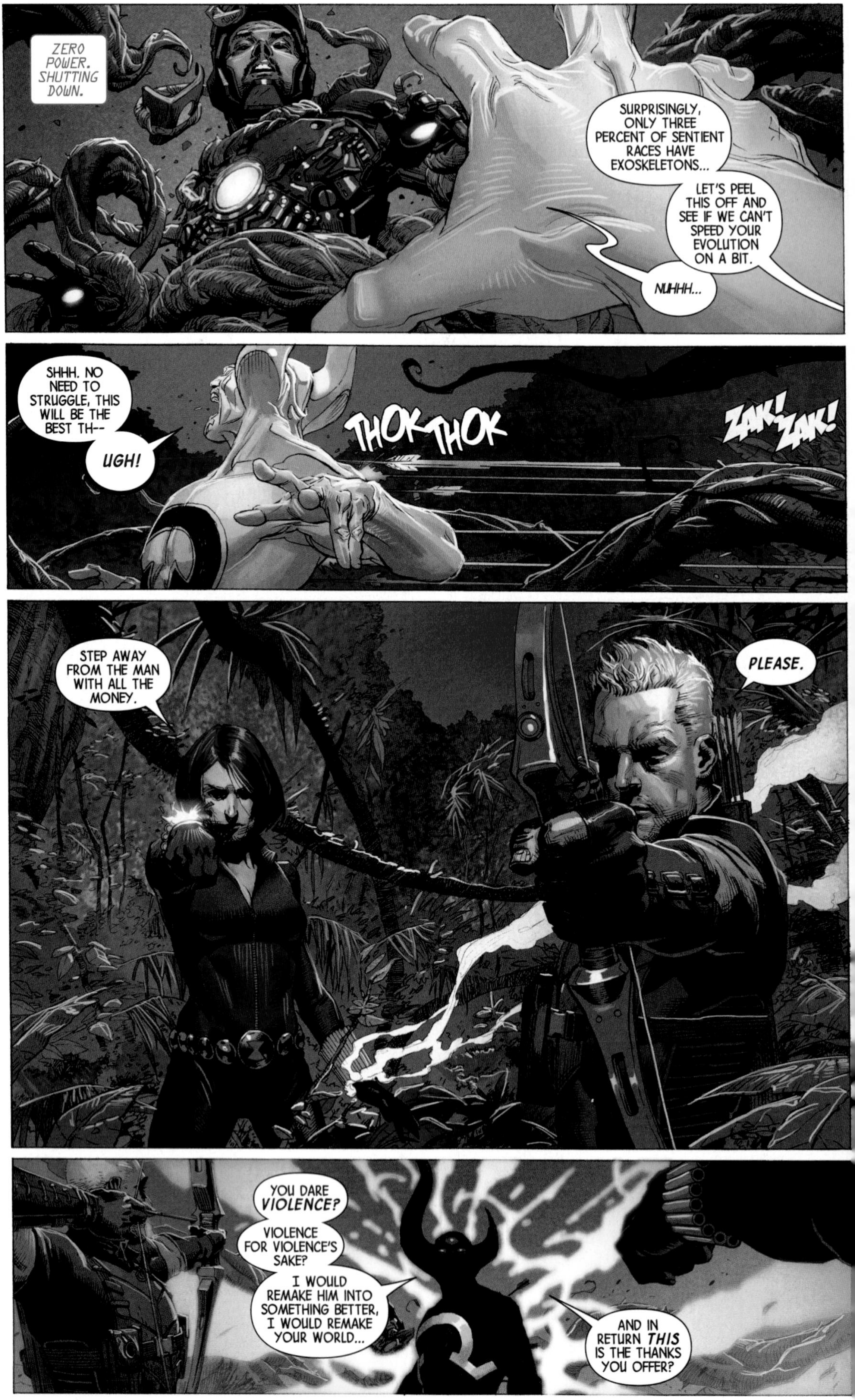
ZERO POWER. SHUTTING DOWN.
SURPRISINGLY, ONLY THREE PERCENT OF SENTIENT RACES HAVE EXOSKELETONS...
LET'S PEEL THIS OFF AND SEE IF WE CAN'T SPEED YOUR EVOLUTION ON A BIT.
NUHHH...
SHHH. NO NEED TO STRUGGLE, THIS WILL BE THE BEST TH--
UGH!
THOK THOK
ZAK! ZAK!
STEP AWAY FROM THE MAN WITH ALL THE MONEY.
PLEASE.
YOU DARE VIOLENCE?
VIOLENCE FOR VIOLENCE'S SAKE?
I WOULD REMAKE HIM INTO SOMETHING BETTER, I WOULD REMAKE YOUR WORLD...
AND IN RETURN THIS IS THE THANKS YOU OFFER?

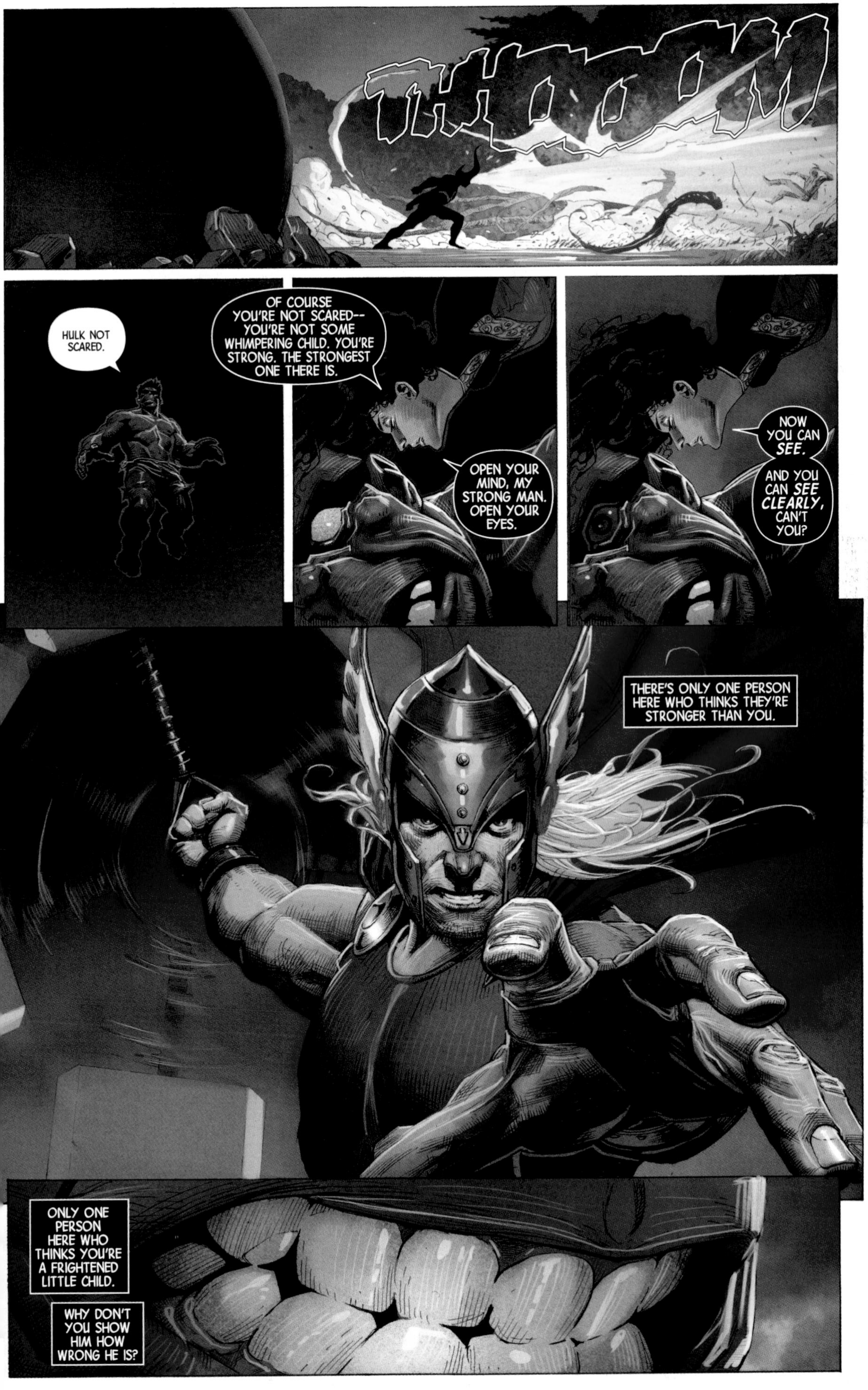
THOOOM
HULK NOT SCARED.
OF COURSE YOU'RE NOT SCARED-- YOU'RE NOT SOME WHIMPERING CHILD. YOU'RE STRONG. THE STRONGEST ONE THERE IS.
OPEN YOUR MIND, MY STRONG MAN. OPEN YOUR EYES.
NOW YOU CAN *SEE.*
AND YOU CAN *SEE CLEARLY,* CAN'T YOU?
THERE'S ONLY ONE PERSON HERE WHO THINKS THEY'RE STRONGER THAN YOU.
ONLY ONE PERSON HERE WHO THINKS YOU'RE A FRIGHTENED LITTLE CHILD.
WHY DON'T YOU SHOW HIM HOW WRONG HE IS?

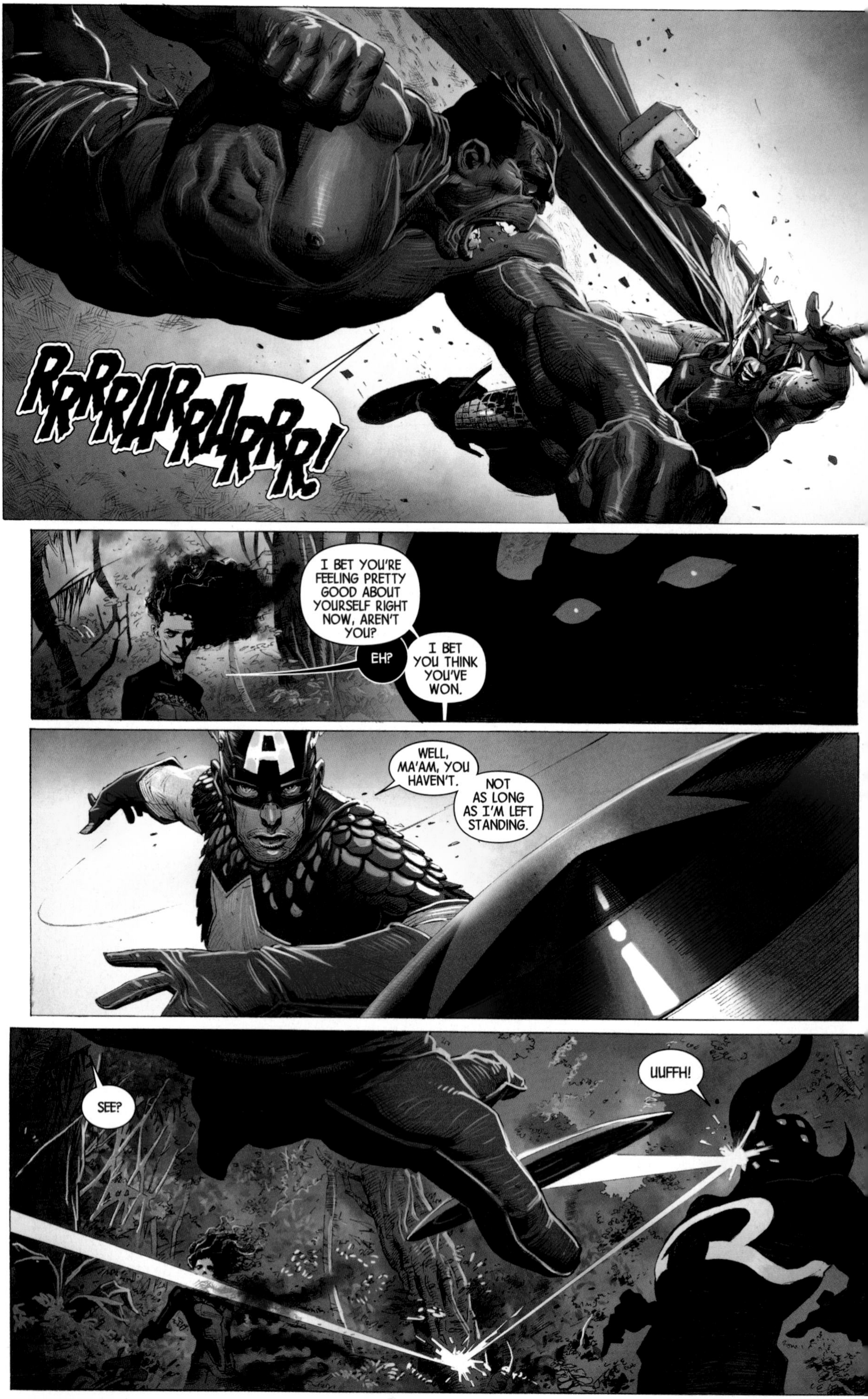
RRRRARRRARRRR!
I BET YOU'RE FEELING PRETTY GOOD ABOUT YOURSELF RIGHT NOW, AREN'T YOU?
EH?
I BET YOU THINK YOU'VE WON.
WELL, MA'AM, YOU HAVEN'T.
NOT AS LONG AS I'M LEFT STANDING.
SEE?
UUFFH!

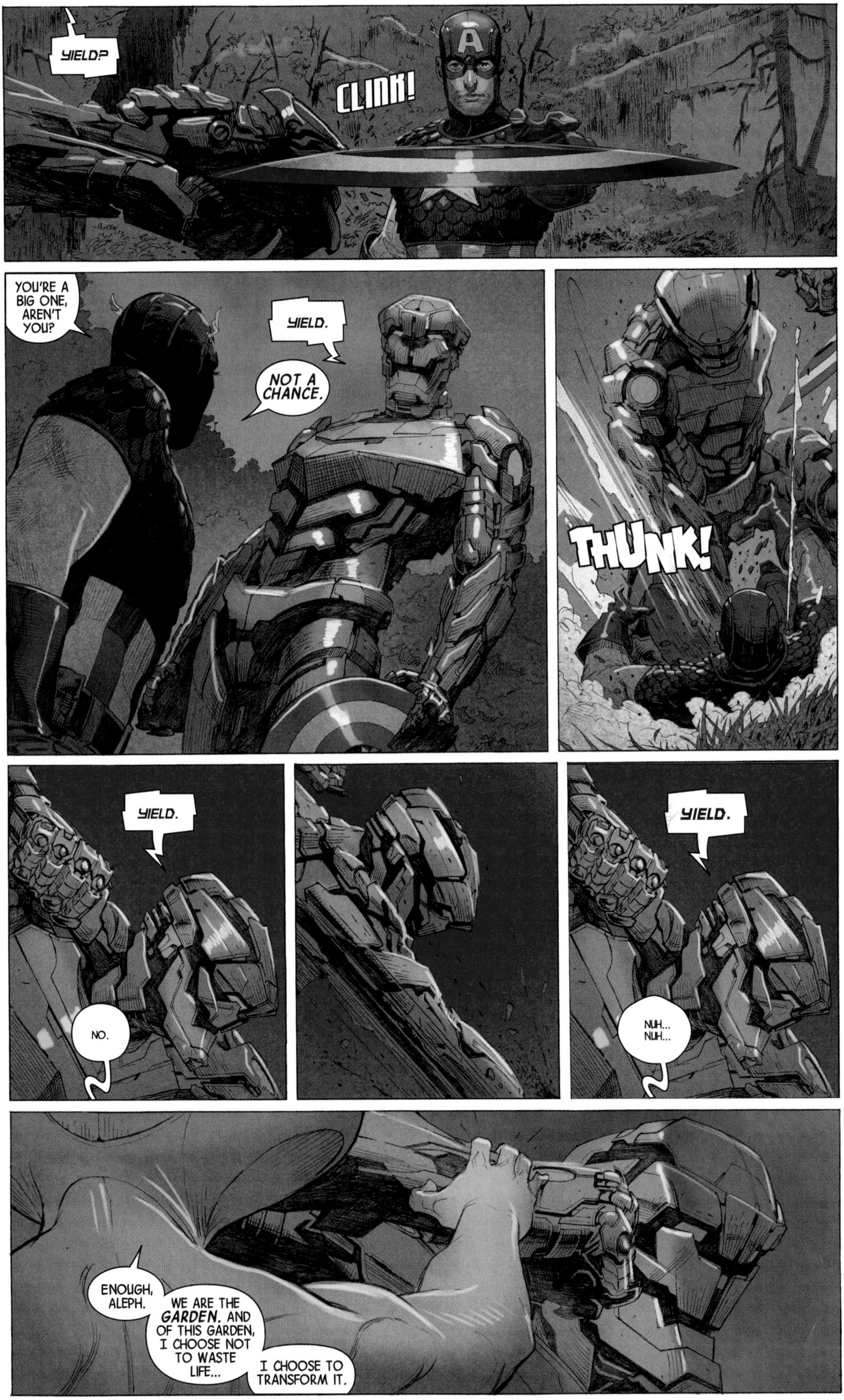
YIELD?
CLINK!
YOU'RE A BIG ONE, AREN'T YOU?
YIELD.
NOT A CHANCE.
THUNK!
YIELD.
NO.
YIELD.
NUH... NUH...
ENOUGH, ALEPH.
WE ARE THE GARDEN. AND OF THIS GARDEN, I CHOOSE NOT TO WASTE LIFE...
I CHOOSE TO TRANSFORM IT.

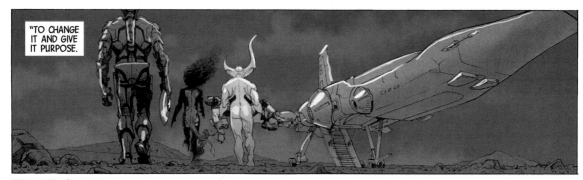

"TO CHANGE IT AND GIVE IT PURPOSE.

"WE WILL USE HIM TO SEND A MESSAGE.

"WE'LL SEND HIM *HOME* TO WRITE A WARNING IN THE HEAVENS.

"HERE, EARTH. HERE IS YOUR CHAMPION.

"WATCH HIM BURN RED THROUGH THE SKY.

"WE HAVE BEEN SENT TO JUDGE YOUR WORLD, AND WE CANNOT BE STOPPED.

"THESE HEROES WERE THE BEST YOU HAD TO OFFER.

"AND THEY WERE FOUND... *WANTING.*"

AVENGERS TOWER.
THREE DAYS LATER.
"WE HAVE TO
GET BIGGER."

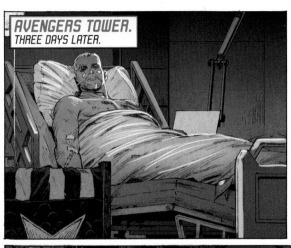

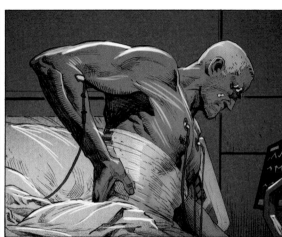

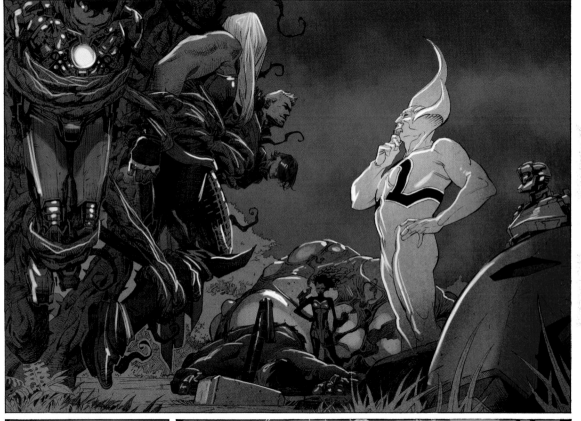

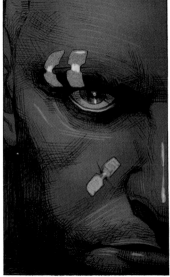

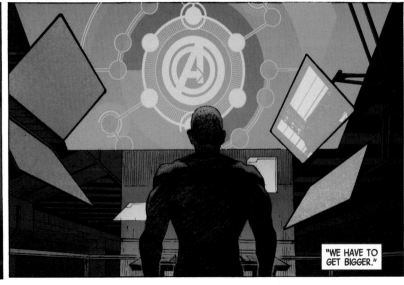

WE HAVE HELD FOR SO LONG, BUT THERE IS SOMETHING LOOMING JUST PAST THE HORIZON.

WE CAN'T SEE IT, BUT IT'S COMING. IT'S GOING TO BE TOO MUCH, AND TOO SOON--AND WE HAVE TO GET READY NOW.

WE'LL KEEP THIS QUIET UNTIL THEY'RE NEEDED-- YOU AND I WILL DO MOST OF THE RECRUITING. SPECIFIC PEOPLE FOR SPECIFIC NEEDS.

BUT THEY'LL BE OUT THERE. READY...

WAITING...

"AND THEN, WHEN THAT DAY COMES, ALL *YOU* HAVE TO DO IS *SAY THE WORDS*."

WAKE THE WORLD

CLICK!

IT WAS A *SUMMONING.*

HE WAS THE FIRST-- *OUR VERY BEST.*

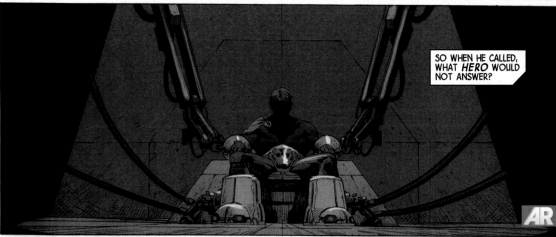

SO WHEN HE CALLED, WHAT *HERO* WOULD NOT ANSWER?

AR

IT STARTED WITH AN IDEA.

THE SPARK THAT STARTED THE FIRE WAS *EXPANSION.*

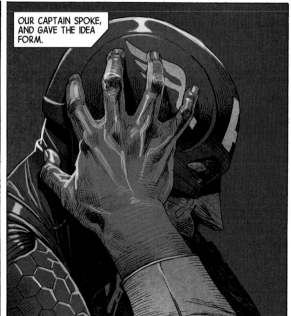

OUR CAPTAIN SPOKE, AND GAVE THE IDEA FORM.

HE SAID THE WORDS, AND MADE IT *REAL.*

HE SAID...

ASSEMBLE AT DAWN.

ASSEMBLE AT DAWN.

AND HOW COULD WE NOT?

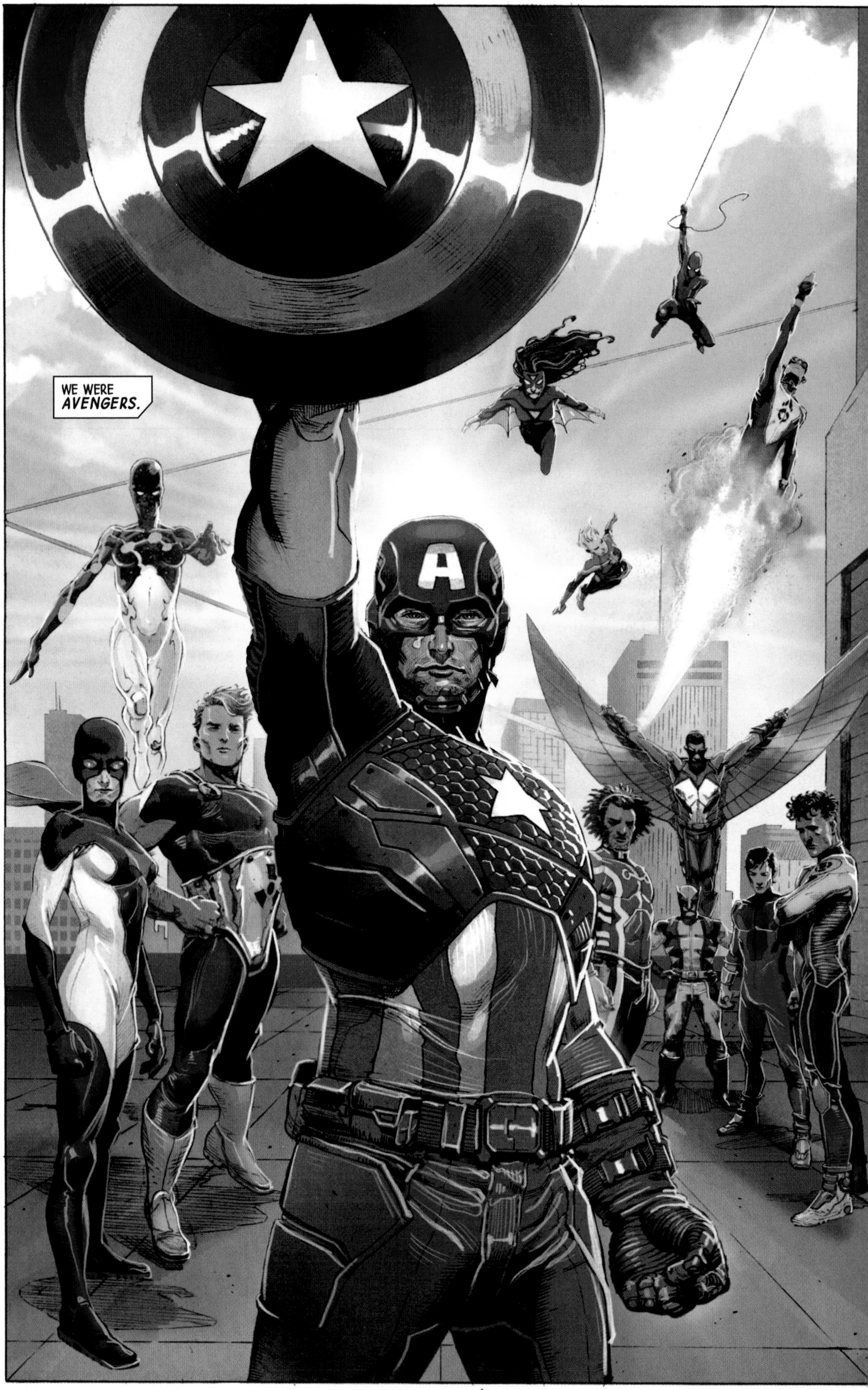
WE WERE AVENGERS.

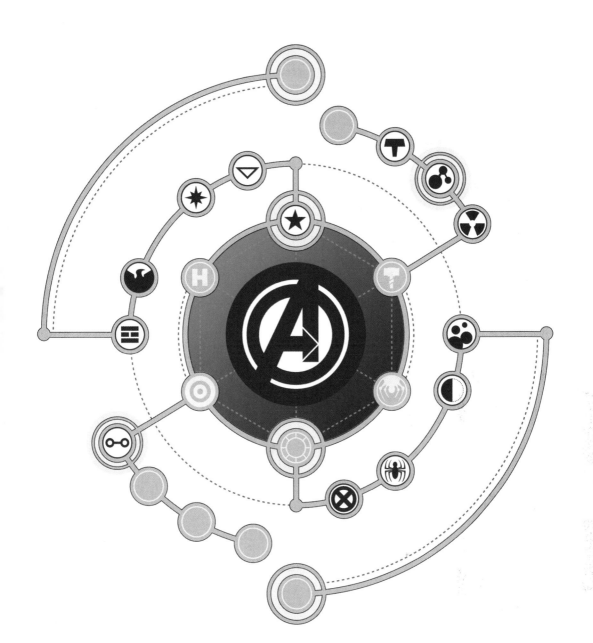

WAKE THE WORLD

AVENGERS #2

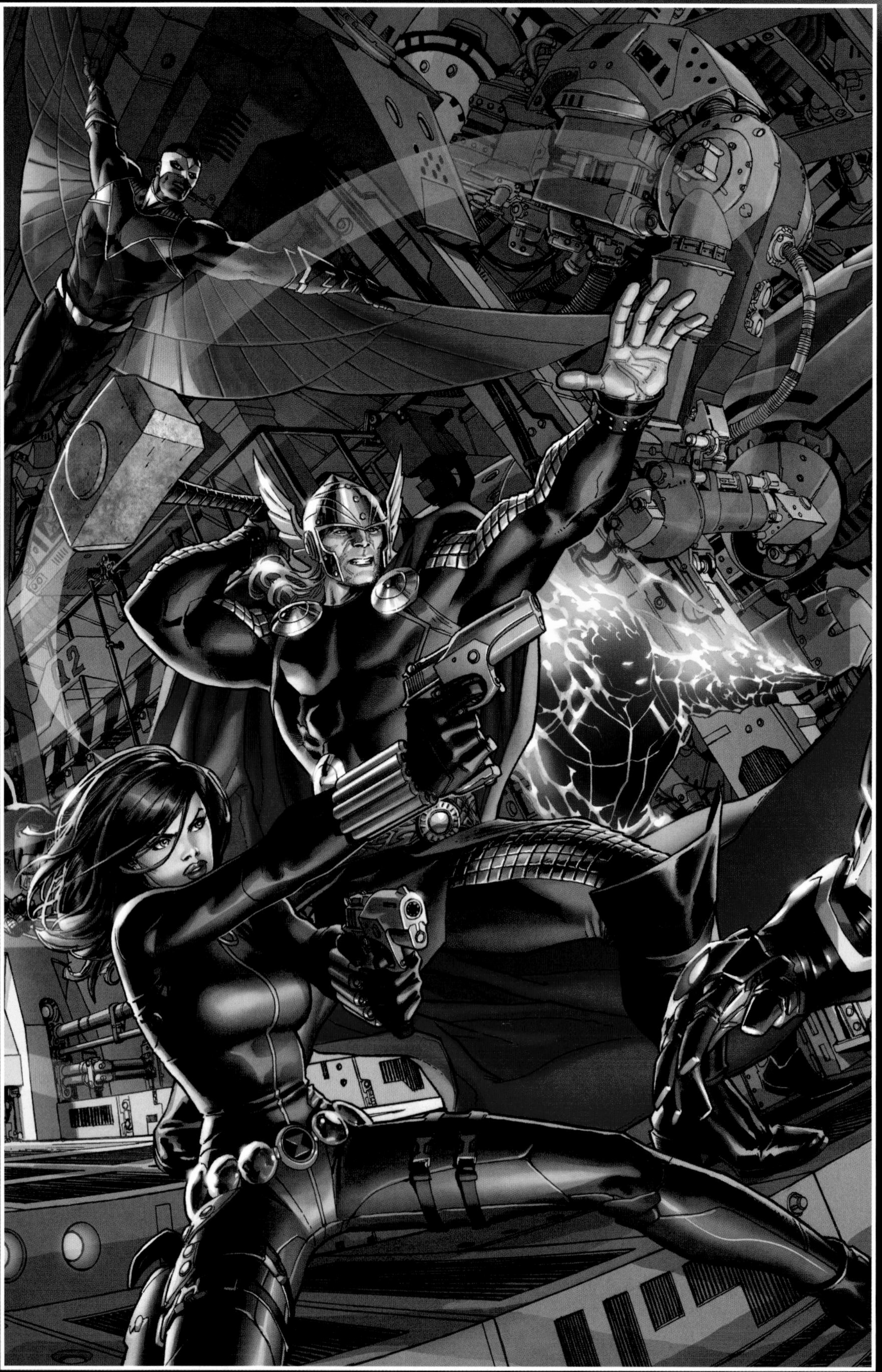

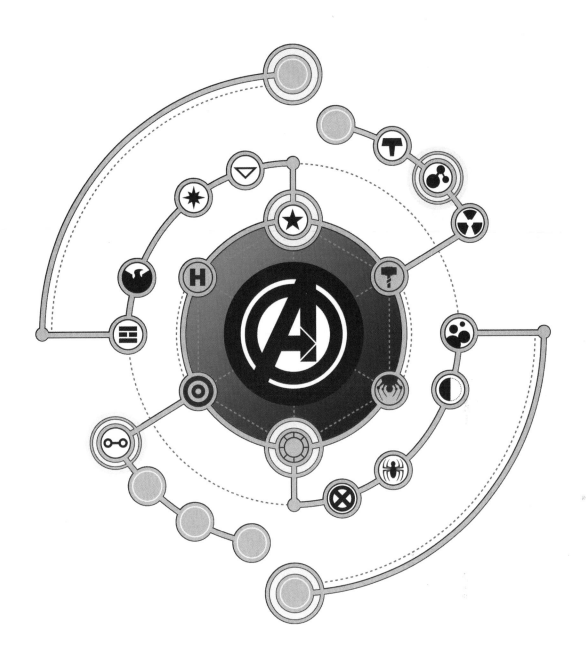

EARTH'S MIGHTIEST HEROES

CAPTAIN AMERICA · IRON MAN · THOR · HAWKEYE · BLACK WIDOW · HULK
WOLVERINE · SPIDER-MAN · CAPTAIN MARVEL · SPIDER-WOMAN
FALCON · SHANG-CHI · SUNSPOT · CANNONBALL · MANIFOLD
SMASHER · CAPTAIN UNIVERSE · HYPERION

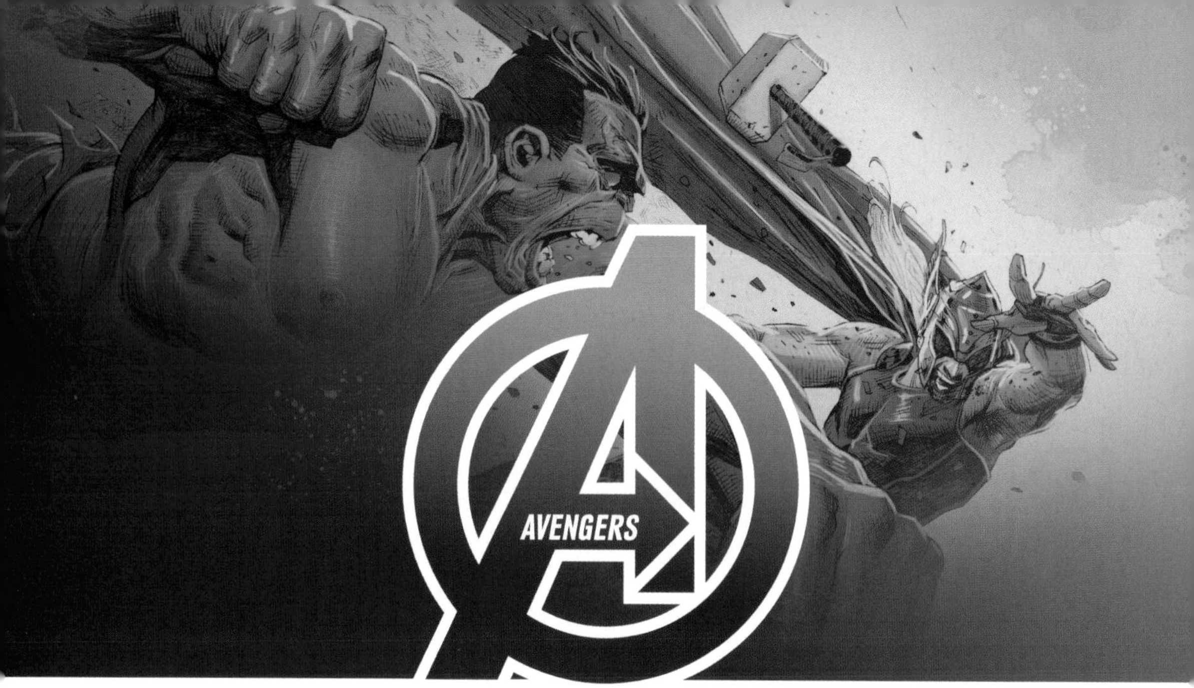
AVENGERS

"WE WERE AVENGERS"

WRITER: JONATHAN HICKMAN
ARTIST: JEROME OPEÑA

COLOR ARTISTS: DEAN WHITE with JUSTIN PONSOR & MORRY HOLLOWELL
LETTERER: VC's CORY PETIT
COVER ART: DUSTIN WEAVER & JUSTIN PONSOR
VARIANT COVER ART: ESAD RIBIC; JOHN ROMITA JR, KLAUS JANSON & DEAN WHITE
ASSISTANT EDITOR: JAKE THOMAS
EDITORS: TOM BREVOORT with LAUREN SANKOVITCH
EDITOR IN CHIEF: AXEL ALONSO
CHIEF CREATIVE OFFICER: JOE QUESADA
PUBLISHER: DAN BUCKLEY
EXECUTIVE PRODUCER: ALAN FINE

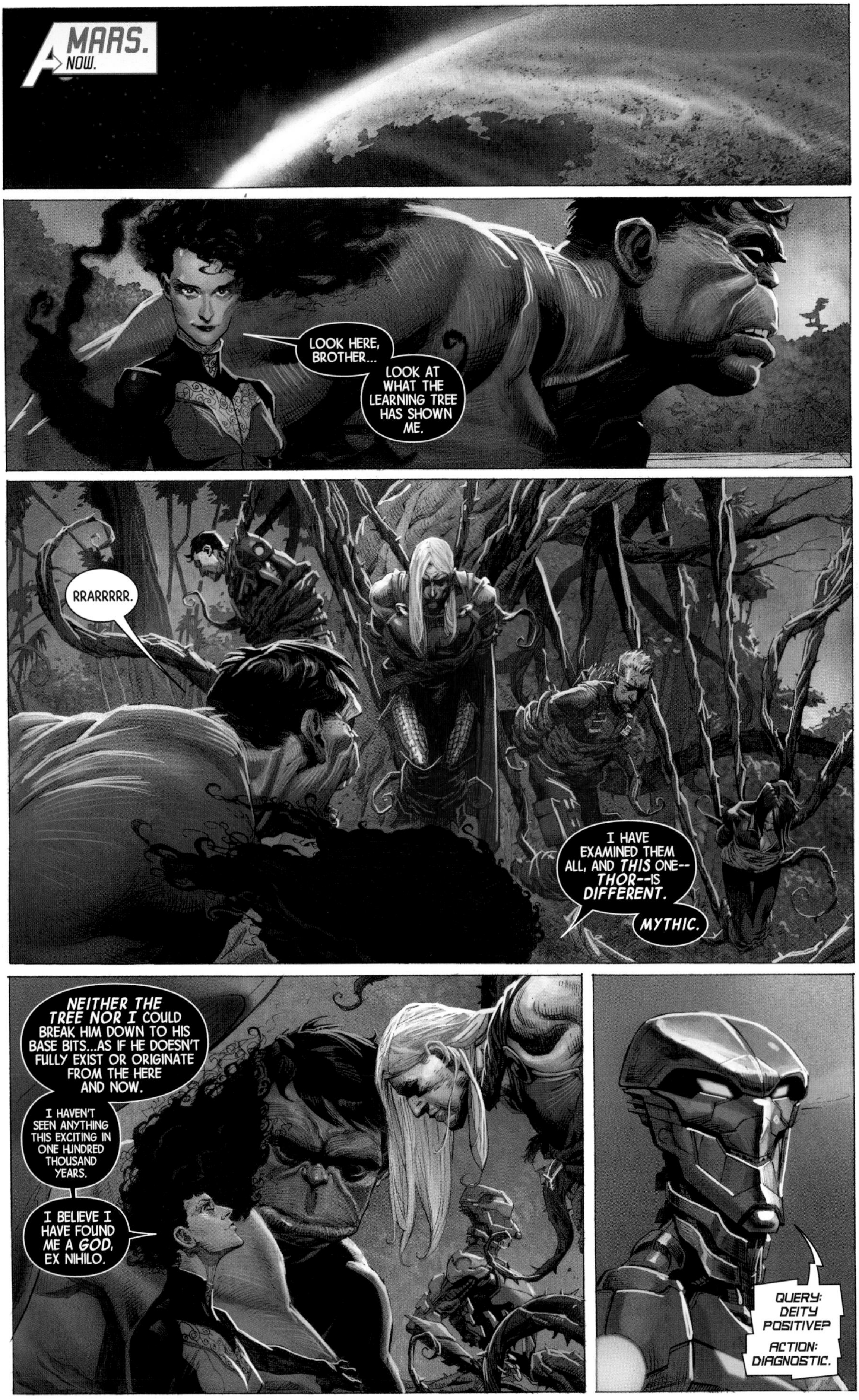

MARS.
NOW.
LOOK HERE, BROTHER...
LOOK AT WHAT THE LEARNING TREE HAS SHOWN ME.
RRARRRRR.
I HAVE EXAMINED THEM ALL, AND THIS ONE--THOR--IS DIFFERENT.
MYTHIC.
NEITHER THE TREE NOR I COULD BREAK HIM DOWN TO HIS BASE BITS...AS IF HE DOESN'T FULLY EXIST OR ORIGINATE FROM THE HERE AND NOW.
I HAVEN'T SEEN ANYTHING THIS EXCITING IN ONE HUNDRED THOUSAND YEARS.
I BELIEVE I HAVE FOUND ME A GOD, EX NIHILO.
QUERY: DEITY POSITIVE?
ACTION: DIAGNOSTIC.

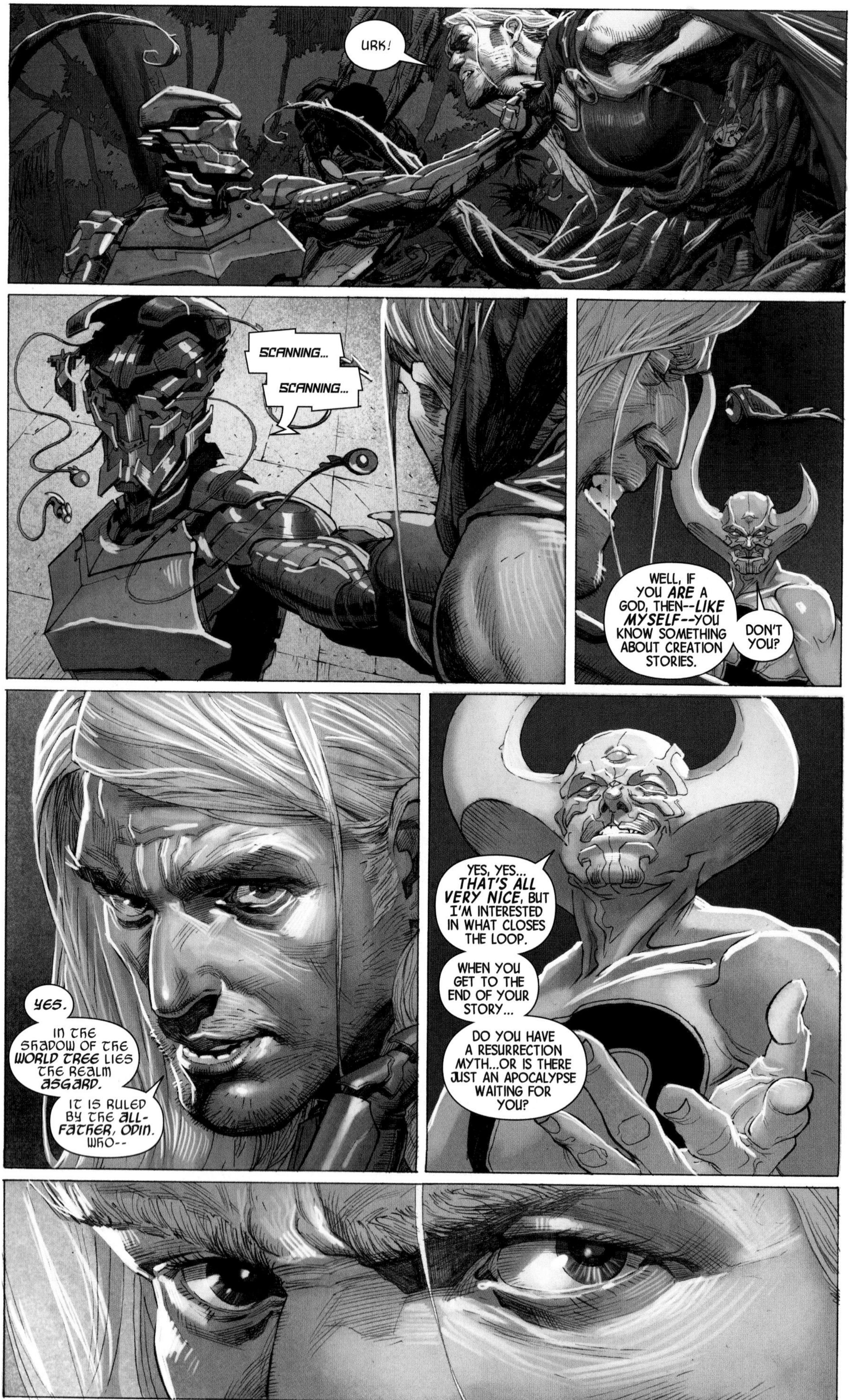
URK!
SCANNING...
SCANNING...
WELL, IF YOU ARE A GOD, THEN--LIKE MYSELF--YOU KNOW SOMETHING ABOUT CREATION STORIES.
DON'T YOU?
YES.
IN THE SHADOW OF THE WORLD TREE LIES THE REALM ASGARD.
IT IS RULED BY THE ALL-FATHER, ODIN. WHO--
YES, YES... THAT'S ALL VERY NICE, BUT I'M INTERESTED IN WHAT CLOSES THE LOOP.
WHEN YOU GET TO THE END OF YOUR STORY...
DO YOU HAVE A RESURRECTION MYTH...OR IS THERE JUST AN APOCALYPSE WAITING FOR YOU?

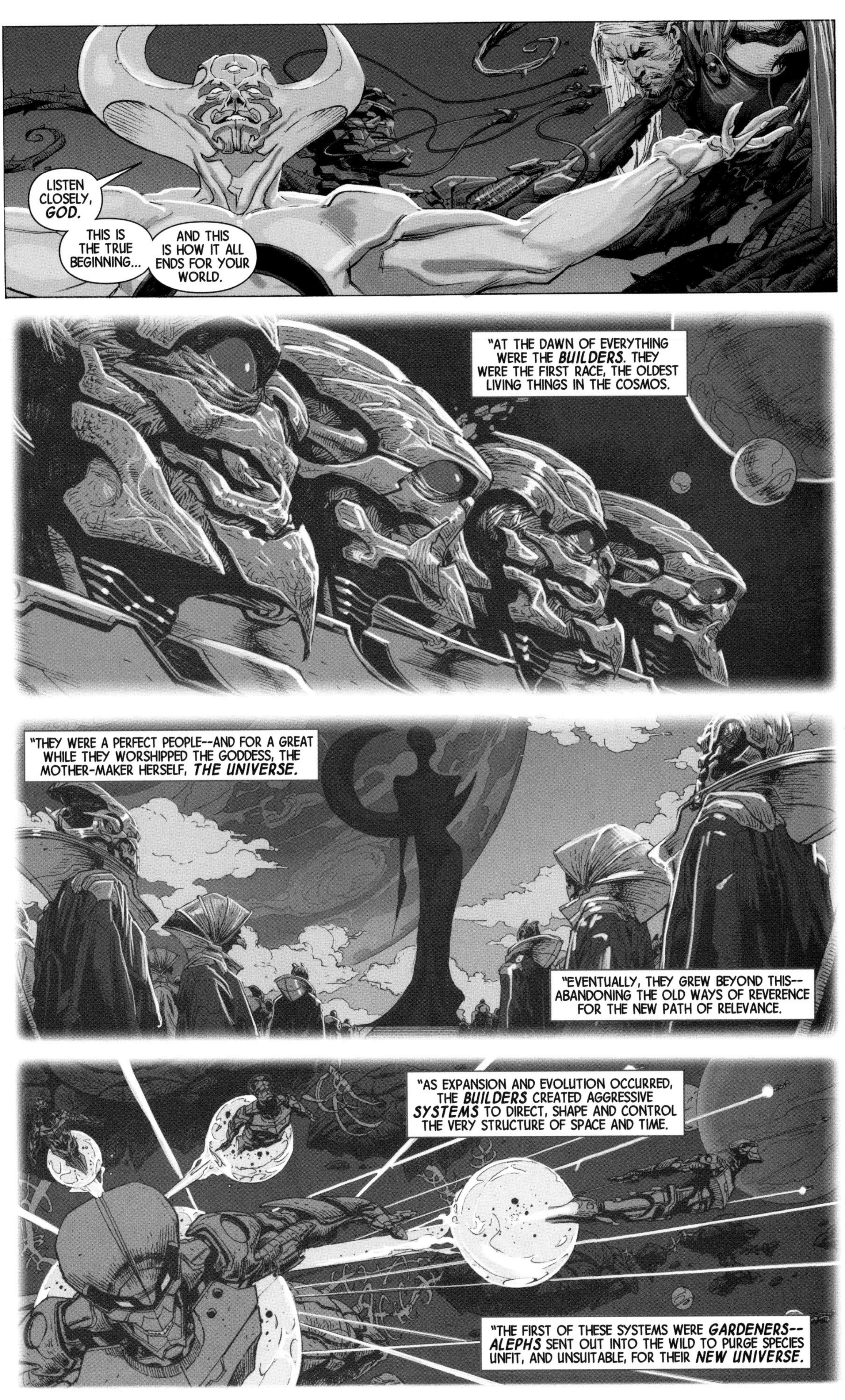
LISTEN CLOSELY, GOD.
THIS IS THE TRUE BEGINNING...
AND THIS IS HOW IT ALL ENDS FOR YOUR WORLD.
"AT THE DAWN OF EVERYTHING WERE THE BUILDERS. THEY WERE THE FIRST RACE, THE OLDEST LIVING THINGS IN THE COSMOS.
"THEY WERE A PERFECT PEOPLE--AND FOR A GREAT WHILE THEY WORSHIPPED THE GODDESS, THE MOTHER-MAKER HERSELF, THE UNIVERSE.
"EVENTUALLY, THEY GREW BEYOND THIS--ABANDONING THE OLD WAYS OF REVERENCE FOR THE NEW PATH OF RELEVANCE.
"AS EXPANSION AND EVOLUTION OCCURRED, THE BUILDERS CREATED AGGRESSIVE SYSTEMS TO DIRECT, SHAPE AND CONTROL THE VERY STRUCTURE OF SPACE AND TIME.
"THE FIRST OF THESE SYSTEMS WERE GARDENERS--ALEPHS SENT OUT INTO THE WILD TO PURGE SPECIES UNFIT, AND UNSUITABLE, FOR THEIR NEW UNIVERSE.

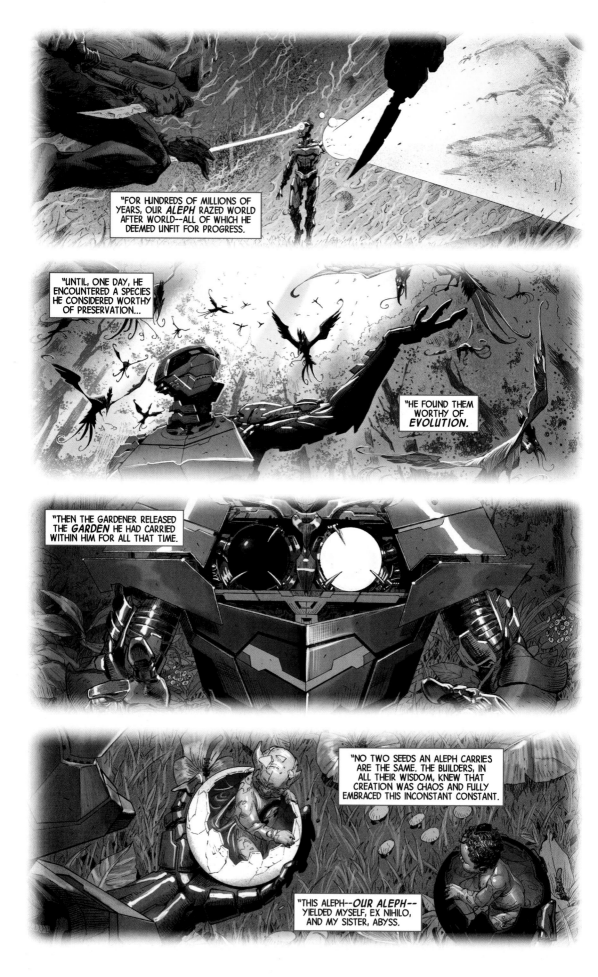

"FOR HUNDREDS OF MILLIONS OF YEARS, OUR *ALEPH* RAZED WORLD AFTER WORLD--ALL OF WHICH HE DEEMED UNFIT FOR PROGRESS.

"UNTIL, ONE DAY, HE ENCOUNTERED A SPECIES HE CONSIDERED WORTHY OF PRESERVATION...

"HE FOUND THEM WORTHY OF *EVOLUTION.*

"THEN THE GARDENER RELEASED THE *GARDEN* HE HAD CARRIED WITHIN HIM FOR ALL THAT TIME.

"NO TWO SEEDS AN ALEPH CARRIES ARE THE SAME. THE BUILDERS, IN ALL THEIR WISDOM, KNEW THAT CREATION WAS CHAOS AND FULLY EMBRACED THIS INCONSTANT CONSTANT.

"THIS ALEPH--*OUR ALEPH*-- YIELDED MYSELF, EX NIHILO, AND MY SISTER, ABYSS.

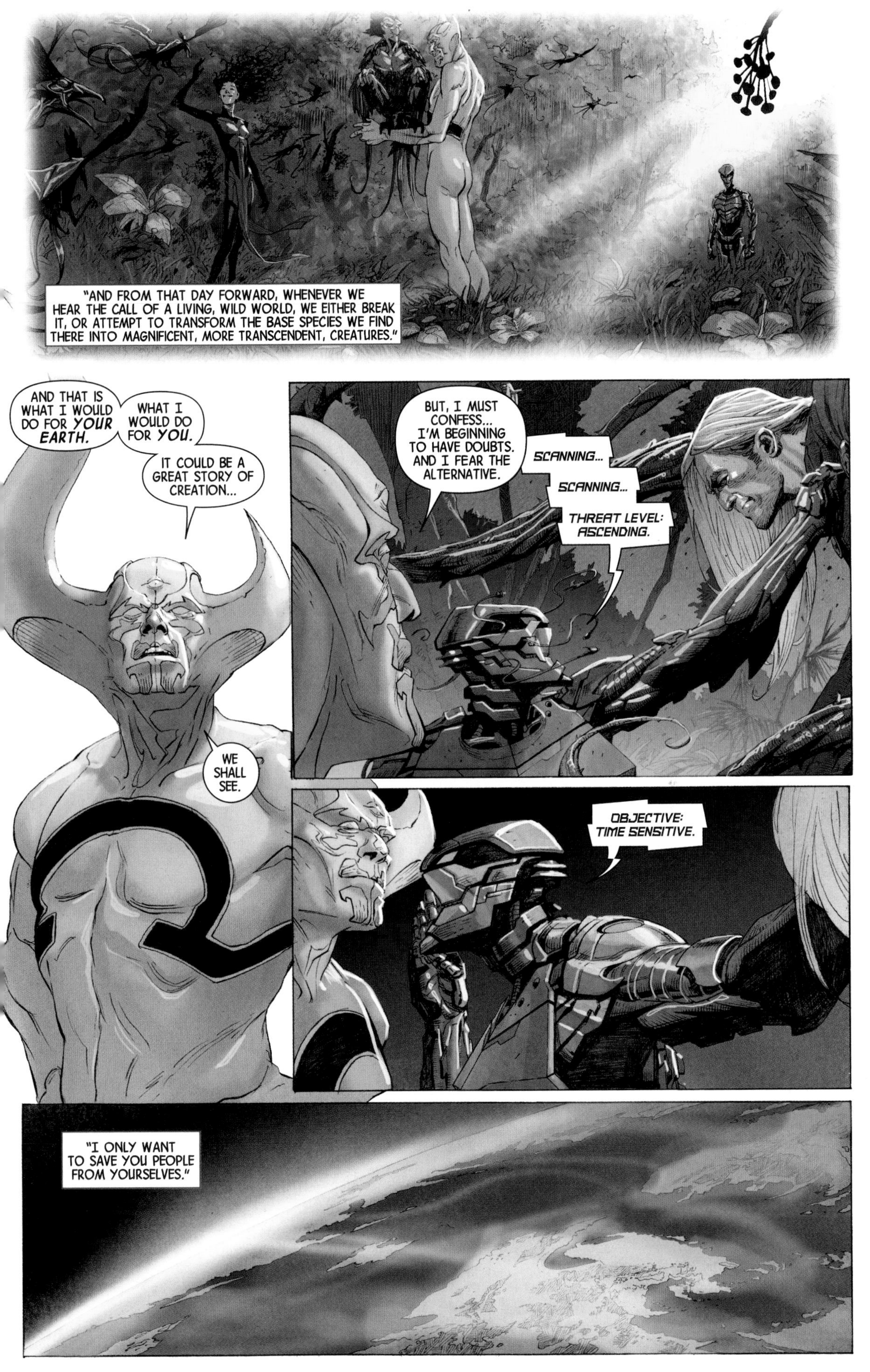
"AND FROM THAT DAY FORWARD, WHENEVER WE HEAR THE CALL OF A LIVING, WILD WORLD, WE EITHER BREAK IT, OR ATTEMPT TO TRANSFORM THE BASE SPECIES WE FIND THERE INTO MAGNIFICENT, MORE TRANSCENDENT, CREATURES."
AND THAT IS WHAT I WOULD DO FOR YOUR EARTH.
WHAT I WOULD DO FOR YOU.
IT COULD BE A GREAT STORY OF CREATION...
WE SHALL SEE.
BUT, I MUST CONFESS... I'M BEGINNING TO HAVE DOUBTS. AND I FEAR THE ALTERNATIVE.
SCANNING...
SCANNING...
THREAT LEVEL: ASCENDING.
OBJECTIVE: TIME SENSITIVE.
"I ONLY WANT TO SAVE YOU PEOPLE FROM YOURSELVES."

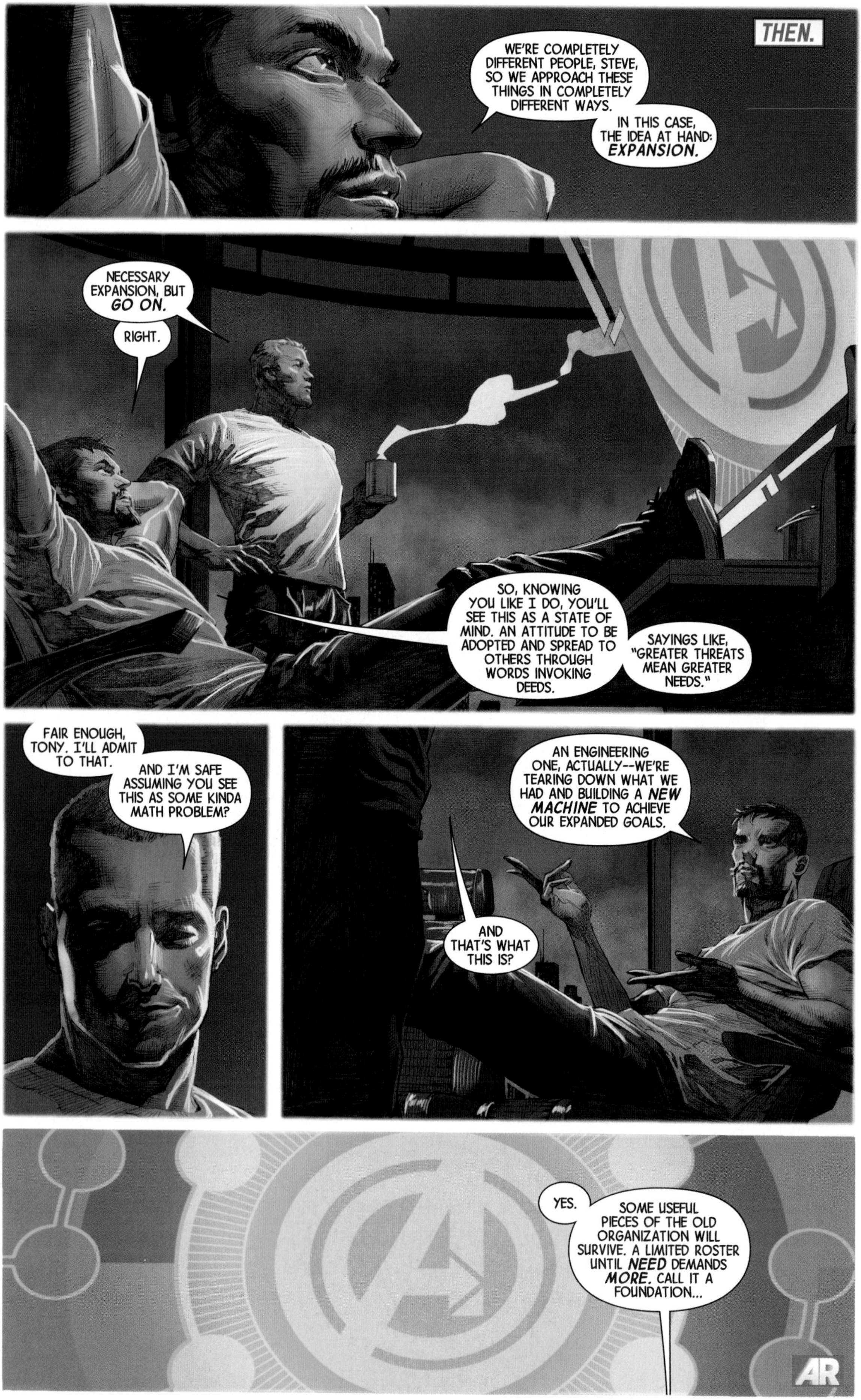
THEN.
WE'RE COMPLETELY DIFFERENT PEOPLE, STEVE, SO WE APPROACH THESE THINGS IN COMPLETELY DIFFERENT WAYS.
IN THIS CASE, THE IDEA AT HAND: EXPANSION.
NECESSARY EXPANSION, BUT GO ON.
RIGHT.
SO, KNOWING YOU LIKE I DO, YOU'LL SEE THIS AS A STATE OF MIND. AN ATTITUDE TO BE ADOPTED AND SPREAD TO OTHERS THROUGH WORDS INVOKING DEEDS.
SAYINGS LIKE, "GREATER THREATS MEAN GREATER NEEDS."
FAIR ENOUGH, TONY. I'LL ADMIT TO THAT.
AND I'M SAFE ASSUMING YOU SEE THIS AS SOME KINDA MATH PROBLEM?
AN ENGINEERING ONE, ACTUALLY--WE'RE TEARING DOWN WHAT WE HAD AND BUILDING A NEW MACHINE TO ACHIEVE OUR EXPANDED GOALS.
AND THAT'S WHAT THIS IS?
YES.
SOME USEFUL PIECES OF THE OLD ORGANIZATION WILL SURVIVE. A LIMITED ROSTER UNTIL NEED DEMANDS MORE. CALL IT A FOUNDATION...
AR

UH-HUH. THE TWO OF US... PLUS THOR, *OF COURSE.*

WE'LL WANT HAWKEYE AND BLACK WIDOW.

AGREED. ALSO, BANNER.

BANNER? *REALLY?*

YOU KNOW HOW THAT ALWAYS ENDS.

IN TIJUANA. OR A MONASTERY. MAYBE SPACE CAMP.

JOKE ALL YOU WANT, BUT WHEN WE SEND OUT THE CALL TO EXPAND, WE'LL WANT A SUPPORT STRUCTURE WITHIN THIS LARGER GROUP--PEOPLE WHO UNDERSTAND OUR *TRADITION* AND OUR *PURPOSE.*

AH, YOU MEAN FORMER MEMBERS TO GO ALONG WITH ANY NEWER ONES.

UH-HUH.

CAPTAIN UNIVERSE

HYPERION

SMASHER

ESPECIALLY IF WE'RE TALKING ABOUT PUSHING THE BOUNDARIES AS FAR AS WE CAN.

• WA... ...MOFF
PI... ...KIMO...
HE...
...LETT
...ORR
...A JONES
...GARRETT
...ROVIK...
...MAQUE...
...RDS
...RM
...MM

• MARC SPECTOR
...ONITA JUÁR...
...S RHODE...
...ARA BAR...
...NICA RAMB...
...FER WALTE...
...N DANVERS
...EL WILSON
...ON WILLIA...
• PA... ...IA WA...
• BRIA... B...DDO...
• MATT... ...RD
DAISY ...
JAMES BA...

00.099

ALREADY THERE.

I'VE DONE THE INITIAL VETTING OF EVERYONE ON THIS LIST. WE'LL WANT TO GET INTO IT A BIT MORE...

BUT FOR NOW, I THINK WE'RE FINE USING THIS AS A LAUNCHING POINT.

ALL RIGHT...

CLICK

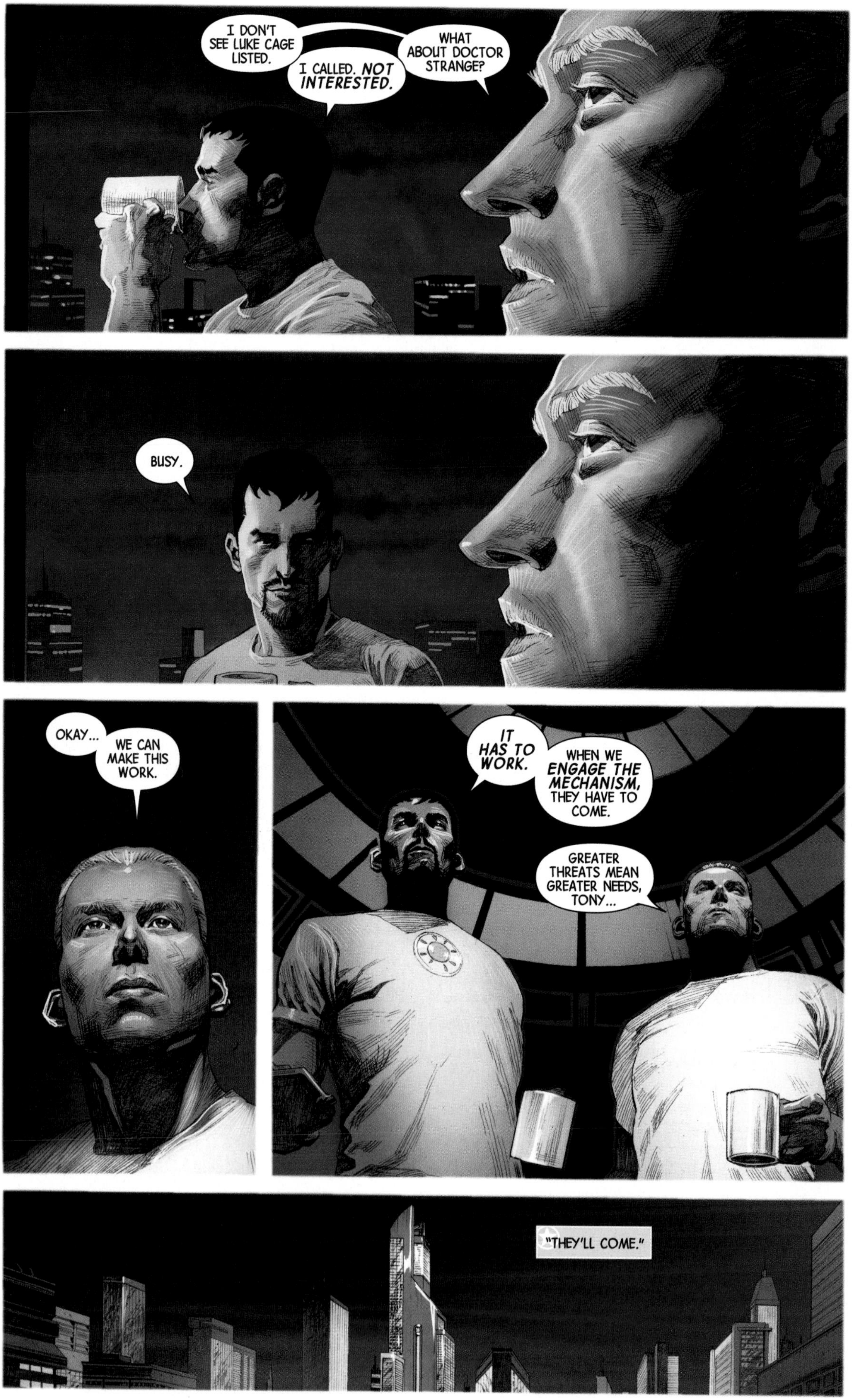
I DON'T SEE LUKE CAGE LISTED.
I CALLED. NOT INTERESTED.
WHAT ABOUT DOCTOR STRANGE?
BUSY.
OKAY...
WE CAN MAKE THIS WORK.
IT HAS TO WORK.
WHEN WE ENGAGE THE MECHANISM, THEY HAVE TO COME.
GREATER THREATS MEAN GREATER NEEDS, TONY...
"THEY'LL COME."

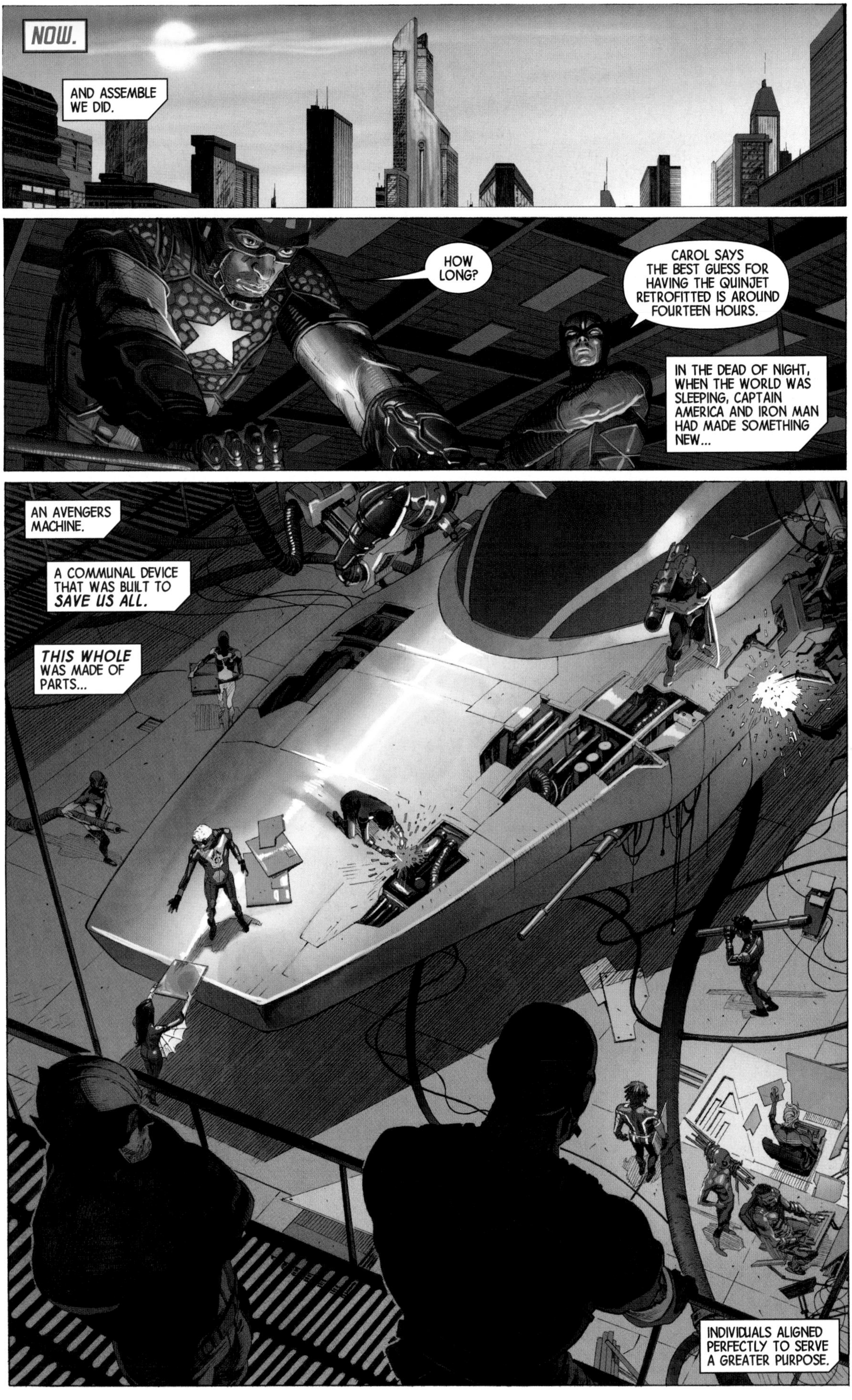
NOW.
AND ASSEMBLE WE DID.
HOW LONG?
CAROL SAYS THE BEST GUESS FOR HAVING THE QUINJET RETROFITTED IS AROUND FOURTEEN HOURS.
IN THE DEAD OF NIGHT, WHEN THE WORLD WAS SLEEPING, CAPTAIN AMERICA AND IRON MAN HAD MADE SOMETHING NEW...
AN AVENGERS MACHINE.
A COMMUNAL DEVICE THAT WAS BUILT TO *SAVE US ALL.*
THIS WHOLE WAS MADE OF PARTS...
INDIVIDUALS ALIGNED PERFECTLY TO SERVE A GREATER PURPOSE.

WHEN CALLED, THEY EACH CAME FOR DIFFERENT REASONS.

WE HAVE BEER.

SOLD.

WOLVERINE.

WE HAVE MONEY.

OH, THANK GOD.

SPIDER-MAN.

I DUNNO... BIRDSEED?

PHSST.

THIS IS ME ASKING, SAM.

THEN YOU ALREADY KNOW.

GOOD. KEEP YOUR PHONE ON.

THE FALCON.

SOME OF US WANTED A NEW CHALLENGE.

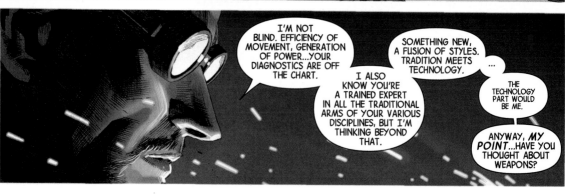

I'M NOT BLIND. EFFICIENCY OF MOVEMENT, GENERATION OF POWER...YOUR DIAGNOSTICS ARE OFF THE CHART.

I ALSO KNOW YOU'RE A TRAINED EXPERT IN ALL THE TRADITIONAL ARMS OF YOUR VARIOUS DISCIPLINES, BUT I'M THINKING BEYOND THAT.

SOMETHING NEW, A FUSION OF STYLES. TRADITION MEETS TECHNOLOGY.

...

THE TECHNOLOGY PART WOULD BE ME.

ANYWAY, MY POINT...HAVE YOU THOUGHT ABOUT WEAPONS?

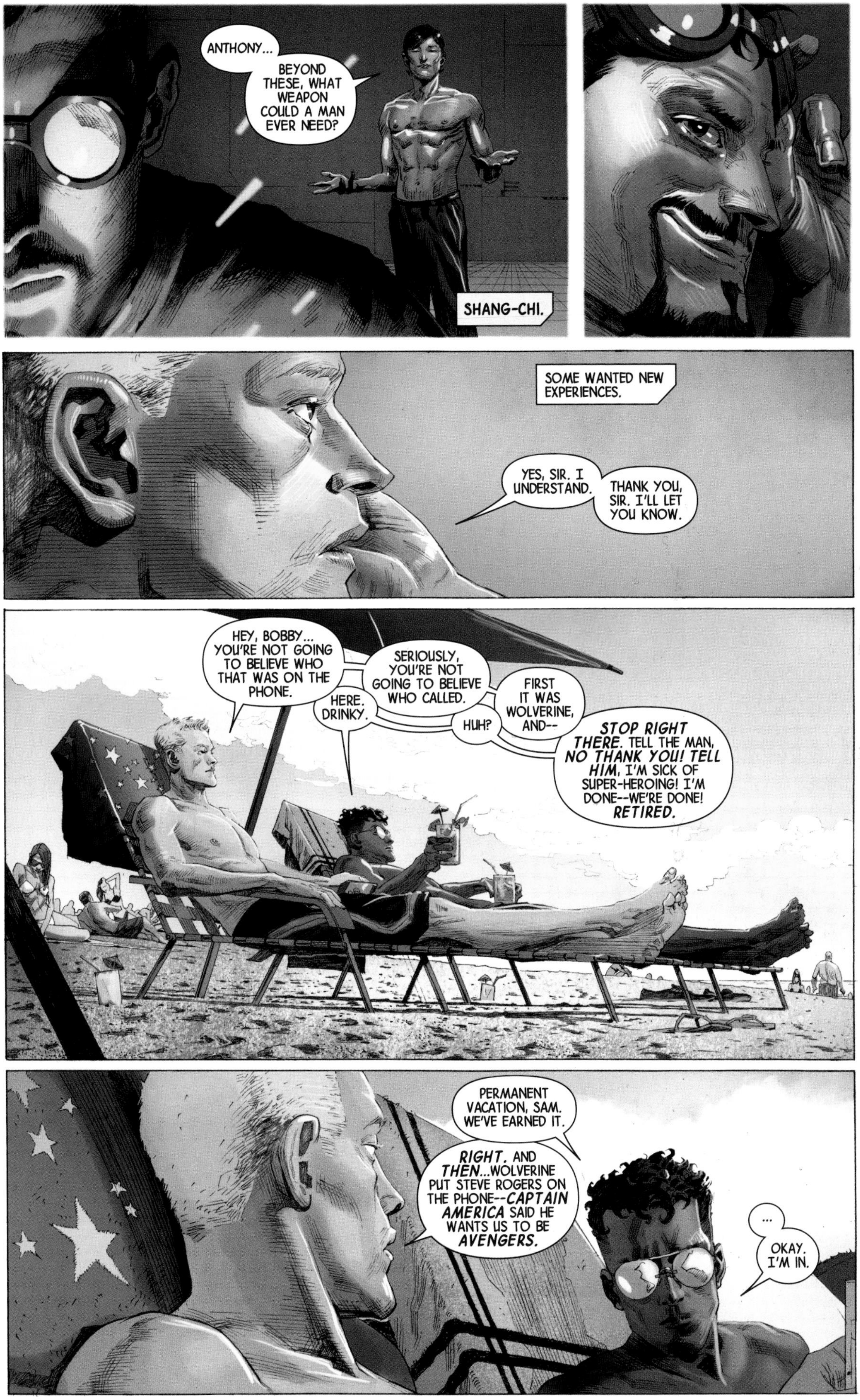
ANTHONY...
BEYOND THESE, WHAT WEAPON COULD A MAN EVER NEED?
SHANG-CHI.
SOME WANTED NEW EXPERIENCES.
YES, SIR. I UNDERSTAND.
THANK YOU, SIR. I'LL LET YOU KNOW.
HEY, BOBBY... YOU'RE NOT GOING TO BELIEVE WHO THAT WAS ON THE PHONE.
SERIOUSLY, YOU'RE NOT GOING TO BELIEVE WHO CALLED.
HERE. DRINKY.
HUH?
FIRST IT WAS WOLVERINE, AND--
STOP RIGHT THERE. TELL THE MAN, NO THANK YOU! TELL HIM, I'M SICK OF SUPER-HEROING! I'M DONE--WE'RE DONE! RETIRED.
PERMANENT VACATION, SAM. WE'VE EARNED IT.
RIGHT. AND THEN...WOLVERINE PUT STEVE ROGERS ON THE PHONE--CAPTAIN AMERICA SAID HE WANTS US TO BE AVENGERS.
...
OKAY. I'M IN.

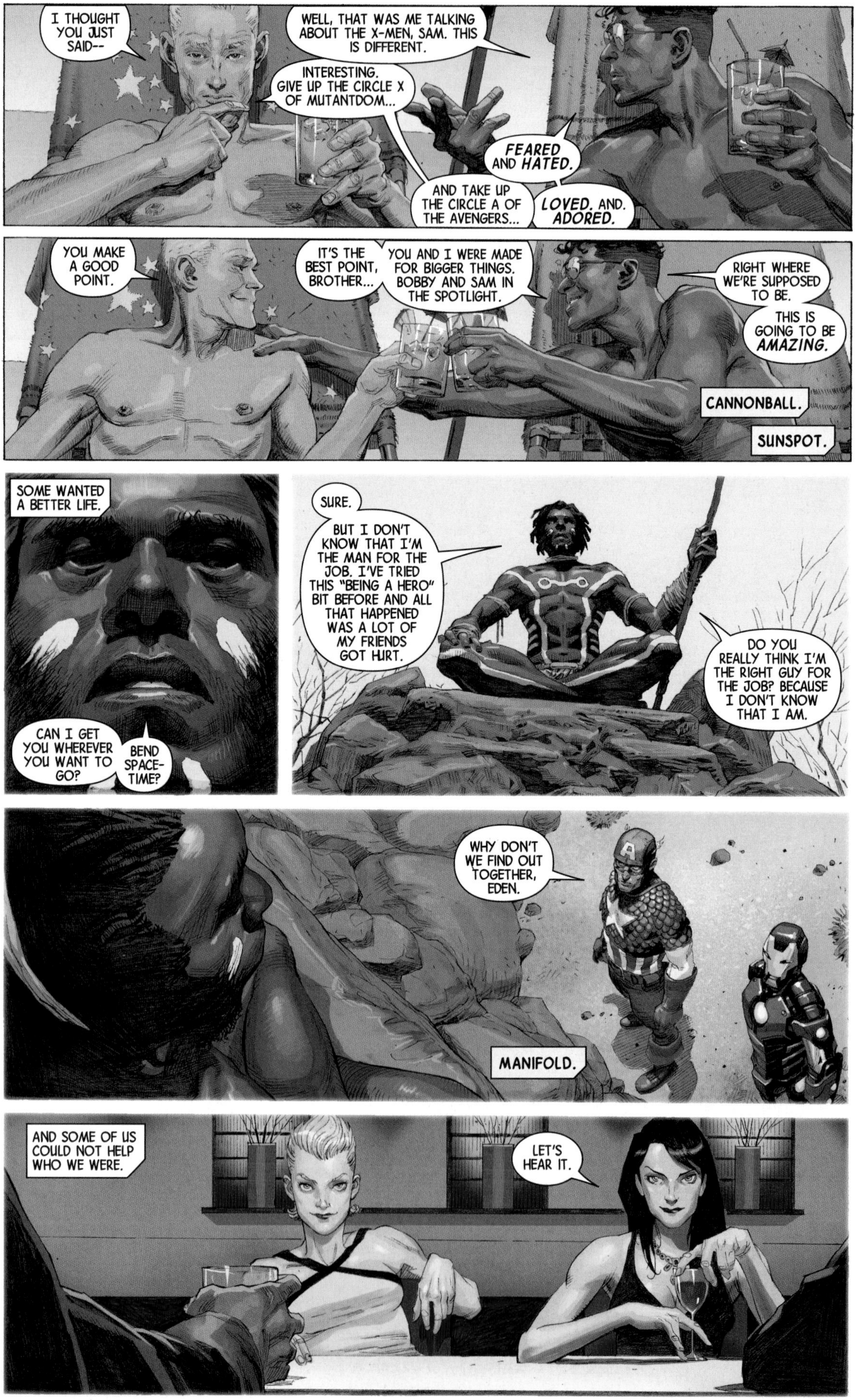
I THOUGHT YOU JUST SAID--
WELL, THAT WAS ME TALKING ABOUT THE X-MEN, SAM. THIS IS DIFFERENT.
INTERESTING. GIVE UP THE CIRCLE X OF MUTANTDOM...
FEARED AND HATED.
AND TAKE UP THE CIRCLE A OF THE AVENGERS...
LOVED. AND. ADORED.
YOU MAKE A GOOD POINT.
IT'S THE BEST POINT, BROTHER...
YOU AND I WERE MADE FOR BIGGER THINGS. BOBBY AND SAM IN THE SPOTLIGHT.
RIGHT WHERE WE'RE SUPPOSED TO BE.
THIS IS GOING TO BE AMAZING.
CANNONBALL.
SUNSPOT.
SOME WANTED A BETTER LIFE.
CAN I GET YOU WHEREVER YOU WANT TO GO?
BEND SPACE-TIME?
SURE.
BUT I DON'T KNOW THAT I'M THE MAN FOR THE JOB. I'VE TRIED THIS "BEING A HERO" BIT BEFORE AND ALL THAT HAPPENED WAS A LOT OF MY FRIENDS GOT HURT.
DO YOU REALLY THINK I'M THE RIGHT GUY FOR THE JOB? BECAUSE I DON'T KNOW THAT I AM.
WHY DON'T WE FIND OUT TOGETHER, EDEN.
MANIFOLD.
AND SOME OF US COULD NOT HELP WHO WE WERE.
LET'S HEAR IT.

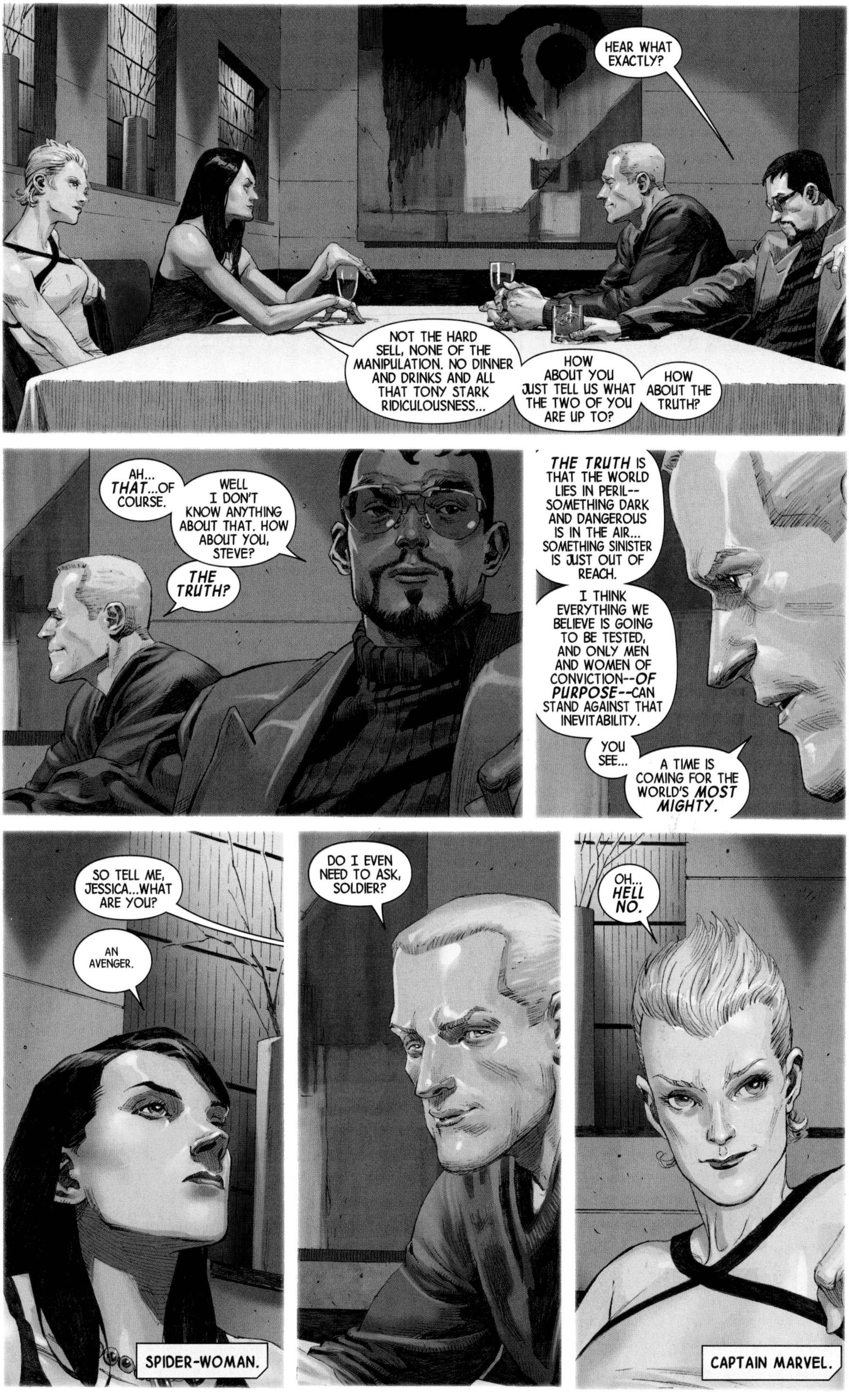
HEAR WHAT EXACTLY?
NOT THE HARD SELL, NONE OF THE MANIPULATION. NO DINNER AND DRINKS AND ALL THAT TONY STARK RIDICULOUSNESS...
HOW ABOUT YOU JUST TELL US WHAT THE TWO OF YOU ARE UP TO?
HOW ABOUT THE TRUTH?
AH... THAT...OF COURSE.
WELL I DON'T KNOW ANYTHING ABOUT THAT. HOW ABOUT YOU, STEVE?
THE TRUTH?
THE TRUTH IS THAT THE WORLD LIES IN PERIL-- SOMETHING DARK AND DANGEROUS IS IN THE AIR... SOMETHING SINISTER IS JUST OUT OF REACH.
I THINK EVERYTHING WE BELIEVE IS GOING TO BE TESTED, AND ONLY MEN AND WOMEN OF CONVICTION--OF PURPOSE--CAN STAND AGAINST THAT INEVITABILITY.
YOU SEE...
A TIME IS COMING FOR THE WORLD'S MOST MIGHTY.
SO TELL ME, JESSICA...WHAT ARE YOU?
AN AVENGER.
SPIDER-WOMAN.
DO I EVEN NEED TO ASK, SOLDIER?
OH... HELL NO.
CAPTAIN MARVEL.

EARTH.
NOW.

CAP! STARKCOMM SATELLITES PICKING UP MULTIPLE INCOMING TARGETS--TRAJECTORY MARKS THEM AS EXTRAPLANETARY...

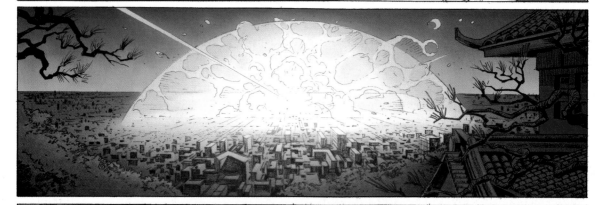

"FROM MARS."

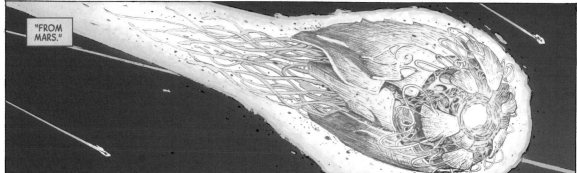

KOBE, JAPAN.
POPULATION: 1,543,091.

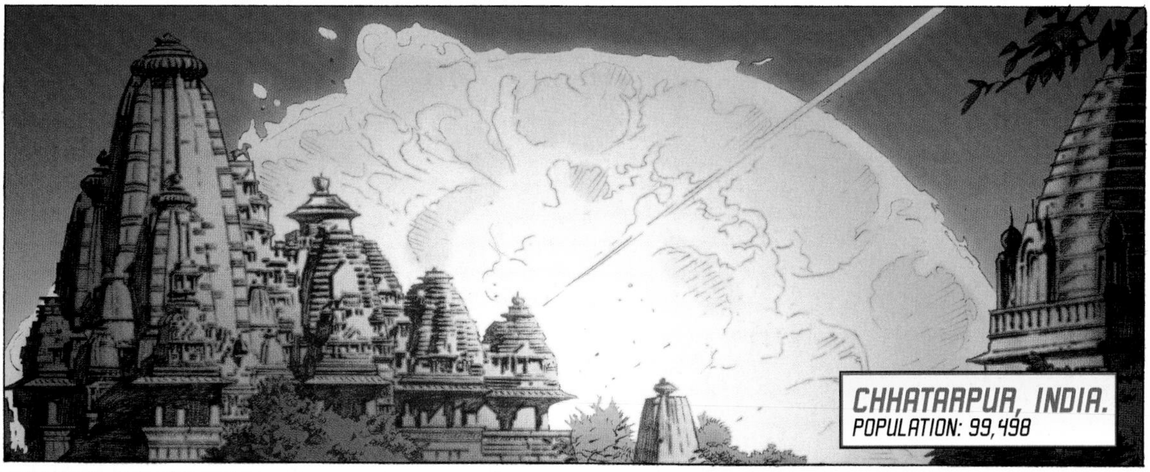
CHHATARPUR, INDIA.
POPULATION: 99,498

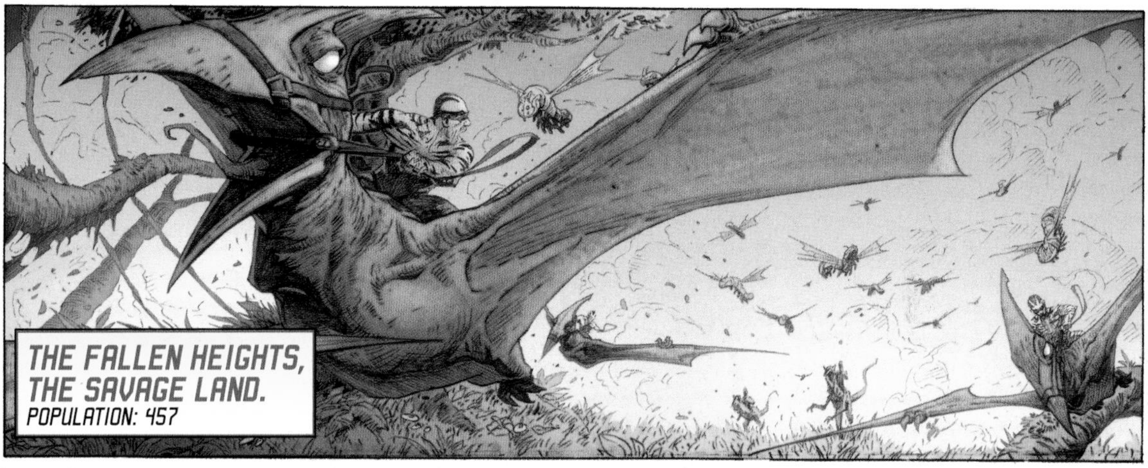
THE FALLEN HEIGHTS, THE SAVAGE LAND.
POPULATION: 457

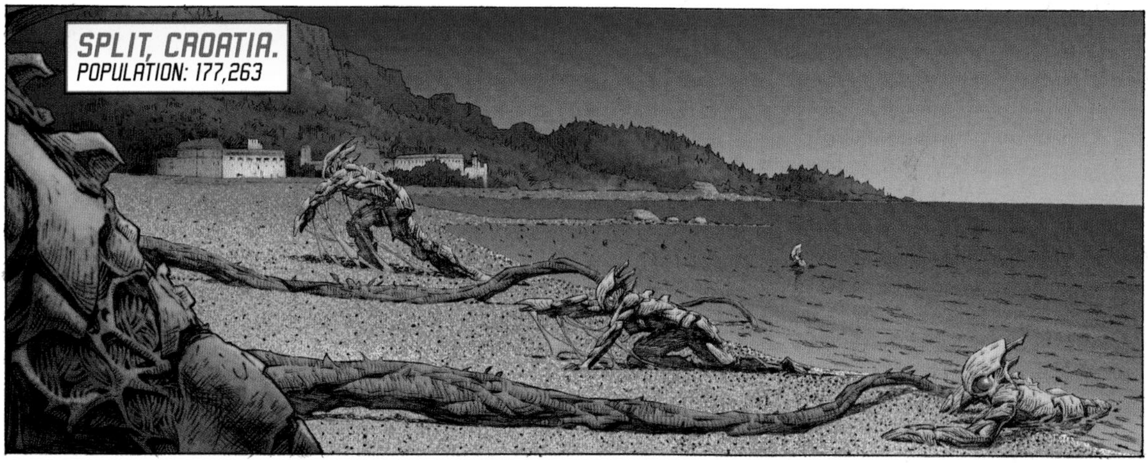
SPLIT, CROATIA.
POPULATION: 177,263

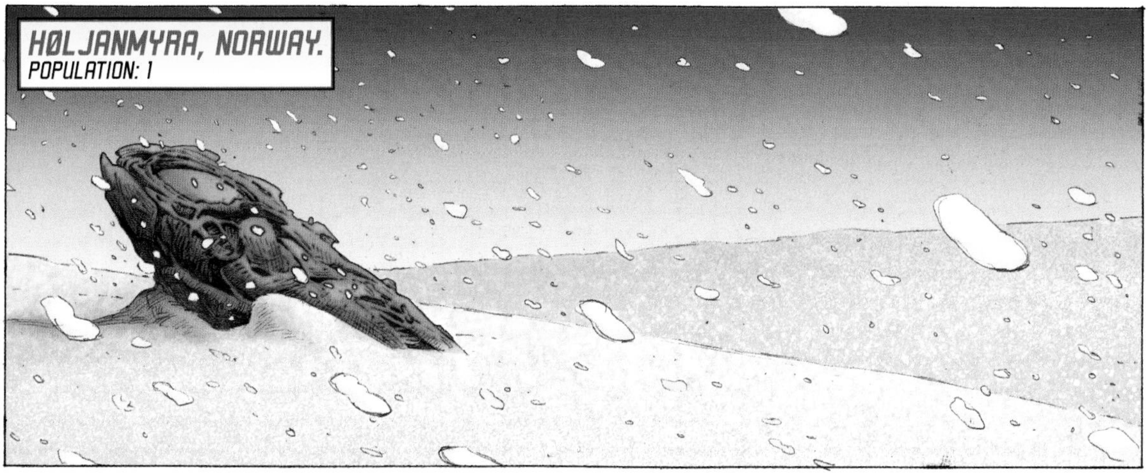
HØLJANMYRA, NORWAY.
POPULATION: 1

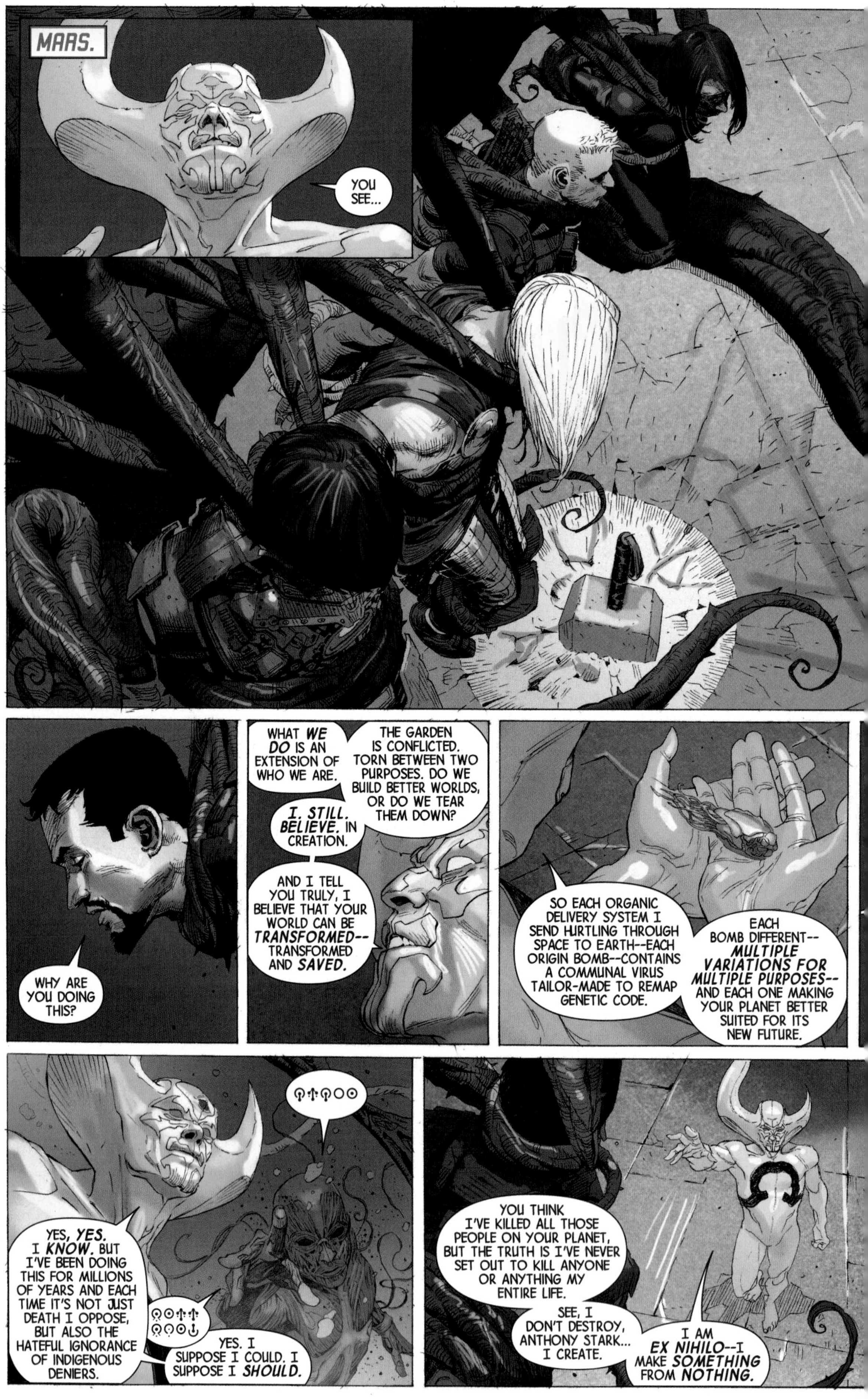
MARS.
YOU SEE...
WHY ARE YOU DOING THIS?
WHAT WE DO IS AN EXTENSION OF WHO WE ARE.
THE GARDEN IS CONFLICTED. TORN BETWEEN TWO PURPOSES. DO WE BUILD BETTER WORLDS, OR DO WE TEAR THEM DOWN?
I. STILL. BELIEVE. IN CREATION.
AND I TELL YOU TRULY, I BELIEVE THAT YOUR WORLD CAN BE TRANSFORMED--TRANSFORMED AND SAVED.
SO EACH ORGANIC DELIVERY SYSTEM I SEND HURTLING THROUGH SPACE TO EARTH--EACH ORIGIN BOMB--CONTAINS A COMMUNAL VIRUS TAILOR-MADE TO REMAP GENETIC CODE.
EACH BOMB DIFFERENT--MULTIPLE VARIATIONS FOR MULTIPLE PURPOSES--AND EACH ONE MAKING YOUR PLANET BETTER SUITED FOR ITS NEW FUTURE.
YES, YES. I KNOW. BUT I'VE BEEN DOING THIS FOR MILLIONS OF YEARS AND EACH TIME IT'S NOT JUST DEATH I OPPOSE, BUT ALSO THE HATEFUL IGNORANCE OF INDIGENOUS DENIERS.
YES. I SUPPOSE I COULD. I SUPPOSE I SHOULD.
YOU THINK I'VE KILLED ALL THOSE PEOPLE ON YOUR PLANET, BUT THE TRUTH IS I'VE NEVER SET OUT TO KILL ANYONE OR ANYTHING MY ENTIRE LIFE.
SEE, I DON'T DESTROY, ANTHONY STARK... I CREATE.
I AM EX NIHILO--I MAKE SOMETHING FROM NOTHING.

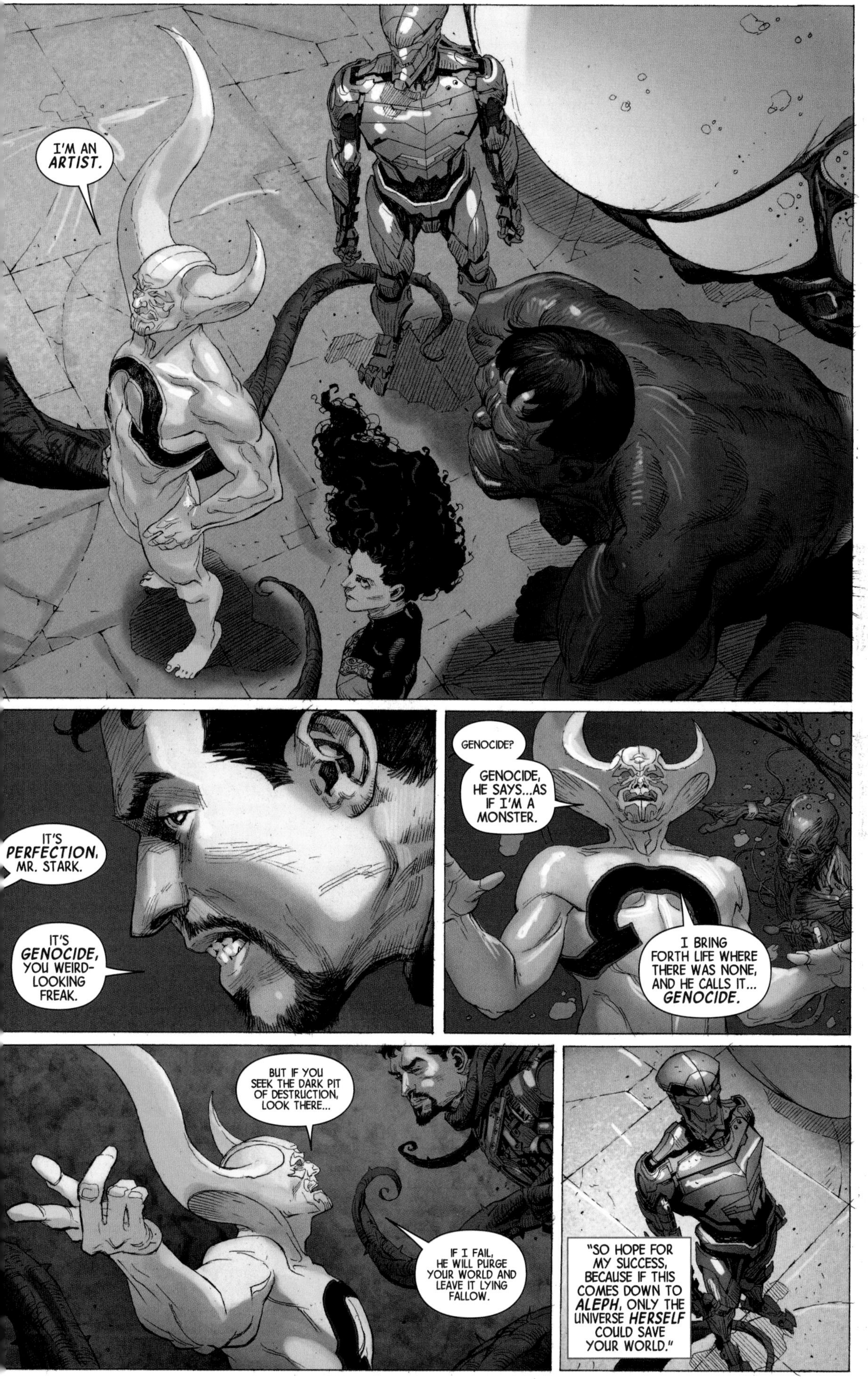

I'M AN ARTIST.
IT'S PERFECTION, MR. STARK.
IT'S GENOCIDE, YOU WEIRD-LOOKING FREAK.
GENOCIDE?
GENOCIDE, HE SAYS...AS IF I'M A MONSTER.
I BRING FORTH LIFE WHERE THERE WAS NONE, AND HE CALLS IT... GENOCIDE.
BUT IF YOU SEEK THE DARK PIT OF DESTRUCTION, LOOK THERE...
IF I FAIL, HE WILL PURGE YOUR WORLD AND LEAVE IT LYING FALLOW.
"SO HOPE FOR MY SUCCESS, BECAUSE IF THIS COMES DOWN TO ALEPH, ONLY THE UNIVERSE HERSELF COULD SAVE YOUR WORLD."

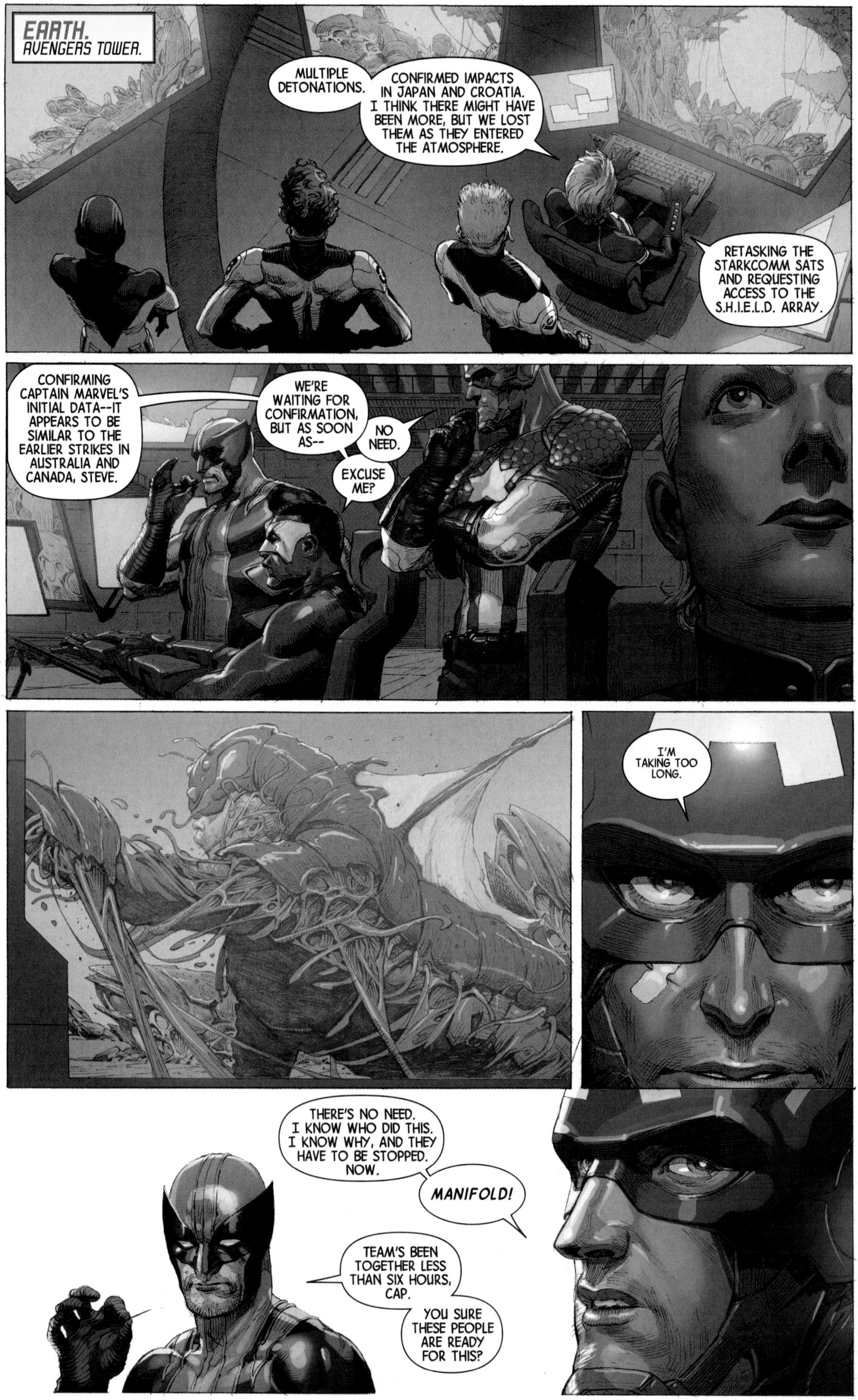
EARTH.
AVENGERS TOWER.
MULTIPLE DETONATIONS.
CONFIRMED IMPACTS IN JAPAN AND CROATIA. I THINK THERE MIGHT HAVE BEEN MORE, BUT WE LOST THEM AS THEY ENTERED THE ATMOSPHERE.
RETASKING THE STARKCOMM SATS AND REQUESTING ACCESS TO THE S.H.I.E.L.D. ARRAY.
CONFIRMING CAPTAIN MARVEL'S INITIAL DATA--IT APPEARS TO BE SIMILAR TO THE EARLIER STRIKES IN AUSTRALIA AND CANADA, STEVE.
WE'RE WAITING FOR CONFIRMATION, BUT AS SOON AS--
NO NEED.
EXCUSE ME?
I'M TAKING TOO LONG.
THERE'S NO NEED. I KNOW WHO DID THIS. I KNOW WHY, AND THEY HAVE TO BE STOPPED. NOW.
MANIFOLD!
TEAM'S BEEN TOGETHER LESS THAN SIX HOURS, CAP.
YOU SURE THESE PEOPLE ARE READY FOR THIS?

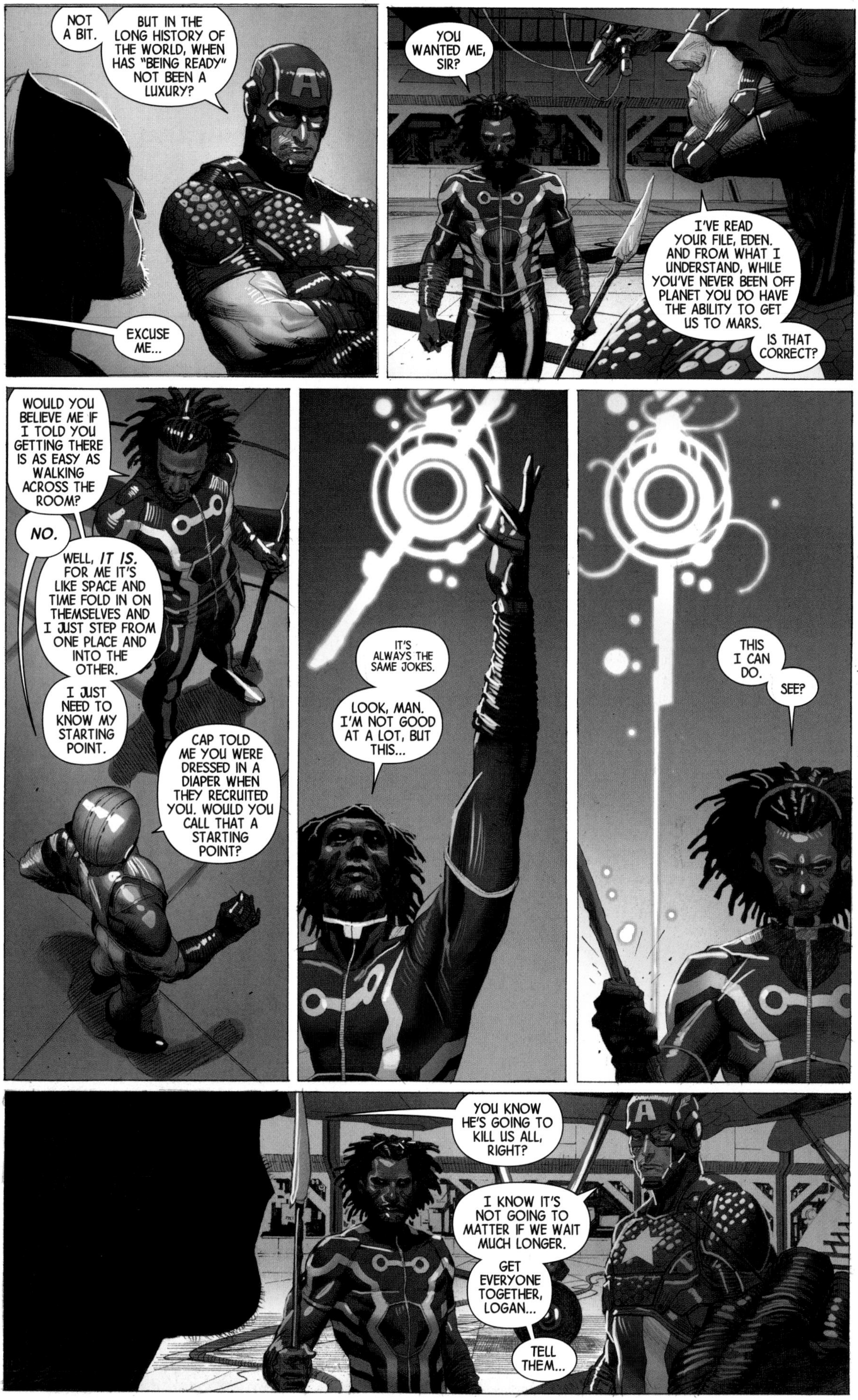
NOT A BIT.
BUT IN THE LONG HISTORY OF THE WORLD, WHEN HAS "BEING READY" NOT BEEN A LUXURY?
EXCUSE ME...
YOU WANTED ME, SIR?
I'VE READ YOUR FILE, EDEN. AND FROM WHAT I UNDERSTAND, WHILE YOU'VE NEVER BEEN OFF PLANET YOU DO HAVE THE ABILITY TO GET US TO MARS.
IS THAT CORRECT?
WOULD YOU BELIEVE ME IF I TOLD YOU GETTING THERE IS AS EASY AS WALKING ACROSS THE ROOM?
NO.
WELL, IT IS. FOR ME IT'S LIKE SPACE AND TIME FOLD IN ON THEMSELVES AND I JUST STEP FROM ONE PLACE AND INTO THE OTHER.
I JUST NEED TO KNOW MY STARTING POINT.
CAP TOLD ME YOU WERE DRESSED IN A DIAPER WHEN THEY RECRUITED YOU. WOULD YOU CALL THAT A STARTING POINT?
IT'S ALWAYS THE SAME JOKES.
LOOK, MAN. I'M NOT GOOD AT A LOT, BUT THIS...
THIS I CAN DO.
SEE?
YOU KNOW HE'S GOING TO KILL US ALL, RIGHT?
I KNOW IT'S NOT GOING TO MATTER IF WE WAIT MUCH LONGER.
GET EVERYONE TOGETHER, LOGAN...
TELL THEM...

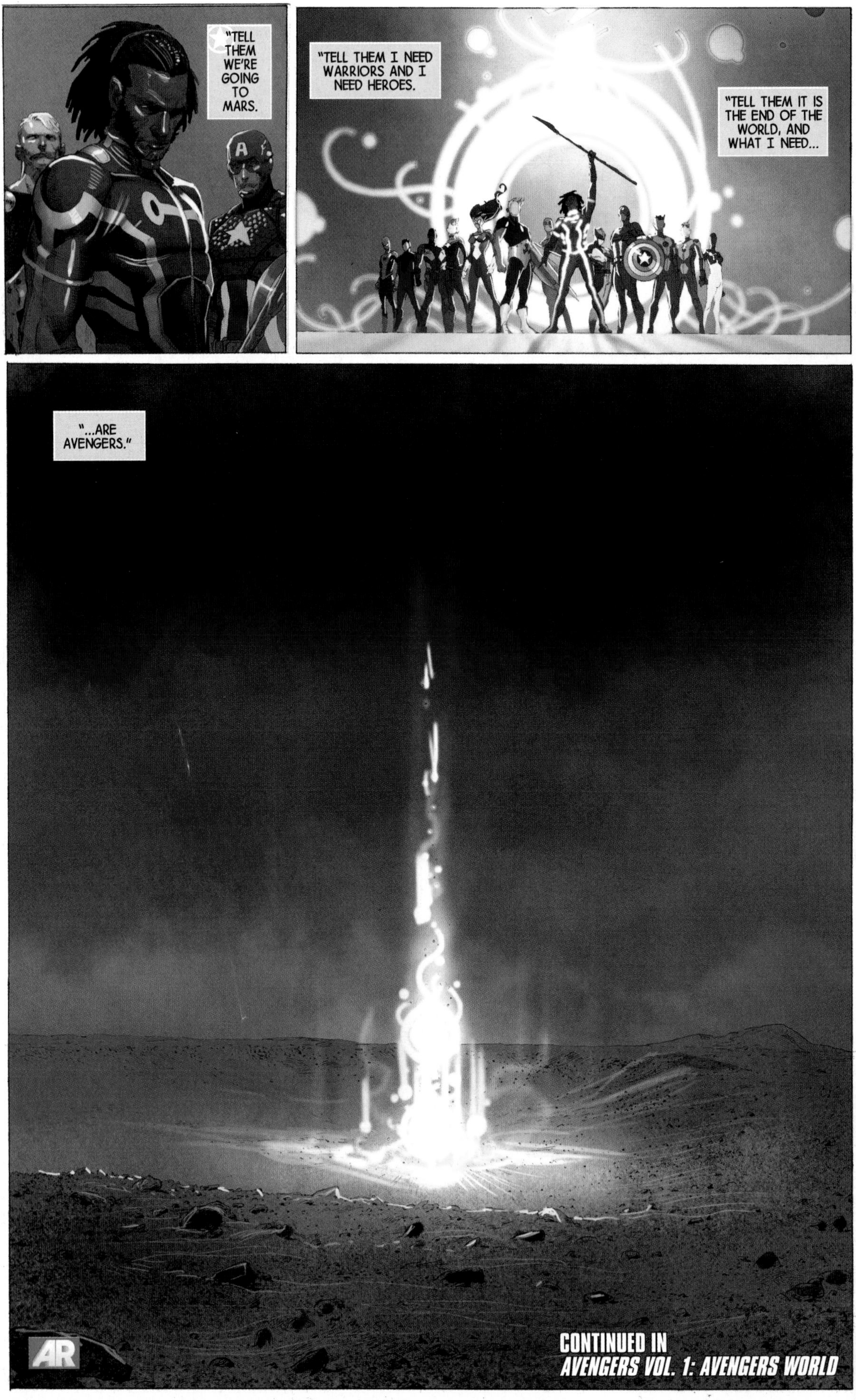
"TELL THEM WE'RE GOING TO MARS.
"TELL THEM I NEED WARRIORS AND I NEED HEROES.
"TELL THEM IT IS THE END OF THE WORLD, AND WHAT I NEED...
"...ARE AVENGERS."
CONTINUED IN
AVENGERS VOL. 1: AVENGERS WORLD

NEW AVENGERS #2

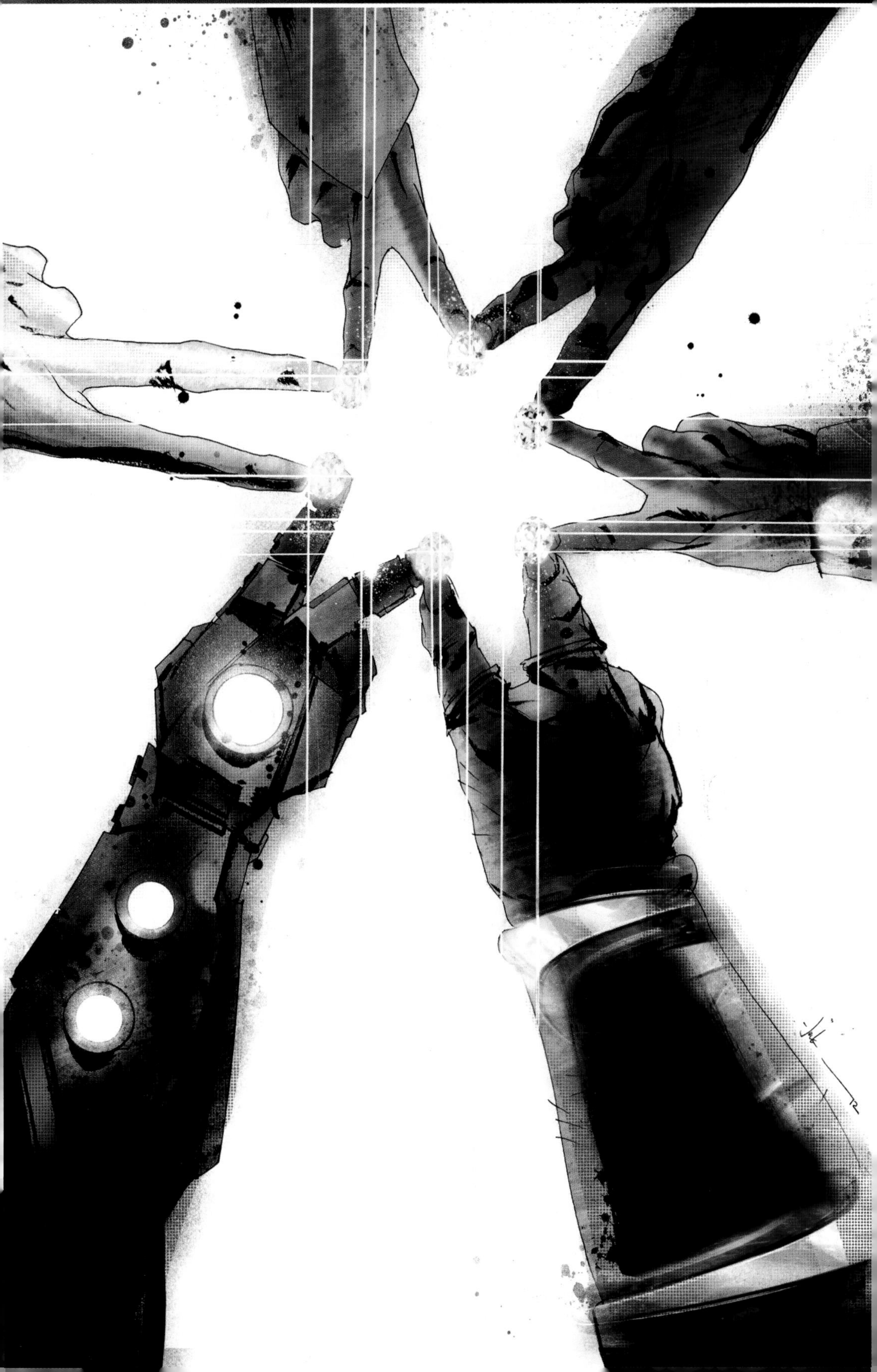

PREVIOUSLY IN NEW AVENGERS

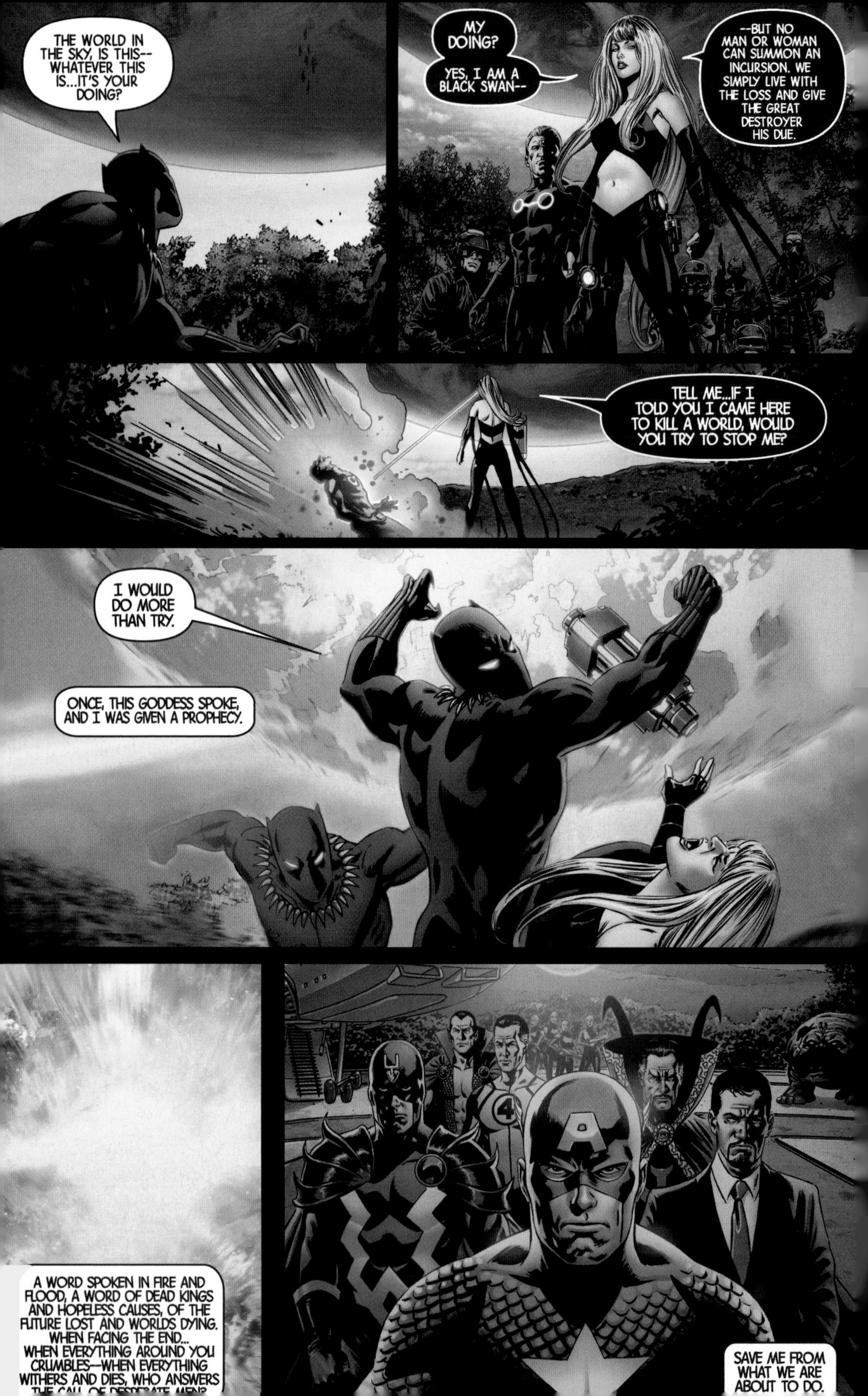
THE WORLD IN THE SKY, IS THIS-- WHATEVER THIS IS...IT'S YOUR DOING?
MY DOING?
YES, I AM A BLACK SWAN--
--BUT NO MAN OR WOMAN CAN SUMMON AN INCURSION. WE SIMPLY LIVE WITH THE LOSS AND GIVE THE GREAT DESTROYER HIS DUE.
TELL ME...IF I TOLD YOU I CAME HERE TO KILL A WORLD, WOULD YOU TRY TO STOP ME?
I WOULD DO MORE THAN TRY.
ONCE, THIS GODDESS SPOKE, AND I WAS GIVEN A PROPHECY.
A WORD SPOKEN IN FIRE AND FLOOD, A WORD OF DEAD KINGS AND HOPELESS CAUSES, OF THE FUTURE LOST AND WORLDS DYING. WHEN FACING THE END... WHEN EVERYTHING AROUND YOU CRUMBLES--WHEN EVERYTHING WITHERS AND DIES, WHO ANSWERS
SAVE ME FROM WHAT WE ARE ABOUT TO DO.

"IN SECRET,
THEY RULE"

WRITER: **JONATHAN HICKMAN**

PENCILER: **STEVE EPTING**

INKERS: **RICK MAGYAR with STEVE EPTING**
COLOR ARTIST: **FRANK D'ARMATA**
LETTERER: **VC's JOE CARAMAGNA**
COVER ART: **JOCK**
VARIANT COVER: **SIMONE BIANCHI and SIMONE PERUZZI**
ASSISTANT EDITOR: **JAKE THOMAS**
EDITORS: **TOM BREVOORT with LAUREN SANKOVITCH**
EDITOR IN CHIEF: **AXEL ALONSO**
CHIEF CREATIVE OFFICER: **JOE QUESADA**
PUBLISHER: **DAN BUCKLEY**
EXECUTIVE PRODUCER: **ALAN FINE**

THE ILLUMINATI

- HOLDERS OF THE INFINITY GEMS -

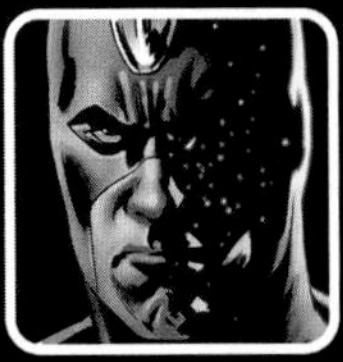

BLACK BOLT
Celestial Messiah

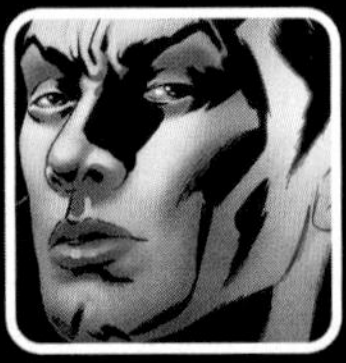

NAMOR
Imperius Rex
(THE POWER GEM)

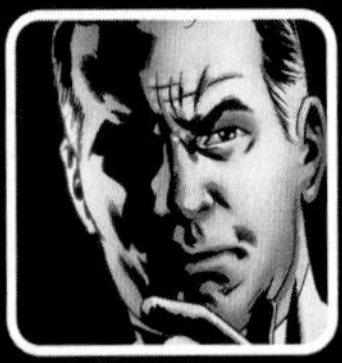

REED RICHARDS
Universal Builder
(THE REALITY GEM)

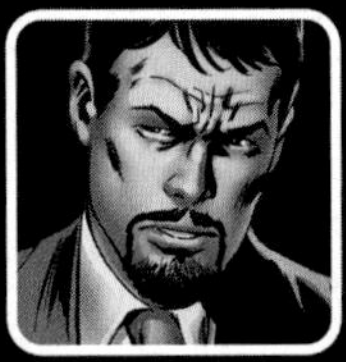

IRON MAN
Master of Machines
(THE SPACE GEM)

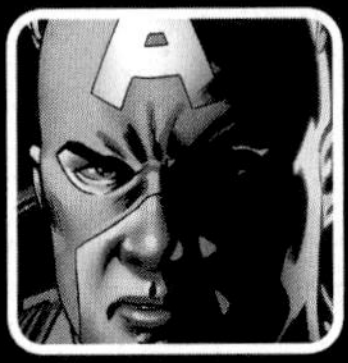

CAPTAIN AMERICA
Hero of Legend
(THE TIME GEM)

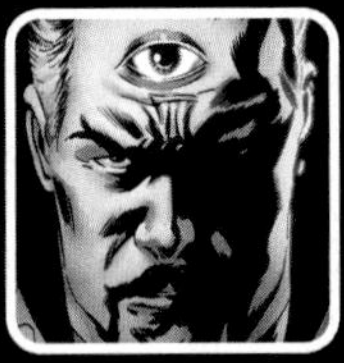

DOCTOR STRANGE
Sorcerer Supreme
(THE SOUL GEM)

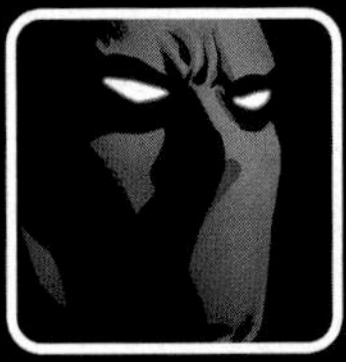

BLACK PANTHER
King of the Dead

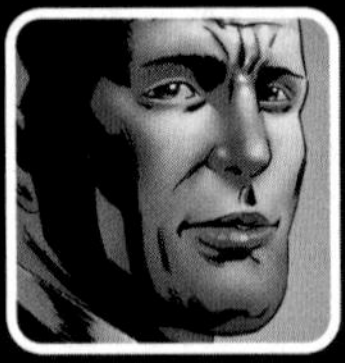

PROFESSOR XAVIER
Deceased
(THE MIND GEM)

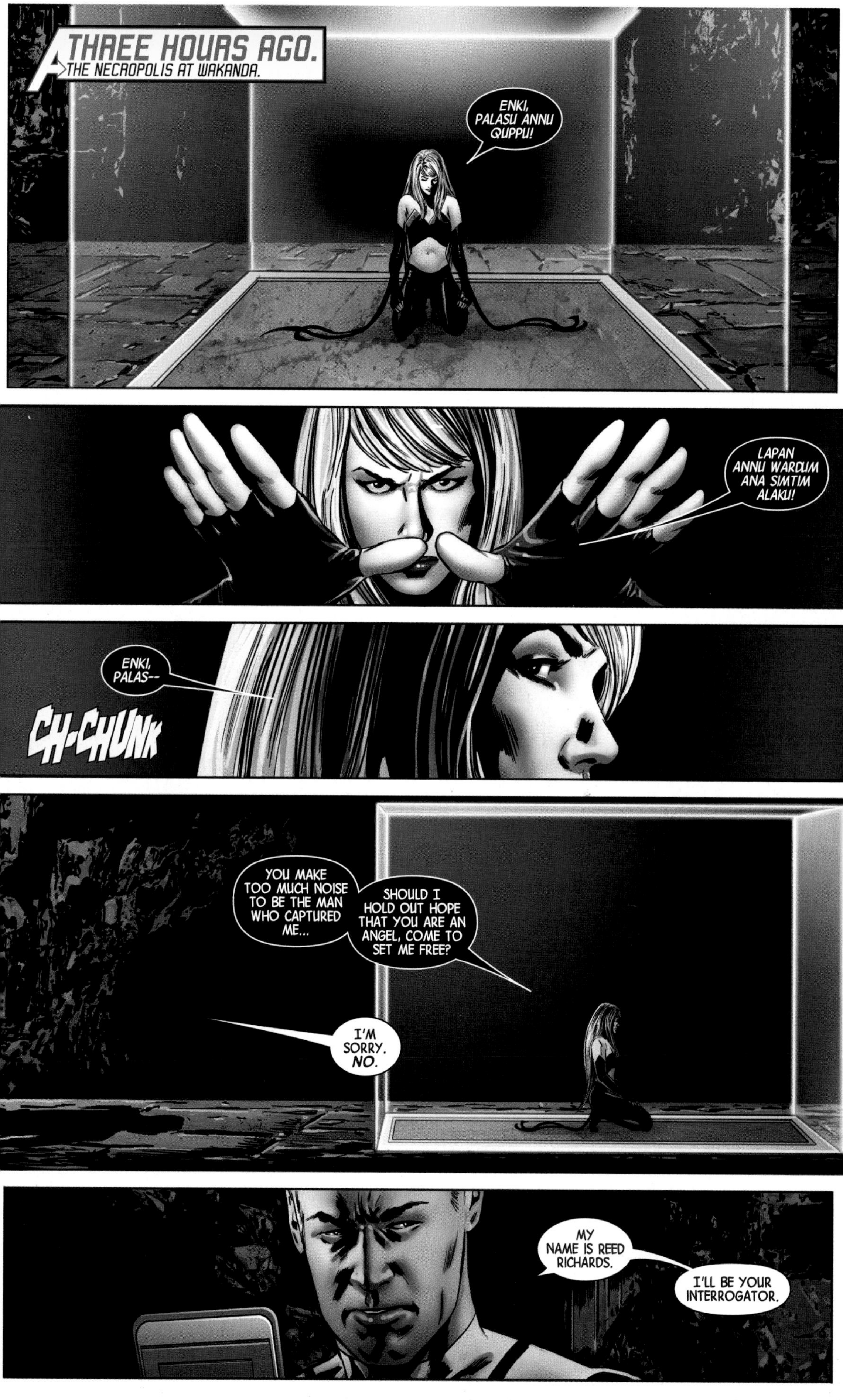
THREE HOURS AGO.
THE NECROPOLIS AT WAKANDA.
ENKI, PALASU ANNU QUPPU!
LAPAN ANNU WARDUM ANA SIMTIM ALAKU!
ENKI, PALAS--
CH-CHUNK
YOU MAKE TOO MUCH NOISE TO BE THE MAN WHO CAPTURED ME...
SHOULD I HOLD OUT HOPE THAT YOU ARE AN ANGEL, COME TO SET ME FREE?
I'M SORRY. NO.
MY NAME IS REED RICHARDS.
I'LL BE YOUR INTERROGATOR.

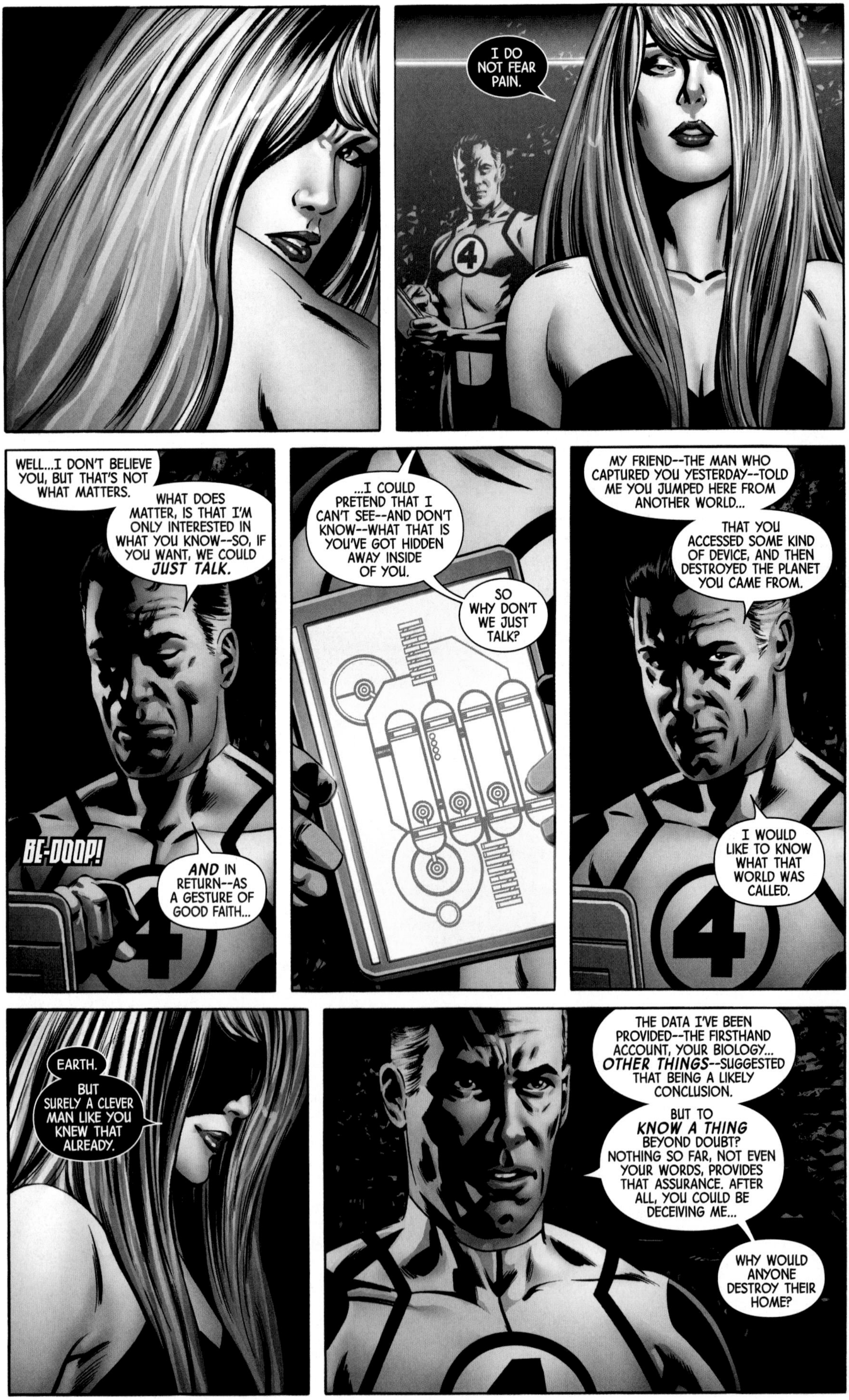
I DO NOT FEAR PAIN.
WELL...I DON'T BELIEVE YOU, BUT THAT'S NOT WHAT MATTERS.
WHAT DOES MATTER, IS THAT I'M ONLY INTERESTED IN WHAT YOU KNOW--SO, IF YOU WANT, WE COULD JUST TALK.
BE-DOOP!
AND IN RETURN--AS A GESTURE OF GOOD FAITH...
...I COULD PRETEND THAT I CAN'T SEE--AND DON'T KNOW--WHAT THAT IS YOU'VE GOT HIDDEN AWAY INSIDE OF YOU.
SO WHY DON'T WE JUST TALK?
MY FRIEND--THE MAN WHO CAPTURED YOU YESTERDAY--TOLD ME YOU JUMPED HERE FROM ANOTHER WORLD...
THAT YOU ACCESSED SOME KIND OF DEVICE, AND THEN DESTROYED THE PLANET YOU CAME FROM.
I WOULD LIKE TO KNOW WHAT THAT WORLD WAS CALLED.
EARTH.
BUT SURELY A CLEVER MAN LIKE YOU KNEW THAT ALREADY.
THE DATA I'VE BEEN PROVIDED--THE FIRSTHAND ACCOUNT, YOUR BIOLOGY... OTHER THINGS--SUGGESTED THAT BEING A LIKELY CONCLUSION.
BUT TO KNOW A THING BEYOND DOUBT? NOTHING SO FAR, NOT EVEN YOUR WORDS, PROVIDES THAT ASSURANCE. AFTER ALL, YOU COULD BE DECEIVING ME...
WHY WOULD ANYONE DESTROY THEIR HOME?

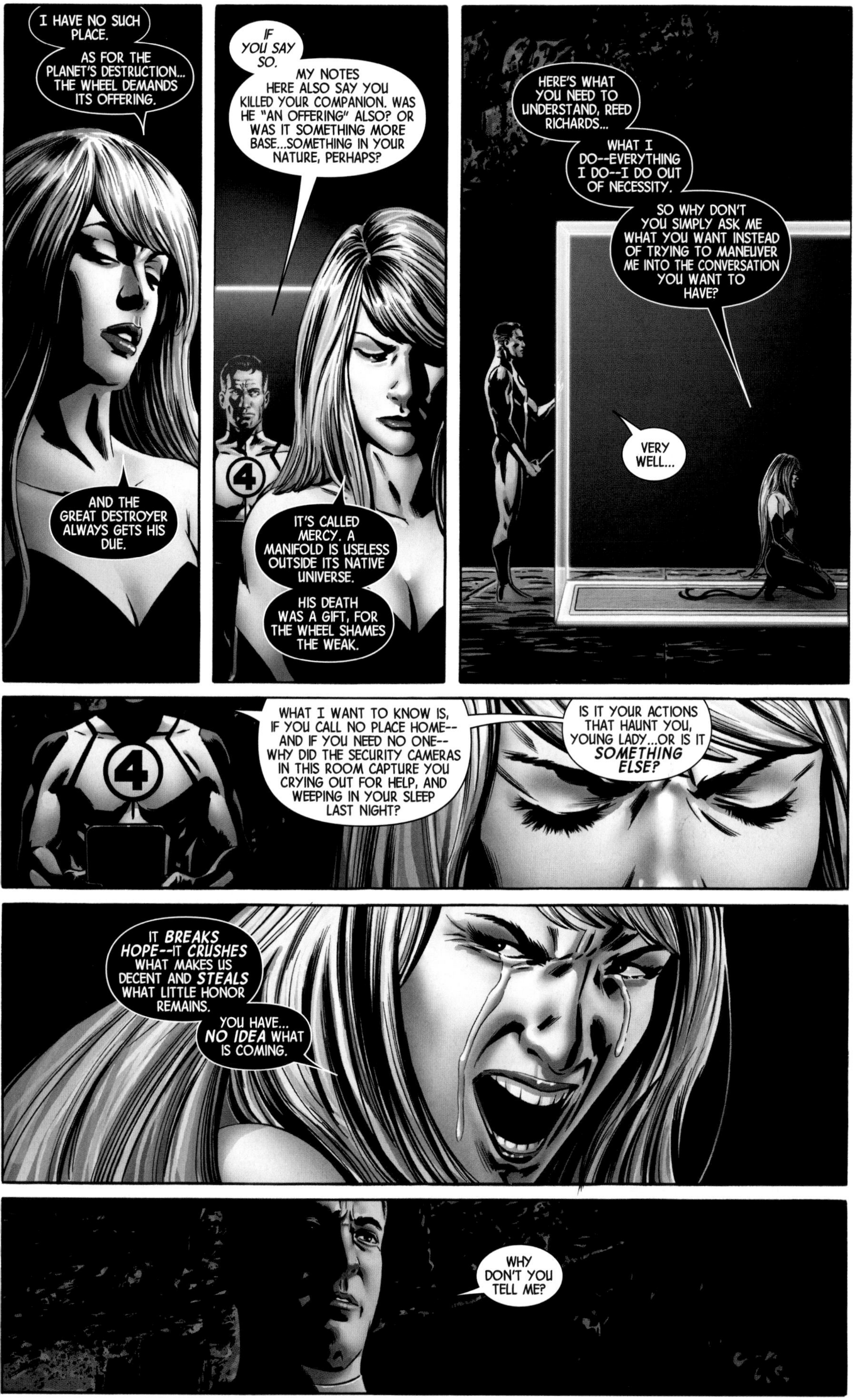

I HAVE NO SUCH PLACE.
AS FOR THE PLANET'S DESTRUCTION... THE WHEEL DEMANDS ITS OFFERING.
AND THE GREAT DESTROYER ALWAYS GETS HIS DUE.
IF YOU SAY SO.
MY NOTES HERE ALSO SAY YOU KILLED YOUR COMPANION. WAS HE "AN OFFERING" ALSO? OR WAS IT SOMETHING MORE BASE...SOMETHING IN YOUR NATURE, PERHAPS?
IT'S CALLED MERCY. A MANIFOLD IS USELESS OUTSIDE ITS NATIVE UNIVERSE.
HIS DEATH WAS A GIFT, FOR THE WHEEL SHAMES THE WEAK.
HERE'S WHAT YOU NEED TO UNDERSTAND, REED RICHARDS...
WHAT I DO--EVERYTHING I DO--I DO OUT OF NECESSITY.
SO WHY DON'T YOU SIMPLY ASK ME WHAT YOU WANT INSTEAD OF TRYING TO MANEUVER ME INTO THE CONVERSATION YOU WANT TO HAVE?
VERY WELL...
WHAT I WANT TO KNOW IS, IF YOU CALL NO PLACE HOME--AND IF YOU NEED NO ONE--WHY DID THE SECURITY CAMERAS IN THIS ROOM CAPTURE YOU CRYING OUT FOR HELP, AND WEEPING IN YOUR SLEEP LAST NIGHT?
IS IT YOUR ACTIONS THAT HAUNT YOU, YOUNG LADY...OR IS IT *SOMETHING ELSE?*
IT *BREAKS HOPE*--IT *CRUSHES* WHAT MAKES US DECENT AND *STEALS* WHAT LITTLE HONOR REMAINS.
YOU HAVE... *NO IDEA* WHAT IS COMING.
WHY DON'T YOU TELL ME?

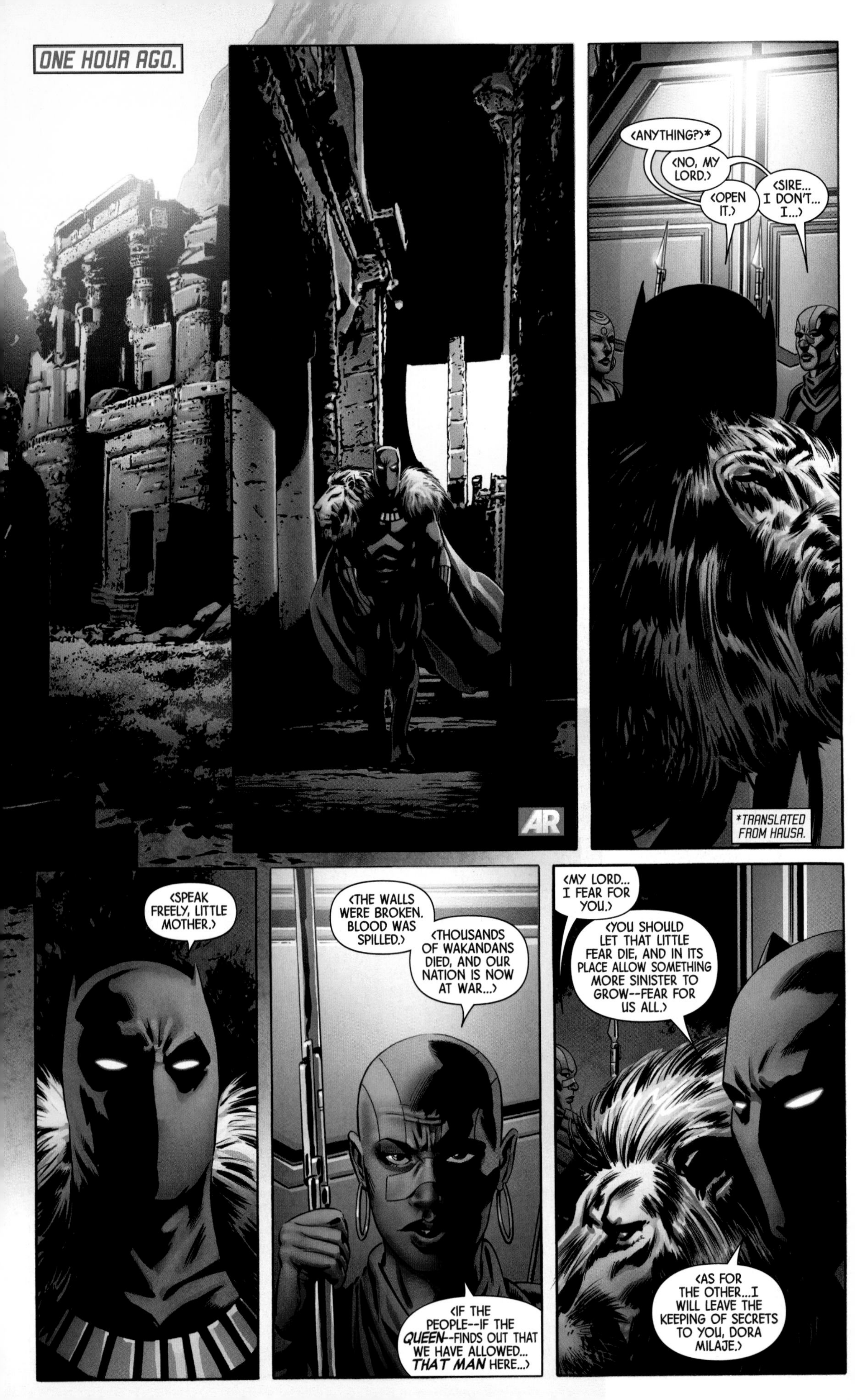
ONE HOUR AGO.
AR
<ANYTHING?>*
<NO, MY LORD.>
<OPEN IT.>
<SIRE... I DON'T... I...>
*TRANSLATED FROM HAUSA.
<SPEAK FREELY, LITTLE MOTHER.>
<THE WALLS WERE BROKEN. BLOOD WAS SPILLED.>
<THOUSANDS OF WAKANDANS DIED, AND OUR NATION IS NOW AT WAR...>
<IF THE PEOPLE--IF THE QUEEN--FINDS OUT THAT WE HAVE ALLOWED... THAT MAN HERE...>
<MY LORD... I FEAR FOR YOU.>
<YOU SHOULD LET THAT LITTLE FEAR DIE, AND IN ITS PLACE ALLOW SOMETHING MORE SINISTER TO GROW--FEAR FOR US ALL.>
<AS FOR THE OTHER...I WILL LEAVE THE KEEPING OF SECRETS TO YOU, DORA MILAJE.>

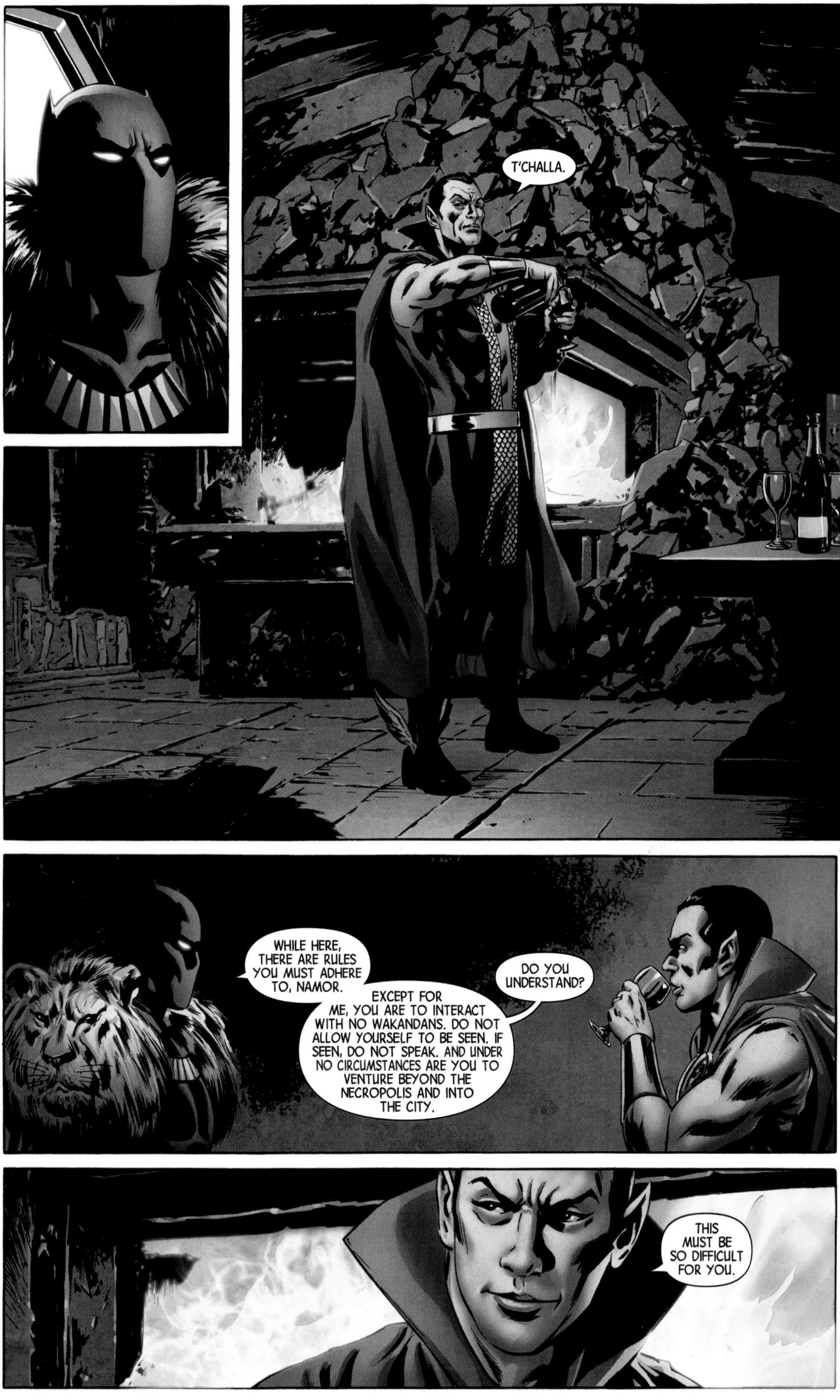
T'CHALLA.
WHILE HERE, THERE ARE RULES YOU MUST ADHERE TO, NAMOR.
EXCEPT FOR ME, YOU ARE TO INTERACT WITH NO WAKANDANS. DO NOT ALLOW YOURSELF TO BE SEEN. IF SEEN, DO NOT SPEAK. AND UNDER NO CIRCUMSTANCES ARE YOU TO VENTURE BEYOND THE NECROPOLIS AND INTO THE CITY.
DO YOU UNDERSTAND?
THIS MUST BE SO DIFFICULT FOR YOU.

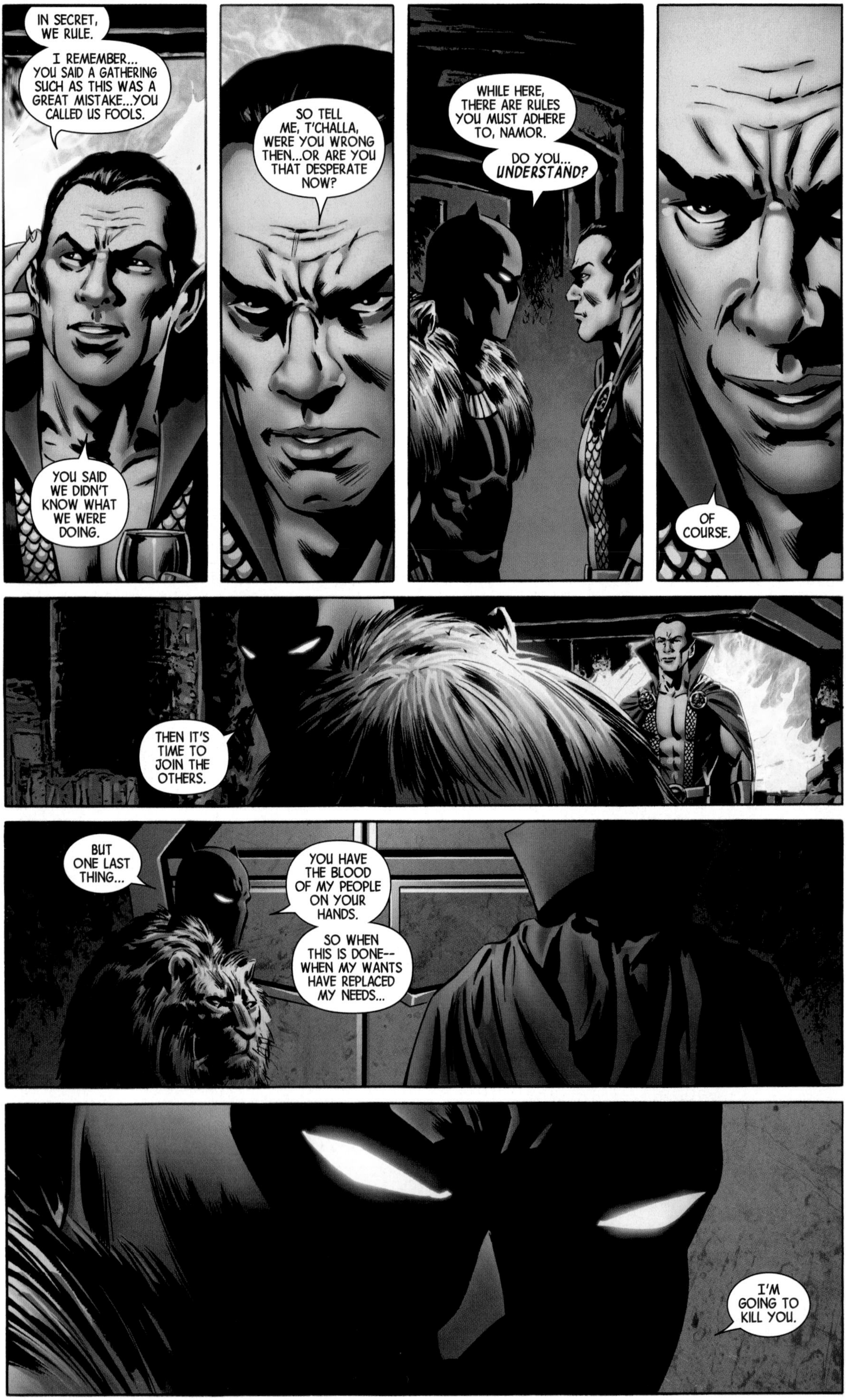
IN SECRET, WE RULE.
I REMEMBER... YOU SAID A GATHERING SUCH AS THIS WAS A GREAT MISTAKE...YOU CALLED US FOOLS.
YOU SAID WE DIDN'T KNOW WHAT WE WERE DOING.
SO TELL ME, T'CHALLA, WERE YOU WRONG THEN...OR ARE YOU THAT DESPERATE NOW?
WHILE HERE, THERE ARE RULES YOU MUST ADHERE TO, NAMOR.
DO YOU... *UNDERSTAND?*
OF COURSE.
THEN IT'S TIME TO JOIN THE OTHERS.
BUT ONE LAST THING...
YOU HAVE THE BLOOD OF MY PEOPLE ON YOUR HANDS.
SO WHEN THIS IS DONE-- WHEN MY WANTS HAVE REPLACED MY NEEDS...
I'M GOING TO KILL YOU.

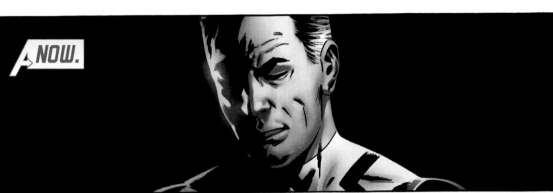

EVERYTHING DIES.

YOU. ME. EVERYONE ON THIS PLANET.

OUR SUN. OUR GALAXY. AND, EVENTUALLY, THE UNIVERSE ITSELF.

THIS IS SIMPLY HOW THINGS ARE.

IT'S INEVITABLE...

AND I ACCEPT IT.

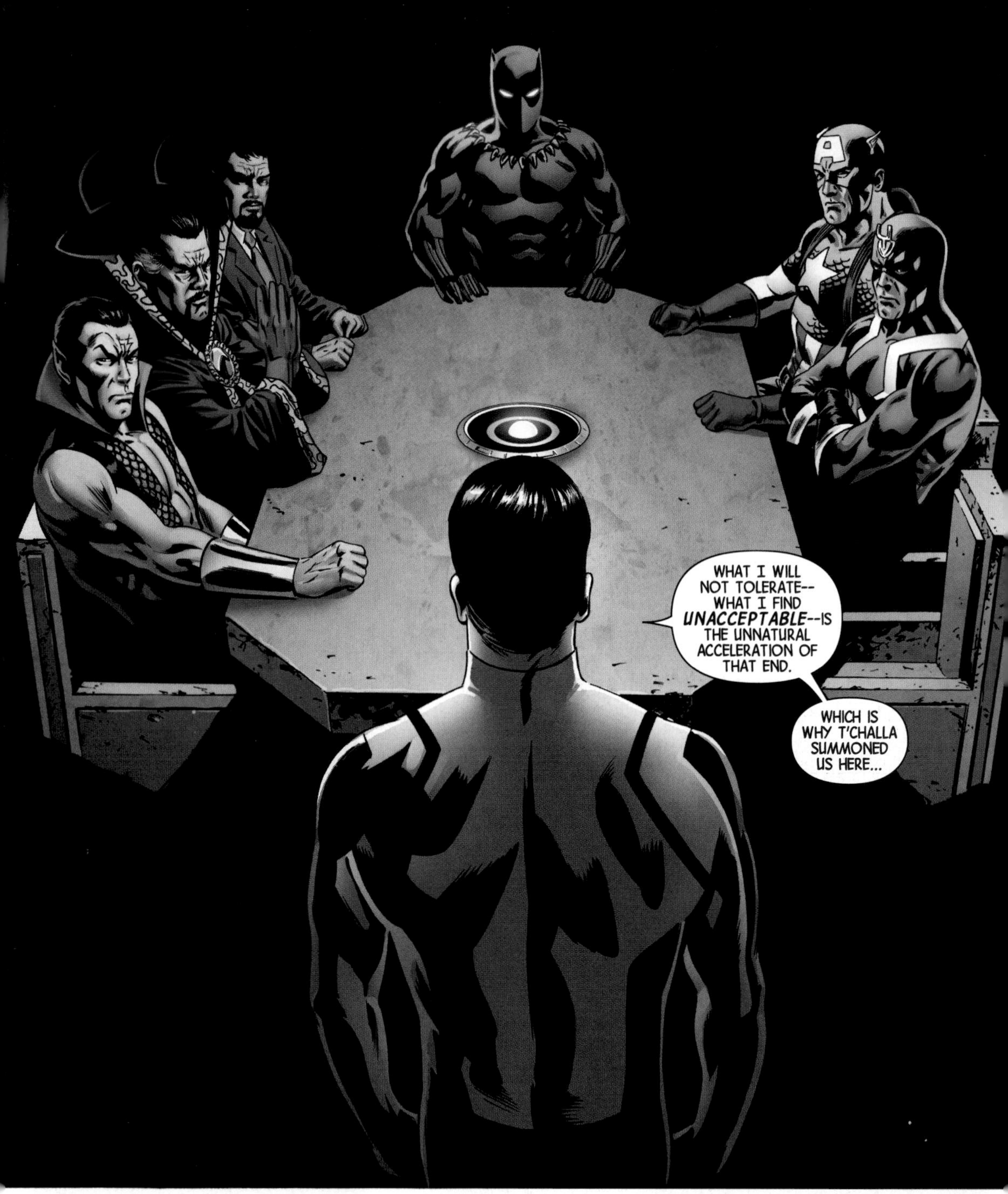
WHAT I WILL NOT TOLERATE-- WHAT I FIND UNACCEPTABLE--IS THE UNNATURAL ACCELERATION OF THAT END.
WHICH IS WHY T'CHALLA SUMMONED US HERE...

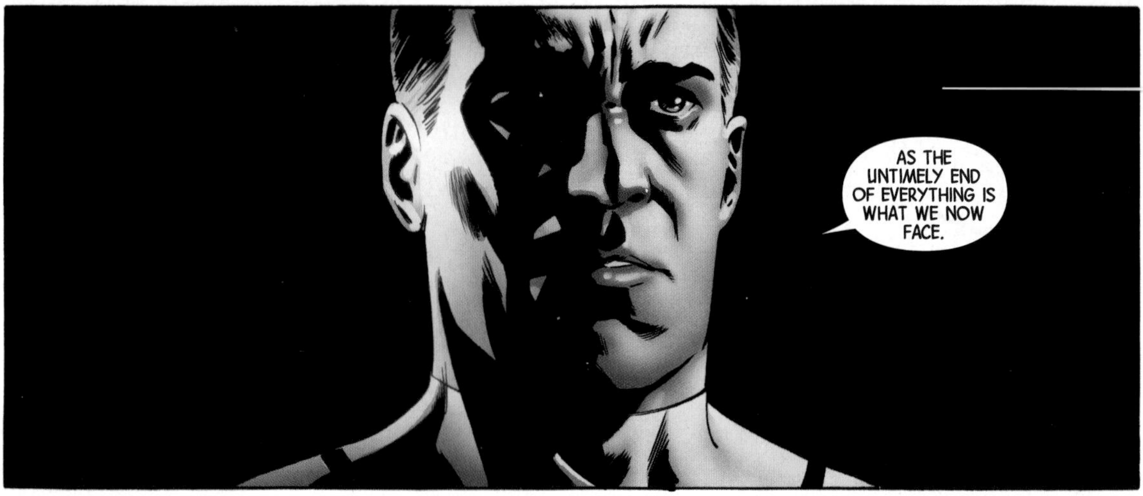
AS THE UNTIMELY END OF EVERYTHING IS WHAT WE NOW FACE.

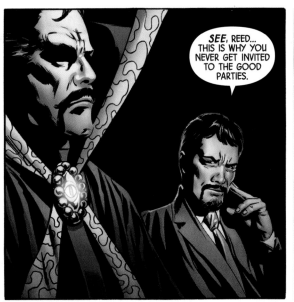
SEE, REED... THIS IS WHY YOU NEVER GET INVITED TO THE GOOD PARTIES.

MANY, MANY TIMES HAVE WE FACED THE WORLD'S END.

AND EACH TIME YOU REFUSED TO ANSWER OUR CALL--YOU REFUSED TO JOIN US...

WHAT MAKES THIS SO DIFFERENT, T'CHALLA?

THE FUTURE OF MY PEOPLE DIED IN MY ARMS YESTERDAY, STEPHEN.

WHAT FOLLOWED...IT DWARFED THAT.

THEN WHAT--

NO. BEFORE WE GET TO WHAT BROUGHT US HERE...

THERE ARE PRECAUTIONS THAT NEED TO BE TAKEN.

WE HAVE BEEN INFILTRATED BEFORE. PLAYED FOR FOOLS.

IF MATTERS ARE THIS GRAVE, I WOULD KNOW IF ONE OF YOU IS NOT WHO YOU SAY YOU ARE...

PROVE YOURSELVES.

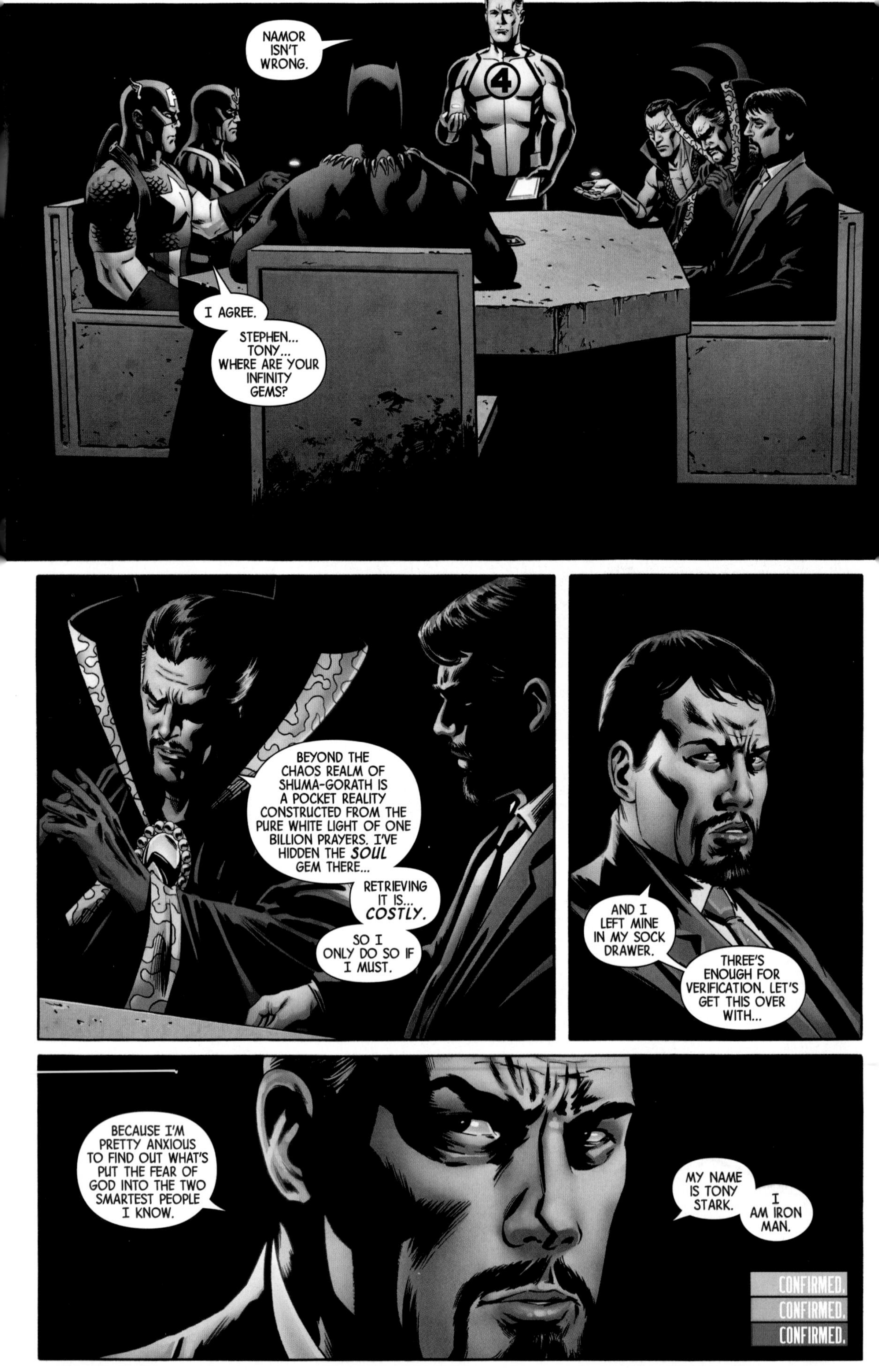
NAMOR ISN'T WRONG.
I AGREE.
STEPHEN... TONY... WHERE ARE YOUR INFINITY GEMS?
BEYOND THE CHAOS REALM OF SHUMA-GORATH IS A POCKET REALITY CONSTRUCTED FROM THE PURE WHITE LIGHT OF ONE BILLION PRAYERS. I'VE HIDDEN THE SOUL GEM THERE...
RETRIEVING IT IS... COSTLY.
SO I ONLY DO SO IF I MUST.
AND I LEFT MINE IN MY SOCK DRAWER.
THREE'S ENOUGH FOR VERIFICATION. LET'S GET THIS OVER WITH...
BECAUSE I'M PRETTY ANXIOUS TO FIND OUT WHAT'S PUT THE FEAR OF GOD INTO THE TWO SMARTEST PEOPLE I KNOW.
MY NAME IS TONY STARK.
I AM IRON MAN.
CONFIRMED.
CONFIRMED.
CONFIRMED.

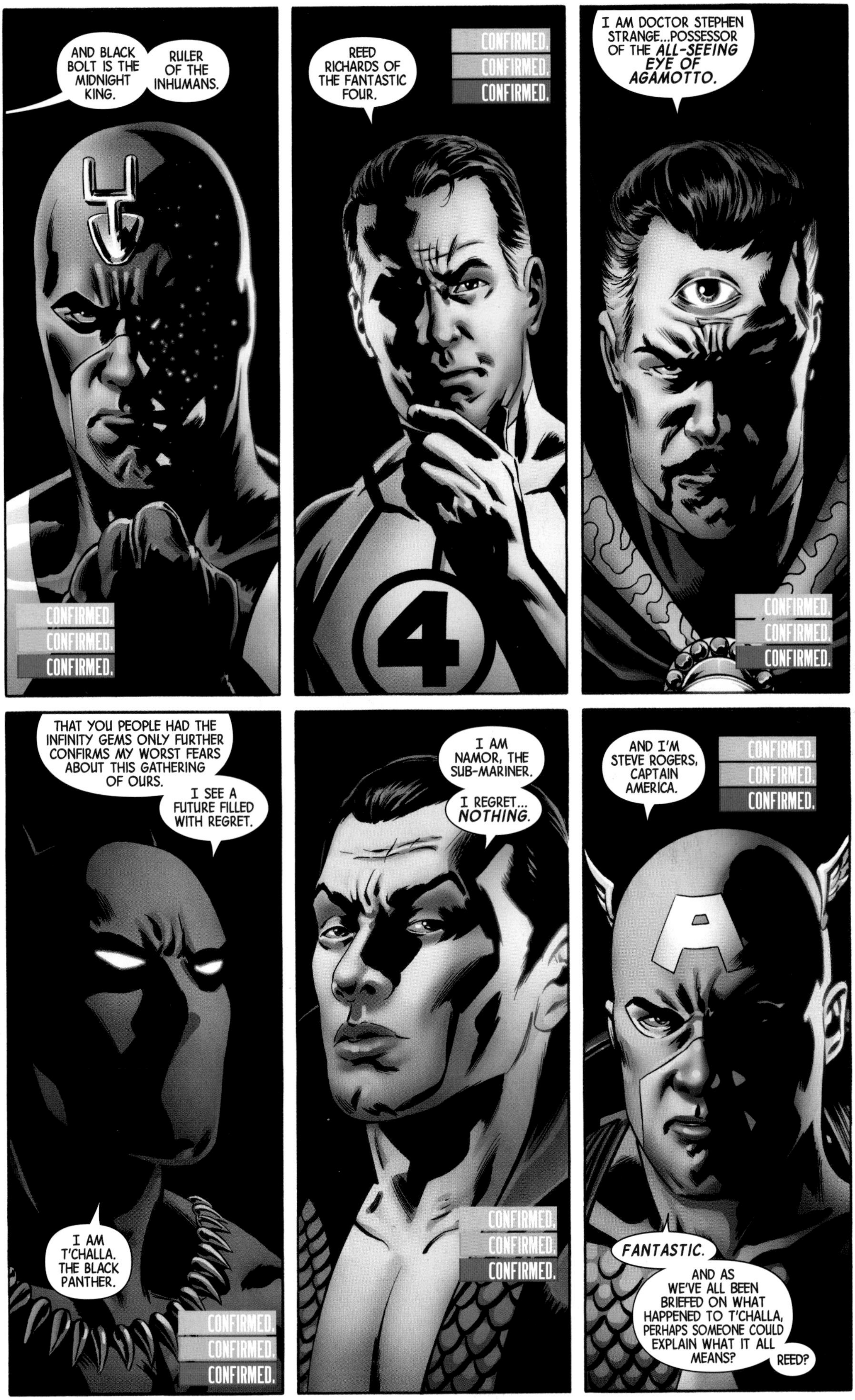
AND BLACK BOLT IS THE MIDNIGHT KING.
RULER OF THE INHUMANS.
CONFIRMED.
CONFIRMED.
CONFIRMED.
REED RICHARDS OF THE FANTASTIC FOUR.
CONFIRMED.
CONFIRMED.
CONFIRMED.
I AM DOCTOR STEPHEN STRANGE...POSSESSOR OF THE ALL-SEEING EYE OF AGAMOTTO.
CONFIRMED.
CONFIRMED.
CONFIRMED.
THAT YOU PEOPLE HAD THE INFINITY GEMS ONLY FURTHER CONFIRMS MY WORST FEARS ABOUT THIS GATHERING OF OURS.
I SEE A FUTURE FILLED WITH REGRET.
I AM T'CHALLA. THE BLACK PANTHER.
CONFIRMED.
CONFIRMED.
CONFIRMED.
I AM NAMOR, THE SUB-MARINER.
I REGRET... NOTHING.
CONFIRMED.
CONFIRMED.
CONFIRMED.
AND I'M STEVE ROGERS, CAPTAIN AMERICA.
CONFIRMED.
CONFIRMED.
CONFIRMED.
FANTASTIC.
AND AS WE'VE ALL BEEN BRIEFED ON WHAT HAPPENED TO T'CHALLA, PERHAPS SOMEONE COULD EXPLAIN WHAT IT ALL MEANS?
REED?

OF COURSE.
BE-DOOP!
IT MIGHT BE BEST IF I START WITH THINGS WE ALL KNOW TO BE TRUE.

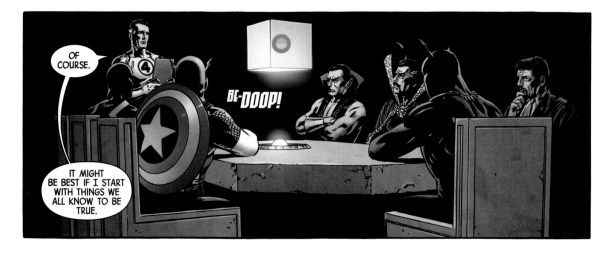

"LIFE AND DEATH.
"THE BIRTH AND HEAT DEATH OF EVERYTHING LIE AT OPPOSITE ENDS ON THE TIMELINE OF THE UNIVERSE.
"THE BEGINNING AND END OF OUR EARTH ALSO EXISTS ON THIS TIMELINE AND, OF COURSE, FALLS WITHIN THESE TWO END POINTS.
"OUR WORLD WAS BORN AFTER THE UNIVERSE'S CREATION, AND OUR WORLD WILL DIE BEFORE THE UNIVERSE ENDS.
"WE ALSO KNOW THERE IS A MULTIVERSE OF REALITIES. AN INFINITE NUMBER OF EARTHS, INSIDE AN INFINITE NUMBER OF UNIVERSES, WHERE ANY MANNER OF DIVERGENT REALITY CAN EXIST.
"ENDLESS POSSIBILITIES...
"HOWEVER, AS I MENTIONED EARLIER... *EVERYTHING DIES.*
"SO, REGARDLESS OF HOW MANY REALITIES THERE ARE, EVENTUALLY THEY ALL END UP IN THE SAME PLACE AND IN THE SAME STATE. EXTINGUISHED AT THE END OF EVERYTHING.
"AND HERE'S WHERE OUR PROBLEM LIES.
"I'VE LEARNED THAT SOMEWHERE, ON ONE OF THESE EARTHS, AN *EVENT* OCCURRED THAT CAUSED THE EARLY DEATH OF ONE OF THESE UNIVERSES.
"THAT *UNTIMELY, UNNATURAL* EVENT THEN CAUSED A TINY CONTRACTION IN THE MULTIVERSE'S TIMELINE.
"NOW, EVERYTHING WOULD DIE EVER-SO-SLIGHTLY SOONER.

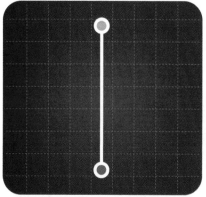

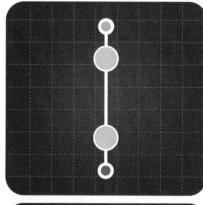

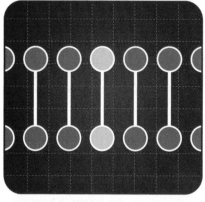

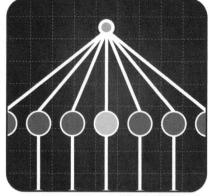

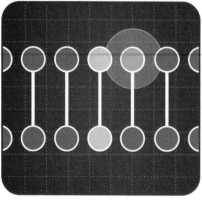

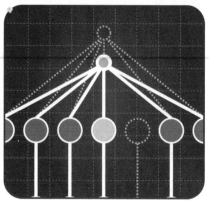

"IN ADDITION, THAT TINY CONTRACTION CAUSED TWO UNIVERSES TO SMASH TOGETHER AT THE *INCURSION POINT* OF THE INITIAL EVENT.

"AND THIS IS WHERE YOU REALLY WANT TO PAY ATTENTION... THAT *POINT* WAS *EARTH*.

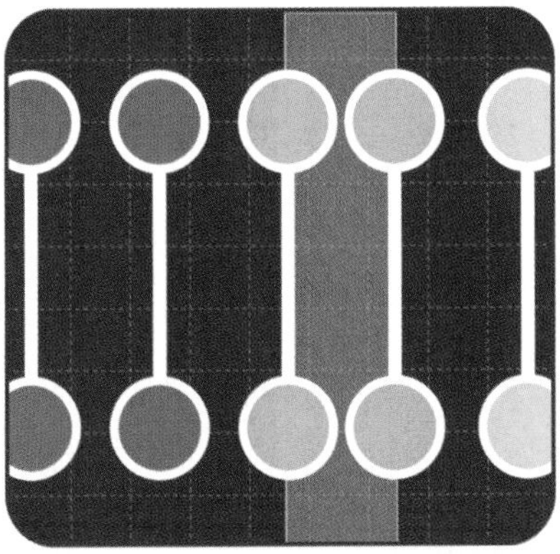

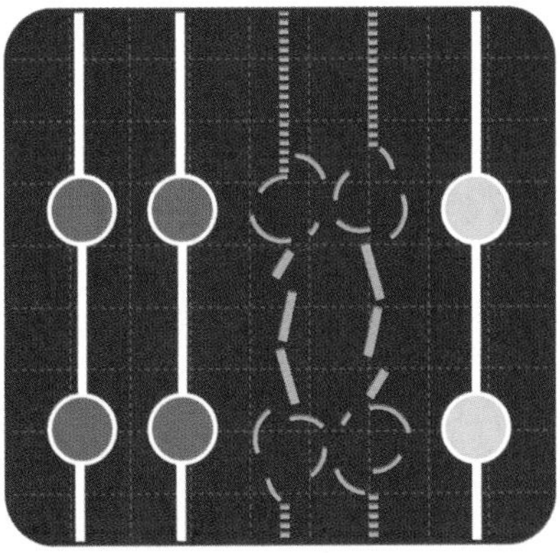

"THEY TOUCHED, AND DESTROYED EACH OTHER--TAKING THEIR UNIVERSES WITH THEM--CAUSING YET ANOTHER CONTRACTION IN THE TIMELINE.

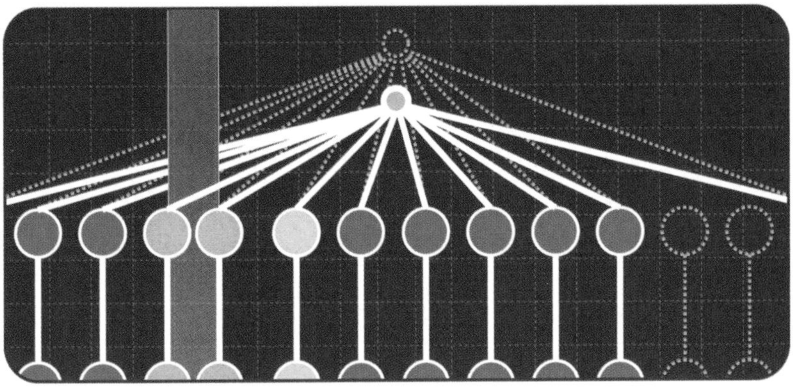

"WHICH IN TURN ACCELERATED THE SMASHING TOGETHER OF EVEN MORE EARTHS AND THEIR RESPECTIVE UNIVERSES.

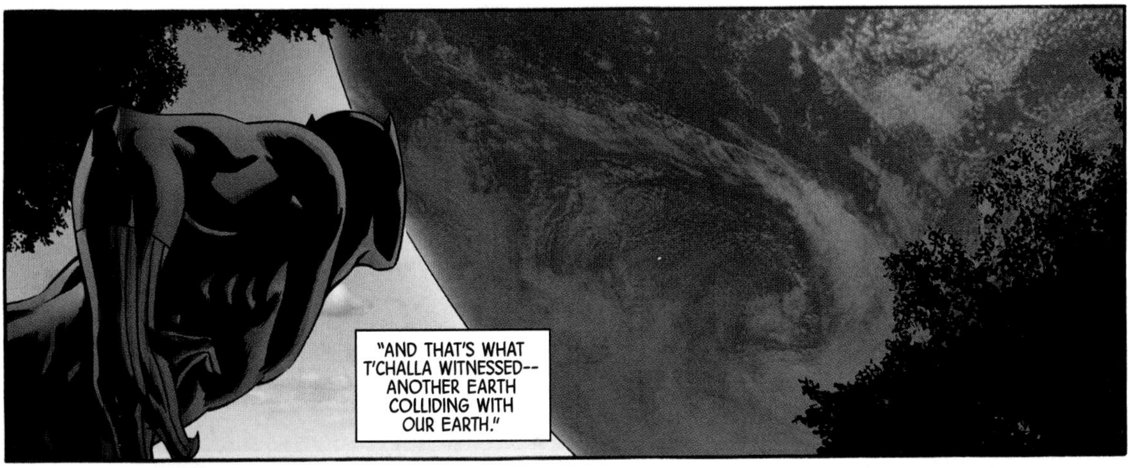
"AND THAT'S WHAT T'CHALLA WITNESSED--ANOTHER EARTH COLLIDING WITH OUR EARTH."

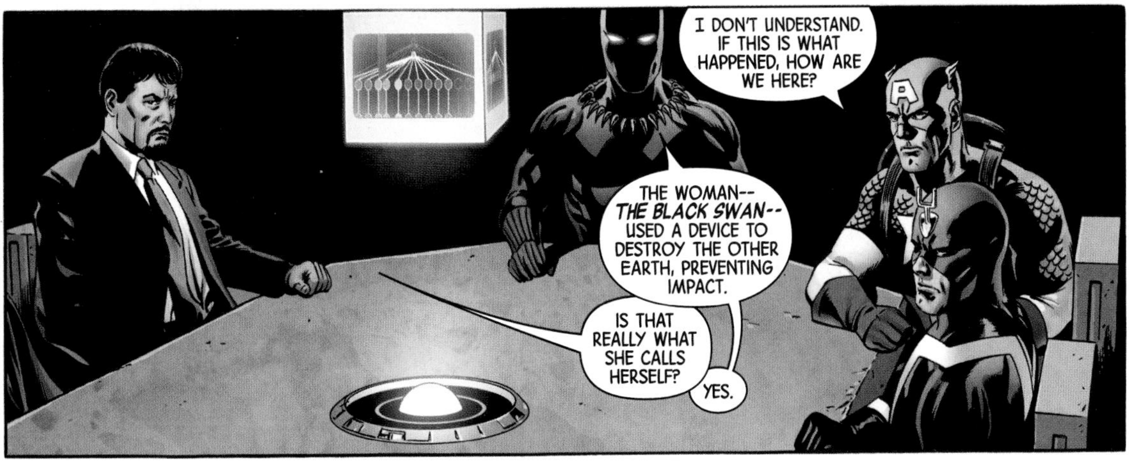
I DON'T UNDERSTAND. IF THIS IS WHAT HAPPENED, HOW ARE WE HERE?
THE WOMAN--*THE BLACK SWAN*--USED A DEVICE TO DESTROY THE OTHER EARTH, PREVENTING IMPACT.
IS THAT REALLY WHAT SHE CALLS HERSELF?
YES.

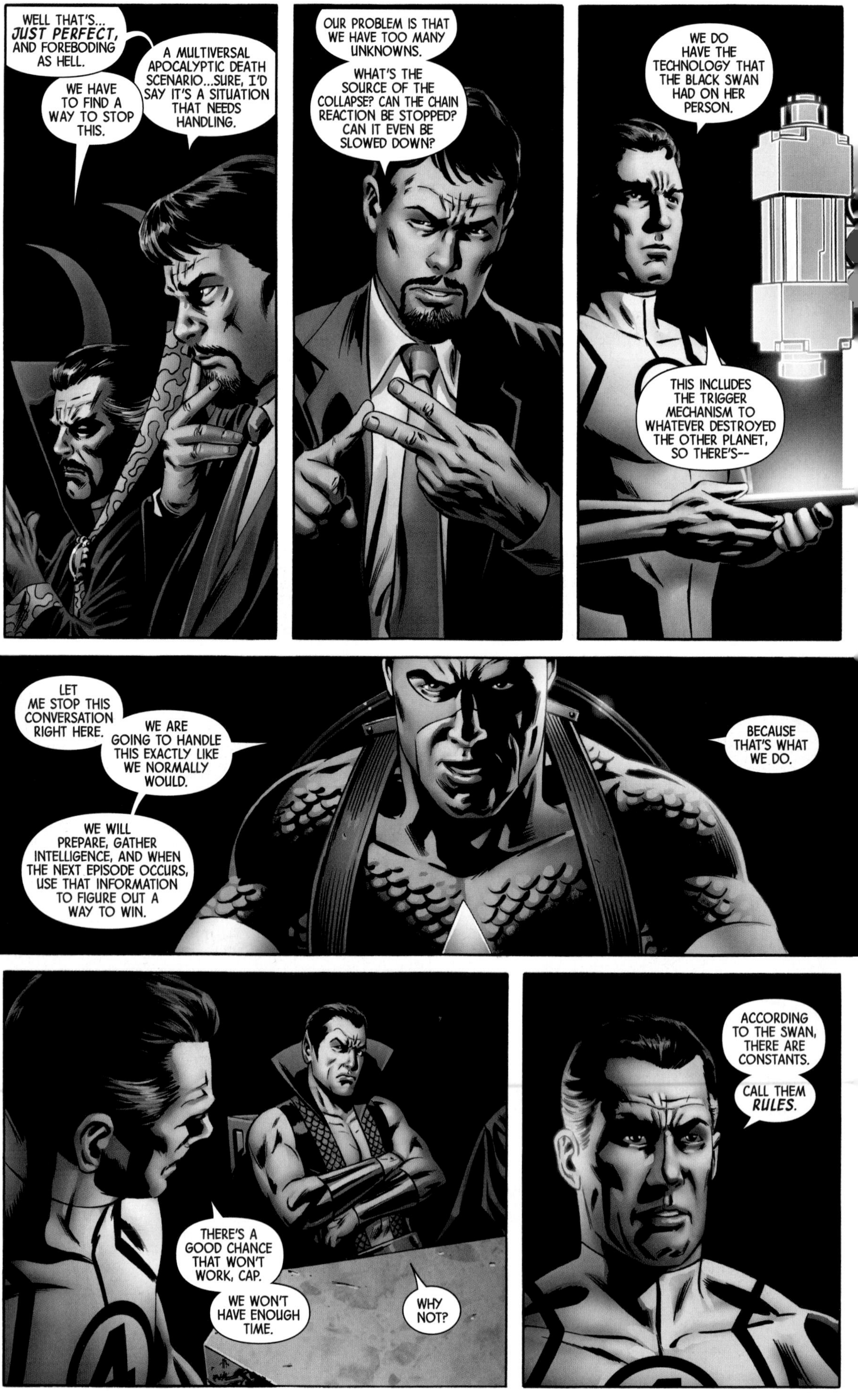
WELL THAT'S... *JUST PERFECT*, AND FOREBODING AS HELL.
A MULTIVERSAL APOCALYPTIC DEATH SCENARIO...SURE, I'D SAY IT'S A SITUATION THAT NEEDS HANDLING.
WE HAVE TO FIND A WAY TO STOP THIS.
OUR PROBLEM IS THAT WE HAVE TOO MANY UNKNOWNS.
WHAT'S THE SOURCE OF THE COLLAPSE? CAN THE CHAIN REACTION BE STOPPED? CAN IT EVEN BE SLOWED DOWN?
WE DO HAVE THE TECHNOLOGY THAT THE BLACK SWAN HAD ON HER PERSON.
THIS INCLUDES THE TRIGGER MECHANISM TO WHATEVER DESTROYED THE OTHER PLANET, SO THERE'S--
LET ME STOP THIS CONVERSATION RIGHT HERE.
WE ARE GOING TO HANDLE THIS EXACTLY LIKE WE NORMALLY WOULD.
WE WILL PREPARE, GATHER INTELLIGENCE, AND WHEN THE NEXT EPISODE OCCURS, USE THAT INFORMATION TO FIGURE OUT A WAY TO WIN.
BECAUSE THAT'S WHAT WE DO.
THERE'S A GOOD CHANCE THAT WON'T WORK, CAP.
WE WON'T HAVE ENOUGH TIME.
WHY NOT?
ACCORDING TO THE SWAN, THERE ARE CONSTANTS.
CALL THEM *RULES*.

"AS I STATED EARLIER, THE TIME WHEN TWO EARTHS BEGIN TO COLLIDE IS CALLED AN *INCURSION*, AND EVERY SINGLE ONE IS EXACTLY THE SAME.

"BEFORE THEY BEGIN, THERE IS A VERY SHORT PERIOD OF HARMONIC ALIGNMENT, WHICH IS WHAT ALLOWS THE TWO EARTHS TO EXIST IN THE SAME SPACE.

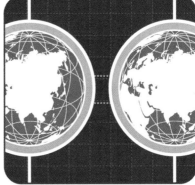

"THE SINGLE BIT OF GOOD NEWS HERE IS THAT WE SHOULD BE ABLE TO DETECT THIS, AND THEREFORE CREATE AN EARLY WARNING SYSTEM. SO, AT LEAST WE'LL KNOW WHEN ONE IS COMING.

"REGARDLESS, ONCE THE *INCURSION* ACTUALLY BEGINS, OUR TIME TO ACT GROWS VERY SHORT...

"AS EACH *INCURSION* LASTS EXACTLY 8 HOURS.

"AT THE END OF THOSE 8 HOURS, WHAT FOLLOWS IS EXTREMELY SIMPLE. EITHER BOTH WORLDS ARE DESTROYED, ALONG WITH THEIR RESPECTIVE UNIVERSES, AS THEY SMASH TOGETHER...

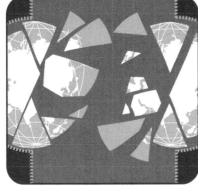

"...OR ONE EARTH IS DESTROYED, WHICH ELIMINATES THE INCURSION POINT BETWEEN THE TWO UNIVERSES, SPARING THEM BOTH.

"EIGHT HOURS. ONE EVENT-- TWO POSSIBLE OUTCOMES."

BE-*DOOP!*

NOW, ADMITTEDLY, THE BLACK SWAN COULD BE LYING--I DID NOT HAVE THAT MUCH TIME WITH HER AND I DEFINITELY THINK SHE'S LEAVING SOME THINGS OUT--BUT BIOMETRICS SHOWED NO SIGNS OF OUTRIGHT DECEPTION.

AND, OF COURSE, THERE'S THE MINOR POINT THAT SHE APPEARED TO DESTROY THE OTHER WORLD, THEREBY SPARING OURS AND SAVING HERSELF.

SO, FOR NOW, HER STORY CHECKS OUT.

EIGHT HOURS. THAT'S ALL WE'LL HAVE.

T'CHALLA?

AR

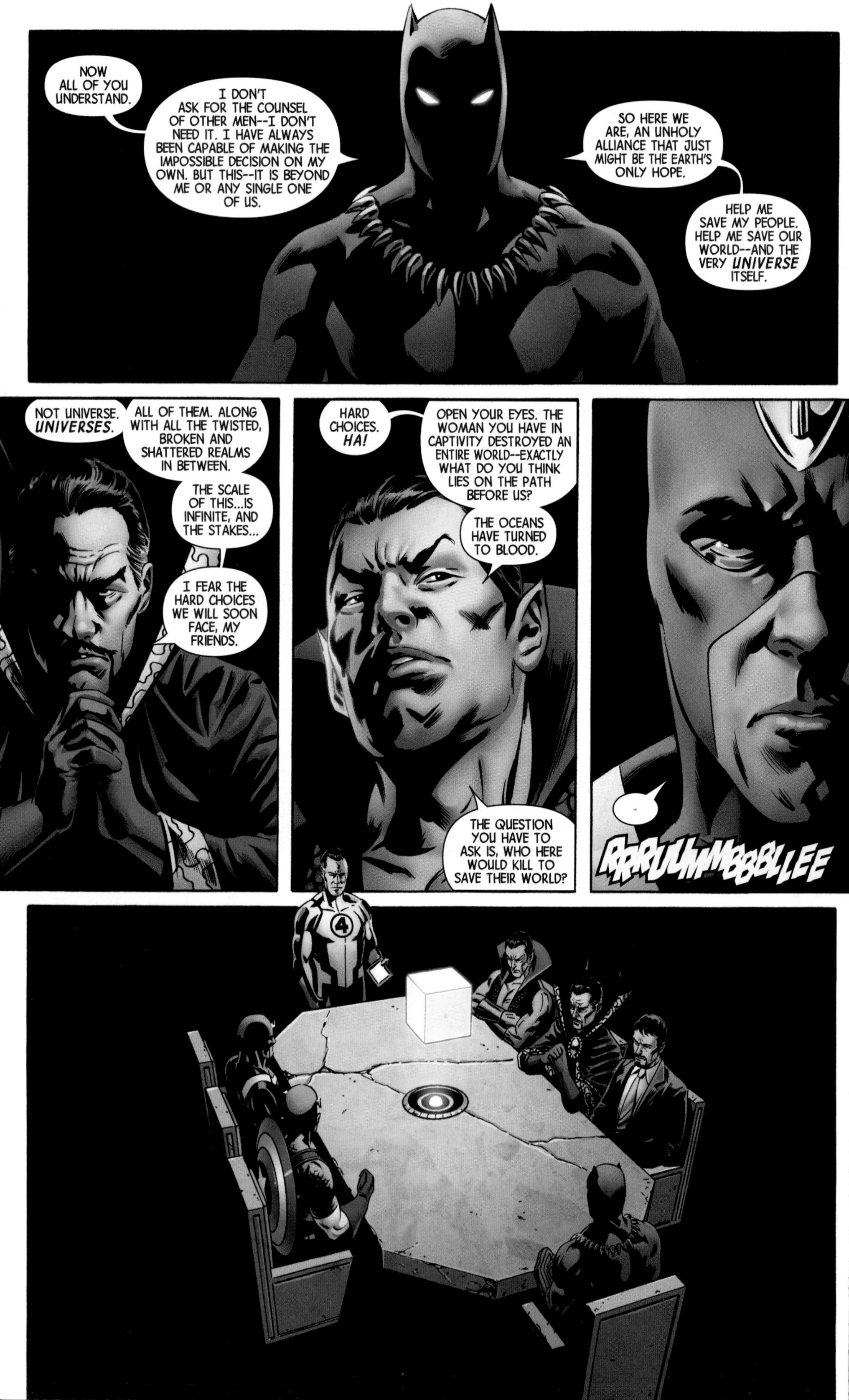
NOW ALL OF YOU UNDERSTAND.
I DON'T ASK FOR THE COUNSEL OF OTHER MEN--I DON'T NEED IT. I HAVE ALWAYS BEEN CAPABLE OF MAKING THE IMPOSSIBLE DECISION ON MY OWN. BUT THIS--IT IS BEYOND ME OR ANY SINGLE ONE OF US.
SO HERE WE ARE, AN UNHOLY ALLIANCE THAT JUST MIGHT BE THE EARTH'S ONLY HOPE.
HELP ME SAVE MY PEOPLE. HELP ME SAVE OUR WORLD--AND THE VERY *UNIVERSE* ITSELF.
NOT UNIVERSE. *UNIVERSES.*
ALL OF THEM. ALONG WITH ALL THE TWISTED, BROKEN AND SHATTERED REALMS IN BETWEEN.
THE SCALE OF THIS...IS INFINITE, AND THE STAKES...
I FEAR THE HARD CHOICES WE WILL SOON FACE, MY FRIENDS.
HARD CHOICES. *HA!*
OPEN YOUR EYES. THE WOMAN YOU HAVE IN CAPTIVITY DESTROYED AN ENTIRE WORLD--EXACTLY WHAT DO YOU THINK LIES ON THE PATH BEFORE US?
THE OCEANS HAVE TURNED TO BLOOD.
THE QUESTION YOU HAVE TO ASK IS, WHO HERE WOULD KILL TO SAVE THEIR WORLD?
RRRUUMMBBBLLEE

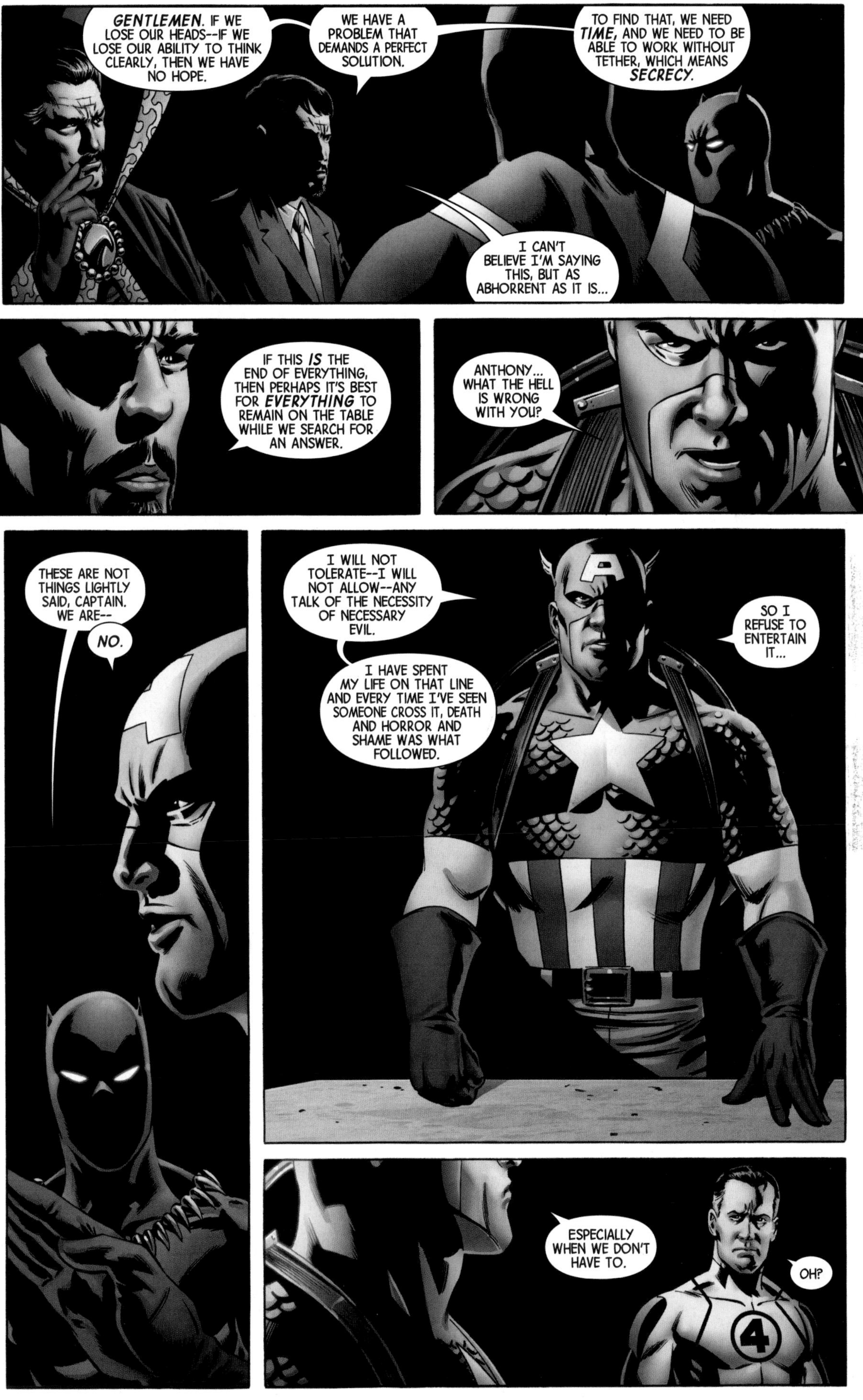
GENTLEMEN. IF WE LOSE OUR HEADS--IF WE LOSE OUR ABILITY TO THINK CLEARLY, THEN WE HAVE NO HOPE.
WE HAVE A PROBLEM THAT DEMANDS A PERFECT SOLUTION.
TO FIND THAT, WE NEED TIME, AND WE NEED TO BE ABLE TO WORK WITHOUT TETHER, WHICH MEANS SECRECY.
I CAN'T BELIEVE I'M SAYING THIS, BUT AS ABHORRENT AS IT IS...
IF THIS IS THE END OF EVERYTHING, THEN PERHAPS IT'S BEST FOR EVERYTHING TO REMAIN ON THE TABLE WHILE WE SEARCH FOR AN ANSWER.
ANTHONY... WHAT THE HELL IS WRONG WITH YOU?
THESE ARE NOT THINGS LIGHTLY SAID, CAPTAIN. WE ARE--
NO.
I WILL NOT TOLERATE--I WILL NOT ALLOW--ANY TALK OF THE NECESSITY OF NECESSARY EVIL.
I HAVE SPENT MY LIFE ON THAT LINE AND EVERY TIME I'VE SEEN SOMEONE CROSS IT, DEATH AND HORROR AND SHAME WAS WHAT FOLLOWED.
SO I REFUSE TO ENTERTAIN IT...
ESPECIALLY WHEN WE DON'T HAVE TO.
OH?

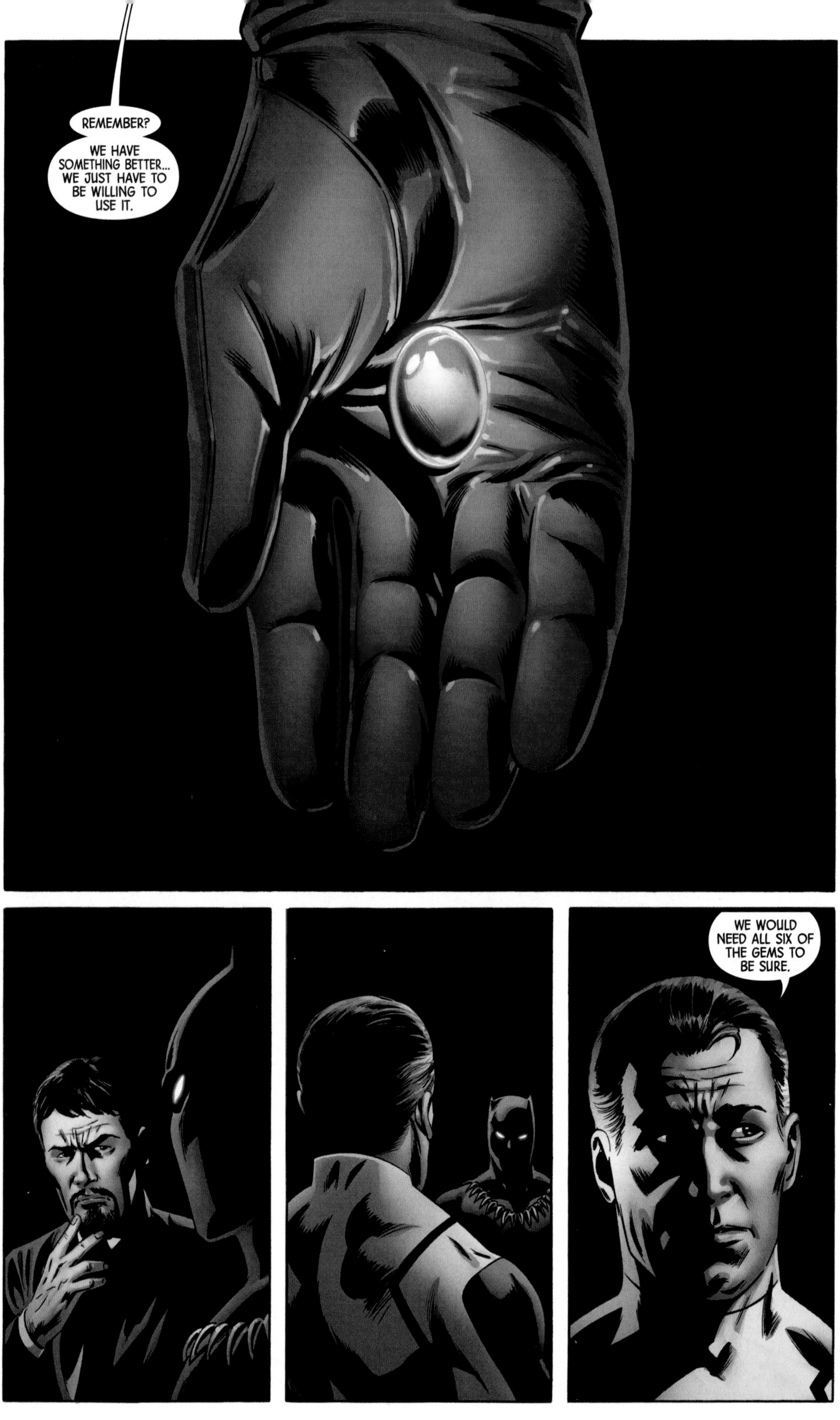
REMEMBER?
WE HAVE SOMETHING BETTER... WE JUST HAVE TO BE WILLING TO USE IT.
WE WOULD NEED ALL SIX OF THE GEMS TO BE SURE.

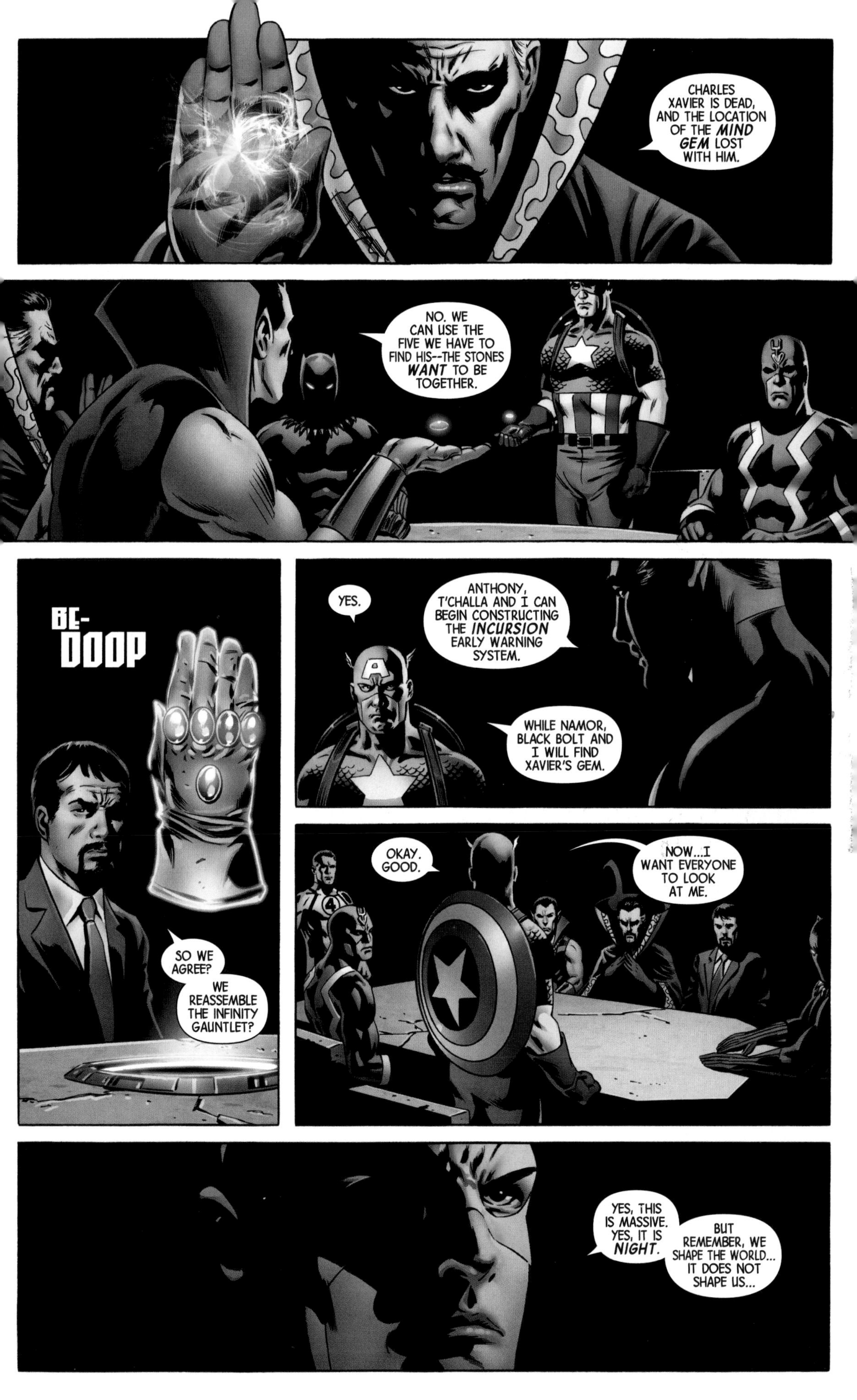
CHARLES XAVIER IS DEAD, AND THE LOCATION OF THE MIND GEM LOST WITH HIM.
NO. WE CAN USE THE FIVE WE HAVE TO FIND HIS--THE STONES WANT TO BE TOGETHER.
BE-DOOP
SO WE AGREE?
WE REASSEMBLE THE INFINITY GAUNTLET?
YES.
ANTHONY, T'CHALLA AND I CAN BEGIN CONSTRUCTING THE INCURSION EARLY WARNING SYSTEM.
WHILE NAMOR, BLACK BOLT AND I WILL FIND XAVIER'S GEM.
OKAY. GOOD.
NOW...I WANT EVERYONE TO LOOK AT ME.
YES, THIS IS MASSIVE. YES, IT IS NIGHT.
BUT REMEMBER, WE SHAPE THE WORLD... IT DOES NOT SHAPE US...

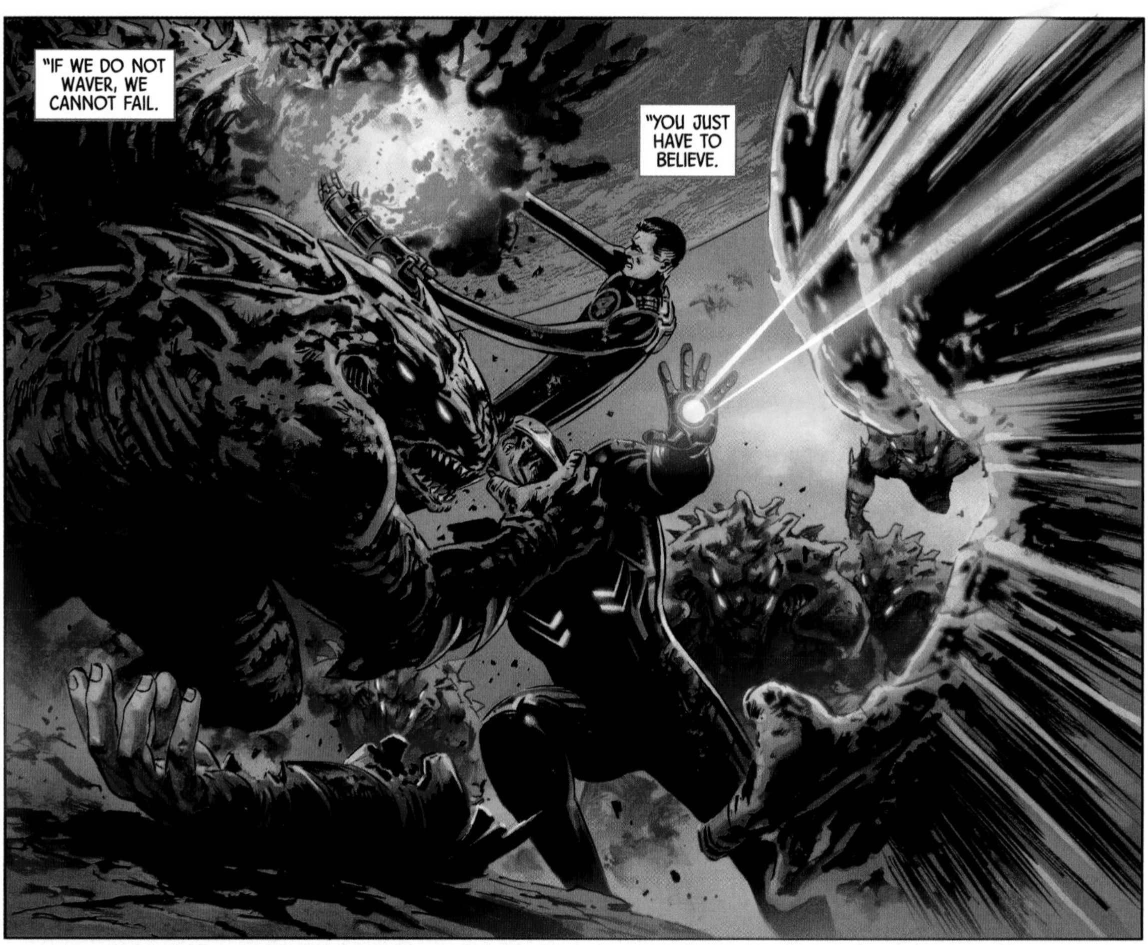
"IF WE DO NOT WAVER, WE CANNOT FAIL.
"YOU JUST HAVE TO BELIEVE.

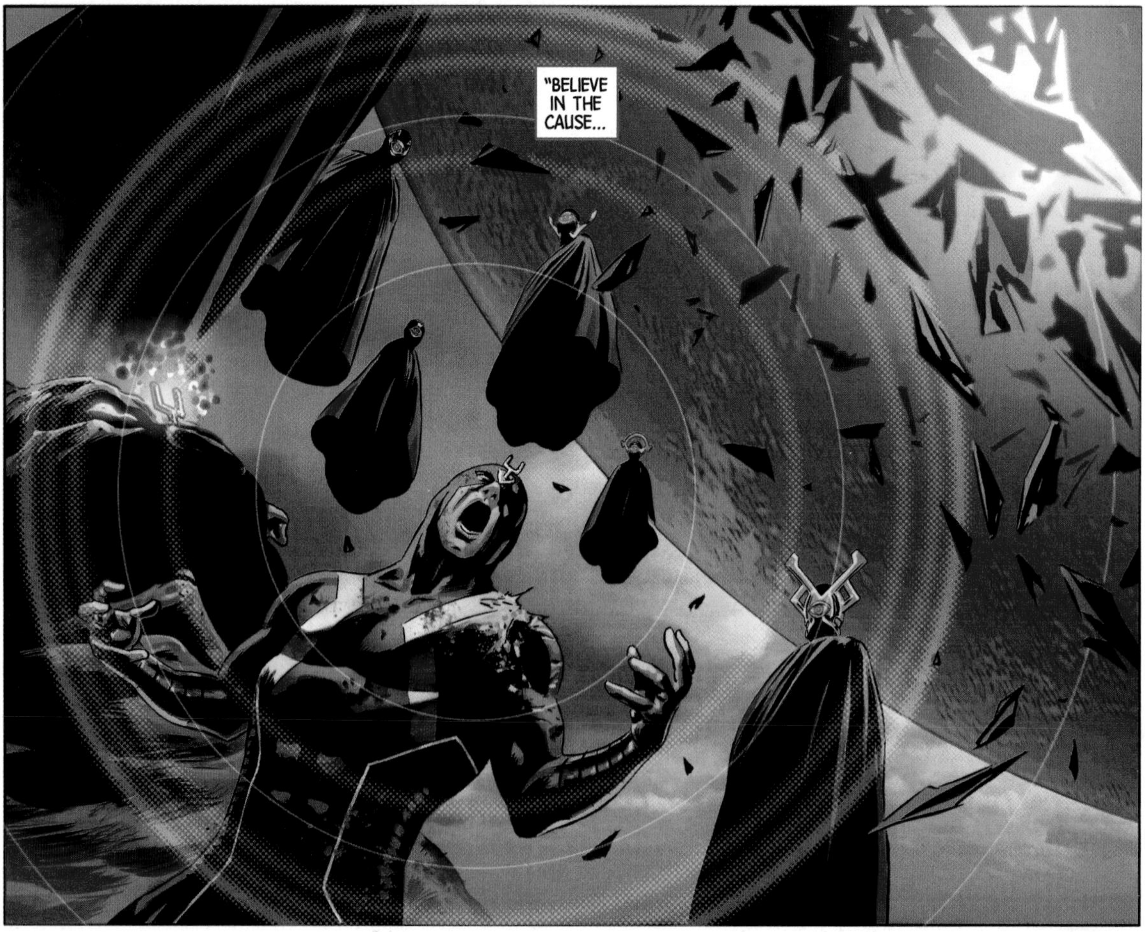
"BELIEVE IN THE CAUSE...

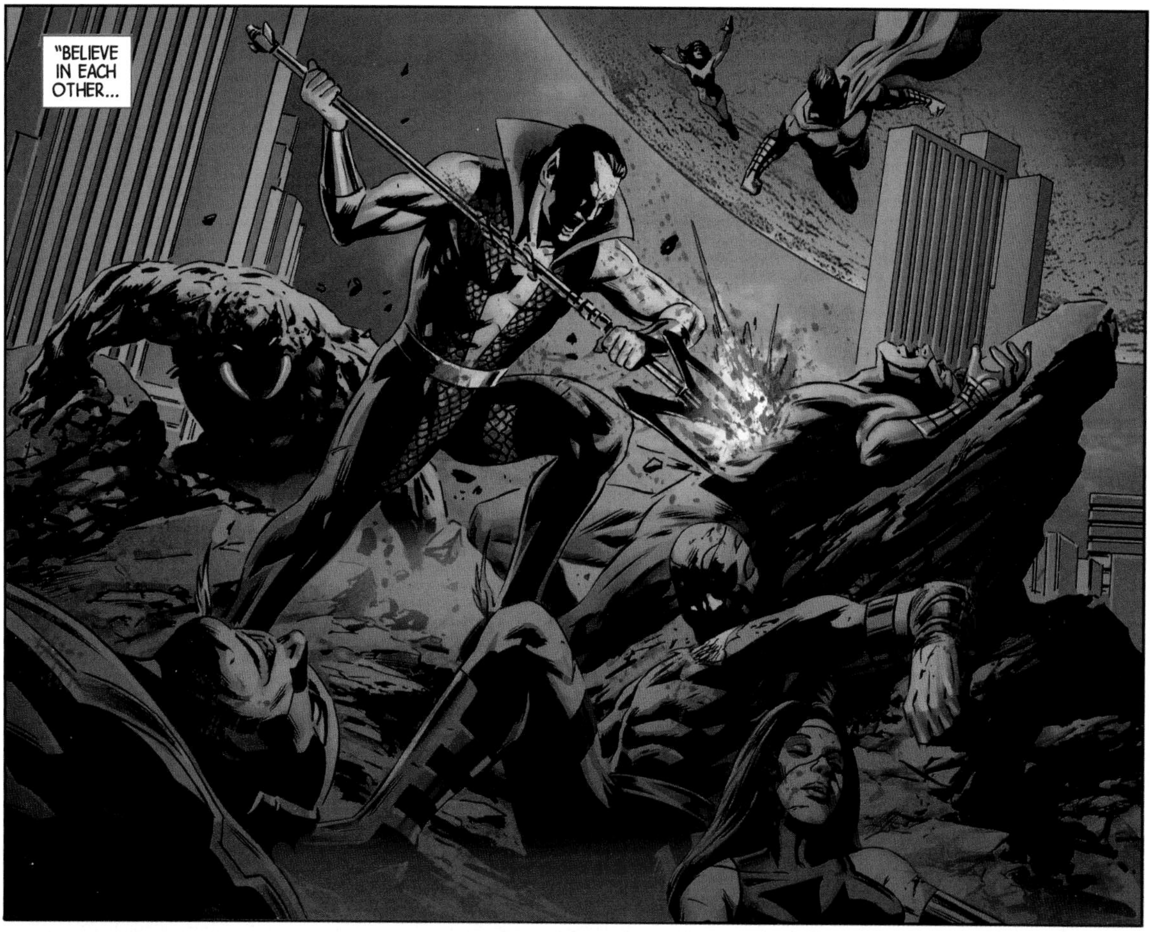
"BELIEVE IN EACH OTHER...

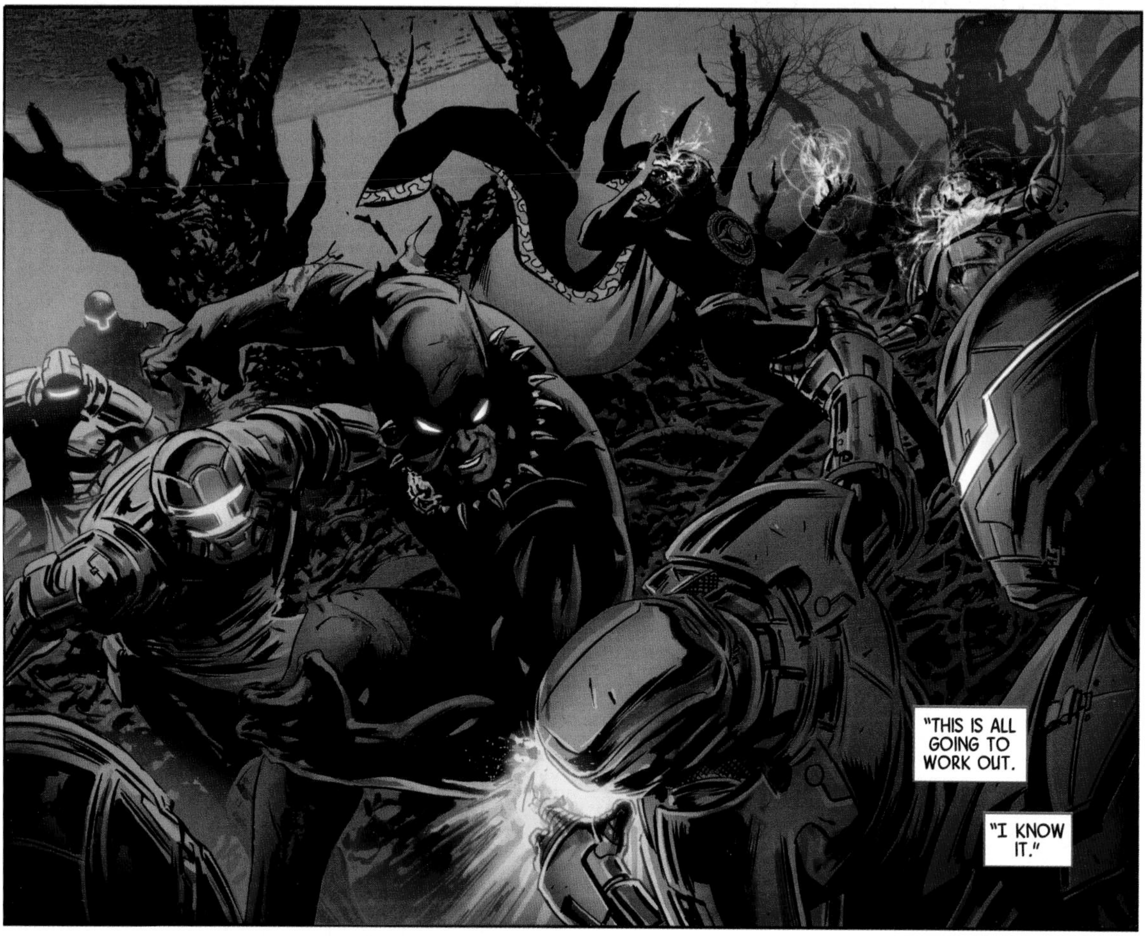
"THIS IS ALL GOING TO WORK OUT.
"I KNOW IT."

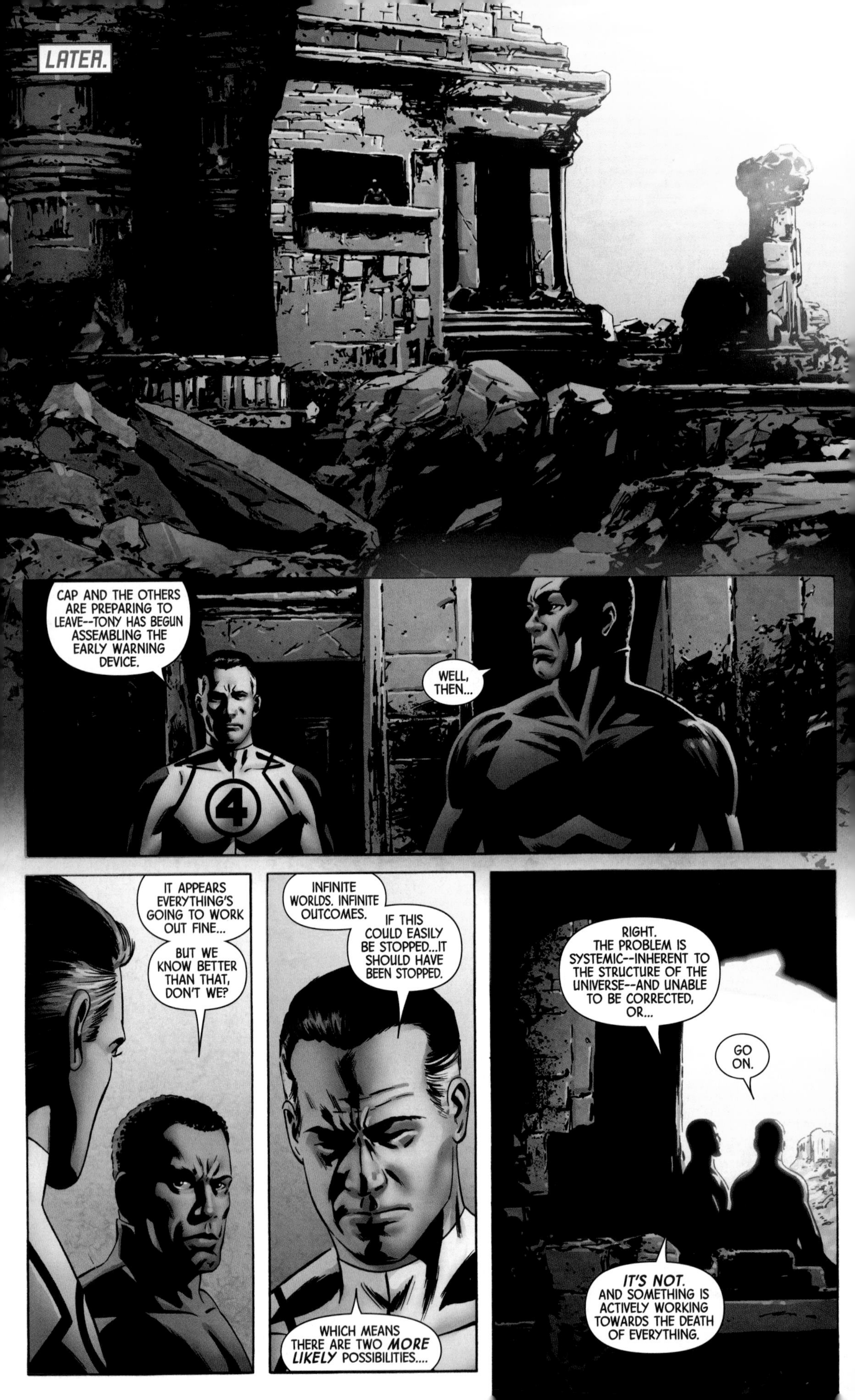
LATER.
CAP AND THE OTHERS ARE PREPARING TO LEAVE--TONY HAS BEGUN ASSEMBLING THE EARLY WARNING DEVICE.
WELL, THEN...
IT APPEARS EVERYTHING'S GOING TO WORK OUT FINE...
BUT WE KNOW BETTER THAN THAT, DON'T WE?
INFINITE WORLDS. INFINITE OUTCOMES.
IF THIS COULD EASILY BE STOPPED...IT SHOULD HAVE BEEN STOPPED.
WHICH MEANS THERE ARE TWO *MORE LIKELY* POSSIBILITIES....
RIGHT. THE PROBLEM IS SYSTEMIC--INHERENT TO THE STRUCTURE OF THE UNIVERSE--AND UNABLE TO BE CORRECTED, OR...
GO ON.
IT'S NOT. AND SOMETHING IS ACTIVELY WORKING TOWARDS THE DEATH OF EVERYTHING.

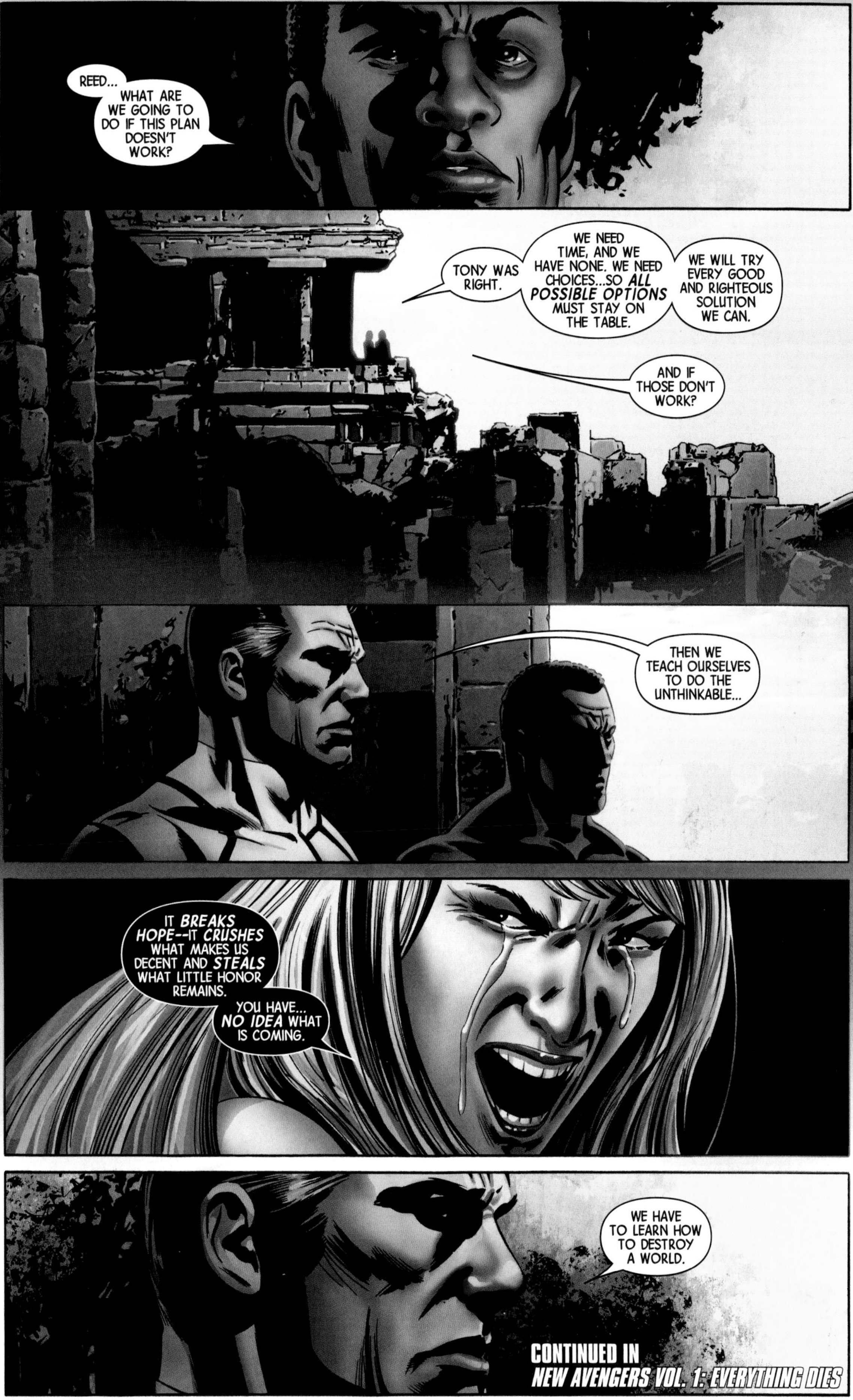
REED... WHAT ARE WE GOING TO DO IF THIS PLAN DOESN'T WORK?
TONY WAS RIGHT.
WE NEED TIME, AND WE HAVE NONE. WE NEED CHOICES...SO ALL POSSIBLE OPTIONS MUST STAY ON THE TABLE.
WE WILL TRY EVERY GOOD AND RIGHTEOUS SOLUTION WE CAN.
AND IF THOSE DON'T WORK?
THEN WE TEACH OURSELVES TO DO THE UNTHINKABLE...
IT BREAKS HOPE--IT CRUSHES WHAT MAKES US DECENT AND STEALS WHAT LITTLE HONOR REMAINS.
YOU HAVE... NO IDEA WHAT IS COMING.
WE HAVE TO LEARN HOW TO DESTROY A WORLD.
CONTINUED IN
NEW AVENGERS VOL. 1: EVERYTHING DIES

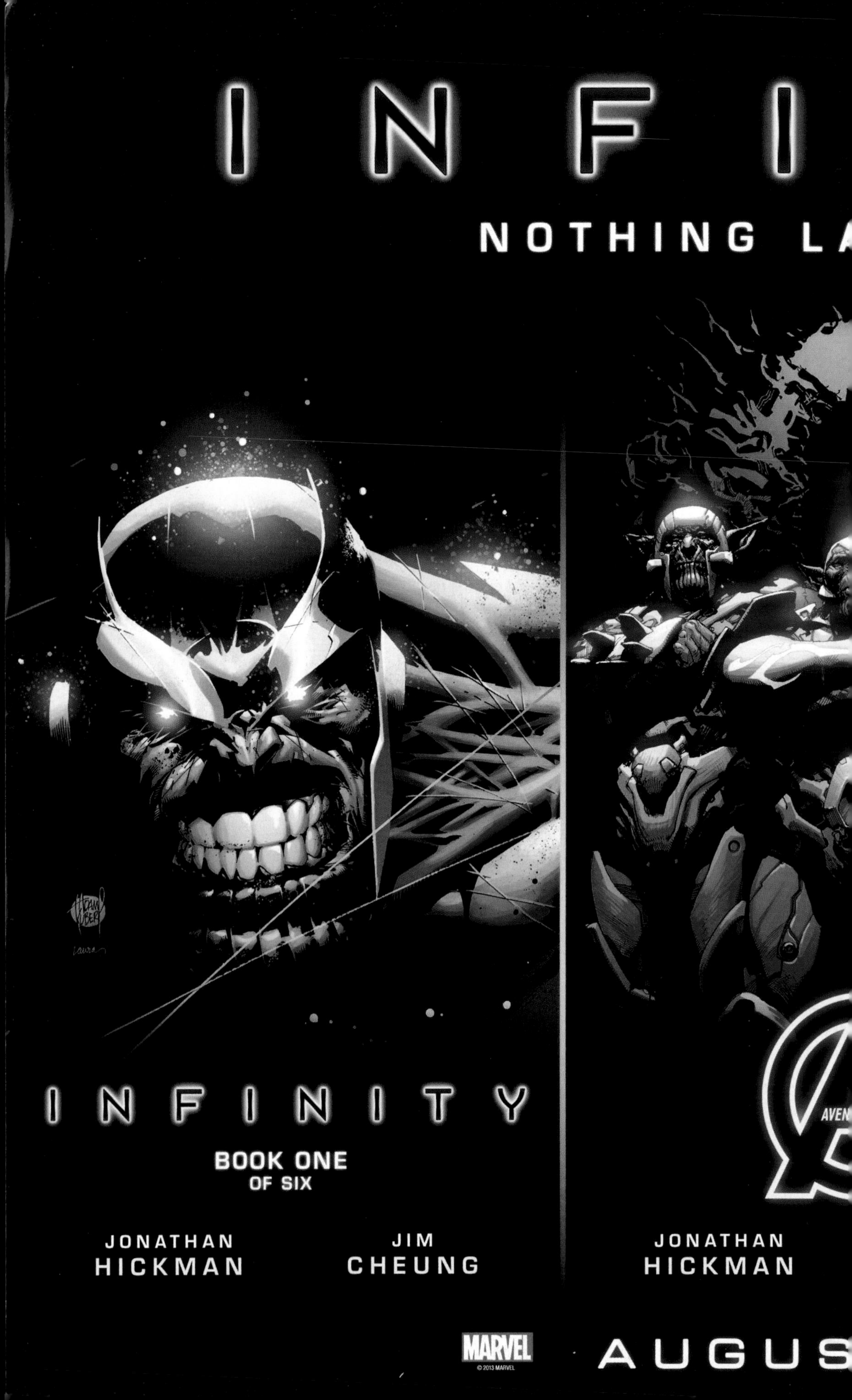
INFI
NOTHING LA
INFINITY
BOOK ONE
OF SIX
JONATHAN
HICKMAN
JIM
CHEUNG
JONATHAN
HICKMAN
MARVEL
© 2013 MARVEL
AUGUS

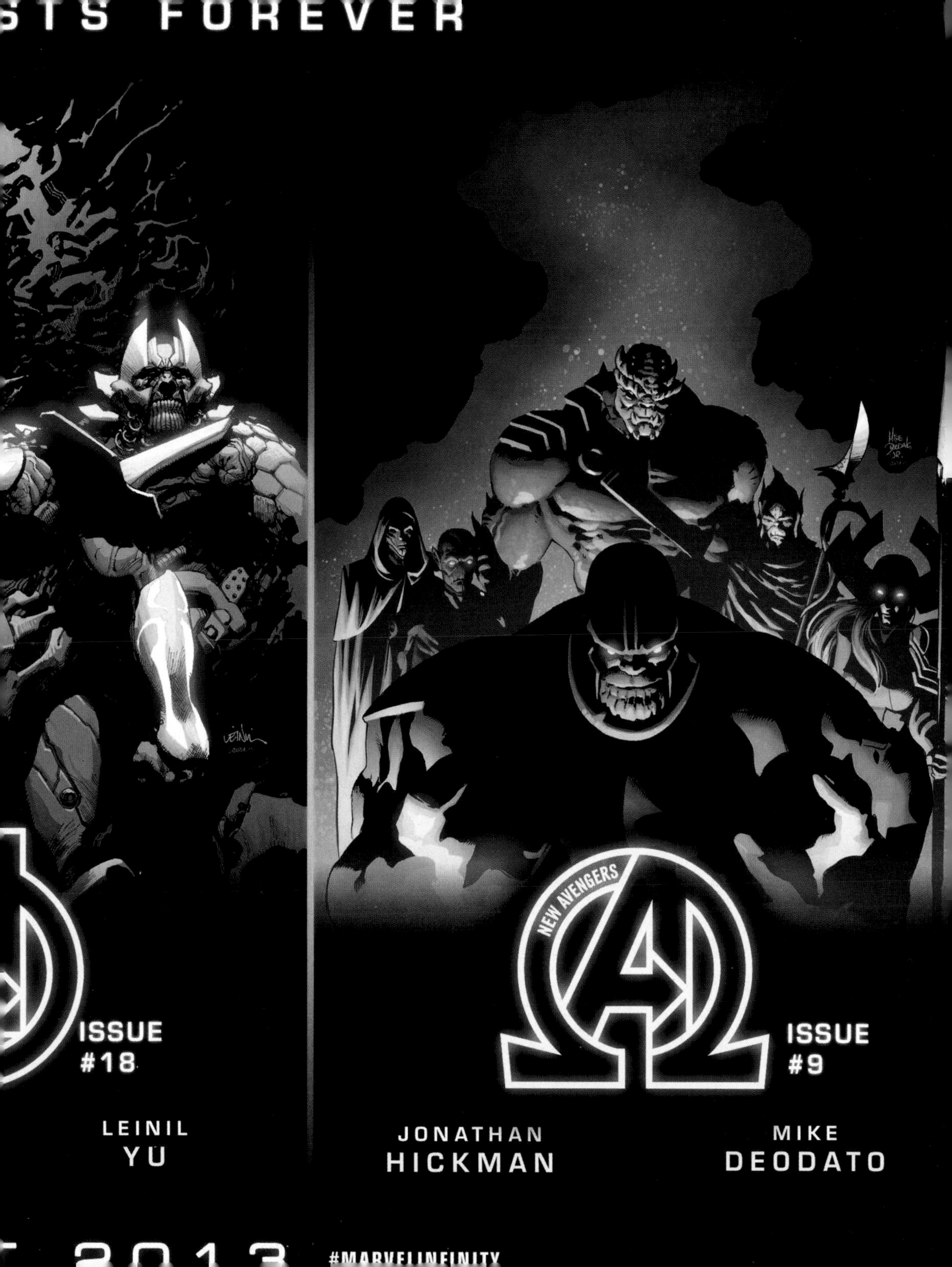

STS FOREVER
ISSUE
#18
LEINIL
YU
NEW AVENGERS
ISSUE
#9
JONATHAN
HICKMAN
MIKE
DEODATO
2013
#MARVELINFINITY

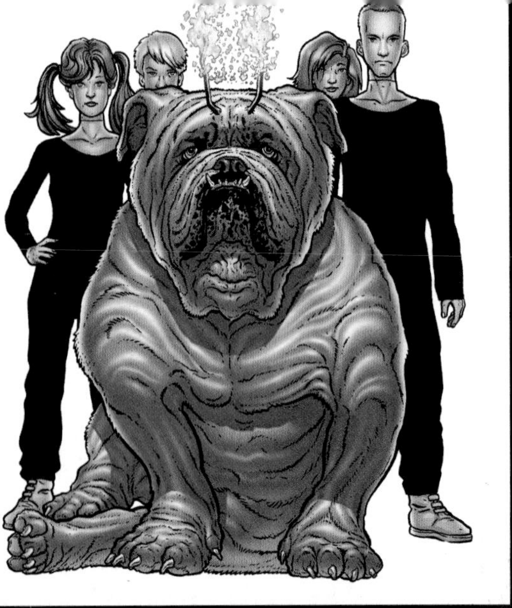

INHUMANS #2 VARIANT
BY JAE LEE & AVALON STUDIOS

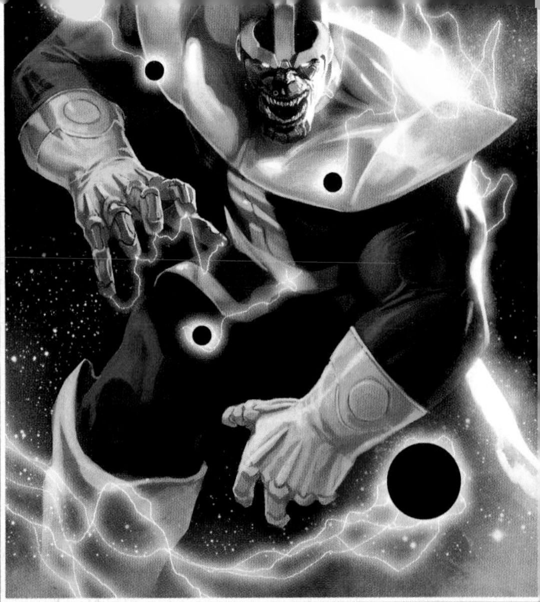

THANOS RISING #1 VARIANT
BY MARKO DJURDJEVIC

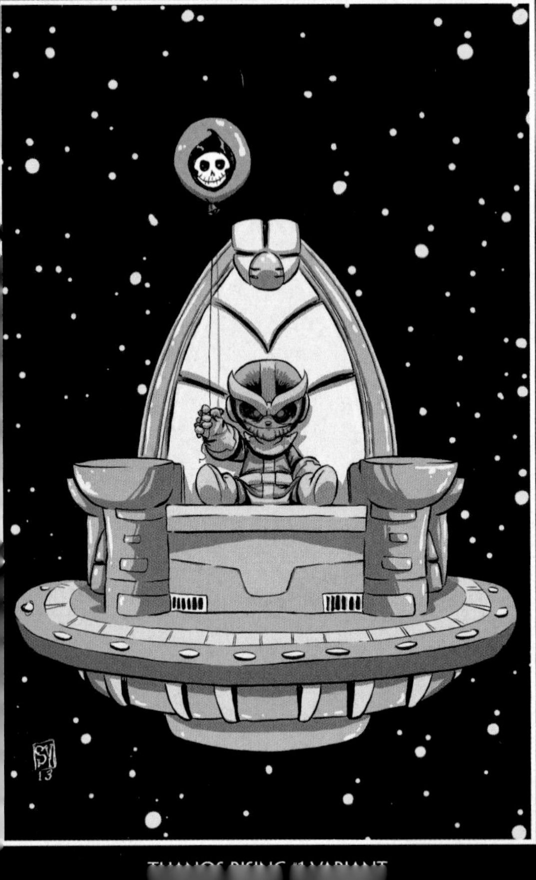

THANOS RISING #1 VARIANT

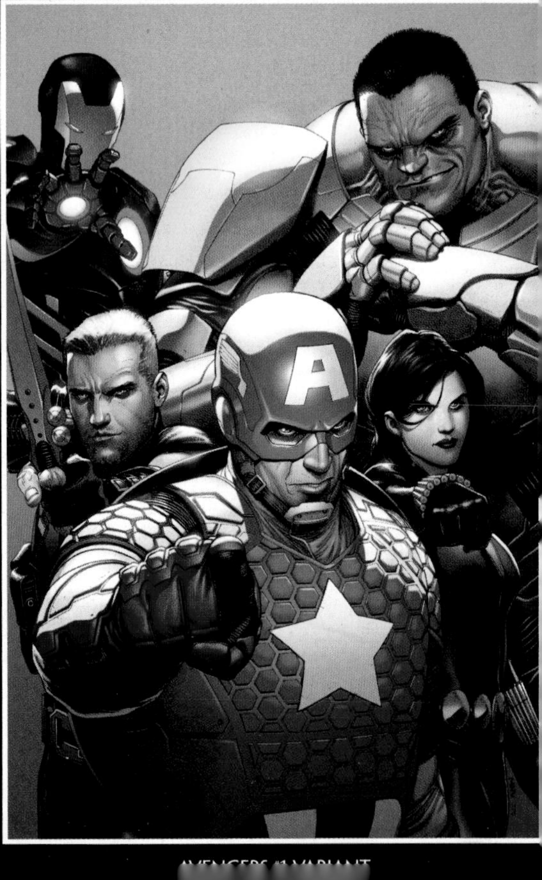

AVENGERS #1 VARIANT